Dad
from
Ron & Teri
Xmas /92

SALMON

THE DECLINE OF THE BRITISH COLUMBIA FISHERY

GEOFF MEGGS

DOUGLAS & McINTYRE
VANCOUVER/TORONTO

Douglas & McIntyre, 1615 Venables Street, Vancouver, BC V5L 2H1

Canadian Cataloguing in Publication Data

Meggs, Geoff, 1951–
    Salmon : the decline of the B.C. fishery

    Includes bibliographical references and index.
    ISBN 0-88894-734-8

    1. Salmon-fisheries—British Columbia—History.   2. Salmon canning industry—British Columbia—History   I. Title.
SH349.M43   1991   338.3'72755'09711
                                                        C91-091522-9
Editing by Saeko Usukawa
Cover & text design by Alexandra Hass
Typeset by The Typeworks
Printed and bound in Canada by D. W. Friesen & Sons Ltd.
Printed on acid-free paper

The author gratefully acknowledges the assistance of the Explorations Program of the Canada Council.

Published with assistance from the British Columbia Heritage Trust.

For Caitlin and Claire

CONTENTS

PREFACE

ALTHOUGH SCORES OF PEOPLE HELPED IN THE PREPARATION of this book, some deserve special thanks.

David Reid, Edith Iglauer Daly and George Brandak offered support and encouragement very early on, as did Duncan Stacey. To four people who had considered these issues before, I owe a particular intellectual debt. They are George North, Harold Griffin, Keith Ralston and Rolf Knight.

The United Fishermen and Allied Workers' Union, its officers and its General Executive Board granted me the time I needed to do research and writing. My association with the union and its members gave this project meaning. The ideas in this book evolved in the course of countless discussions with many people, but union members above all. Five whose friendship and patience were especially appreciated were Dennis Brown, Frank Cox, John Sutcliffe, Mike James and Joy Thorkelson.

Finally, thanks to Jan O'Brien, who helped make the whole project possible.

SALMON, OUR COMMON HERITAGE

THE STORY OF THE PACIFIC SALMON IS ONE OF ABUNDANCE
and destruction, wealth and poverty, development and decline. In Canada, we
see salmon as our common heritage and a symbol of our apparently inexhaustible natural wealth. But the image is hollow: our wild salmon runs are threatened with destruction. Although some major runs remain strong, uncounted
minor races already have been wiped out and each season brings formerly
bountiful stocks closer to elimination. Even those runs that remain strong can
fluctuate unaccountably from season to season, showering the coast in a windfall of wealth one year only to struggle back in ragged remnants in the next
turn of the cycle.

Europeans walked into British Columbia on the backs of salmon. Had the
native people of the Interior not provided fur trader and explorer Simon Fraser
with fish, he likely would have died on his way to the Pacific. When the fur
trade proved mediocre, the Hudson's Bay Company (HBC) turned to the salt
salmon trade and reaped monopoly profits. When gold was discovered glittering in the spawning beds of the Fraser, the HBC purchased enormous supplies
of salmon from native people to feed the miners whose rush to the gravel bars
transformed the province. When those with fortunes from the gold rush
looked for another source of easy cash, the salmon canning trade offered itself
as a ticket to wealth.

The history of the Pacific salmon fishery in British Columbia is that of a
century-long struggle for control of the resource. A brutal, no-holds-barred
war for a monopoly on the profits of the salmon industry began with the arrival of Europeans on the coast. The existing fisheries of native people were
brushed aside, then suppressed by legislation. Within a decade of the creation

of the canning industry on the Fraser River, cannery operators had raised the cry of overfishing despite their inability to catch and preserve even a fraction of the runs that surged passed their docks. It was conservation of profits, not fish, that concerned them. They fought tooth and nail against any restriction of their packs. With solemn resolutions and pious briefs to Ottawa, they sought and won guaranteed access to the wealth of rivers. The province's cannery entrepreneurs gorged on the salmon with a rapacious abandon that sickened the general public. Outrage over the canners' depredations forced the imposition of the first fisheries regulations, but more importantly won for the average citizen—provided he was a white British subject—the right to participate in the harvest of what was a public resource. Canadians considered it fundamental in a democratic society that the wealth of country's resources should be shared by all, not controlled by a few.

The ostensible concern of canners about conservation died down briefly as runs increased and revenues rose, only to erupt once more at the turn of the century when the Fraser produced the greatest returns since record-keeping began in 1880. Scores of canneries vied to pile up the largest pack, and the collapse of profits that resulted produced new warnings of depleted runs. Drastic measures were proposed, including a four-year total closure of the Fraser River. It was only in their private correspondence that the pro-closure canners developed their plans to move operations across the line to the United States, where they could continue to crop the runs with traps while the newly unionized independent fishermen of B.C. starved on the beach. Public opinion backed the fishermen and saved the salmon from the canners' onslaught, but confirmed the government commitment to hatcheries rather than fisheries management and habitat protection to conserve the runs.

It is more than coincidence that every major public controversy about conservation of B.C. salmon—in 1893, 1900, 1928, 1968, 1982 and again in 1990—was accompanied by massive corporate concentration and new measures to control access to the resource. When the corporate sector cried depletion, governments hurried to restore the flood of cash into the canners' coffers. When a crisis was declared, it was always the workers of the industry who were called upon to make sacrifices in the interests of all through reduced prices, employment and wages. It was always the workers in the industry, often prompted by native people still dependent on the runs, who offered real conservation policies and opposed a complete surrender of the resource to corporate imperatives.

It was not until 1919 that open entry for white British subjects was achieved coastwide and not until after the Second World War that formal racial barriers to the commercial fishery were eliminated to guarantee the right of Japanese Canadians to fish. Native fishing rights still remain locked in legal controversy. Only in the past twenty years has the century-old demand of fishing industry workers for real conservation of the stocks been partially realized with the creation of a salmonid enhancement program and the defeat of several projects to dam the Fraser. Thanks to the Hell's Gate fishways, the effects of the devastating slide of 1913, which brought the Fraser's salmon runs to their knees, have been overcome, and the river is rising once more to its former glory. Yet this recovery of individual elements of the salmon's ecosystem masks an erosion of its foundations. Toxic waste, water diversion, elimination of estuary rearing areas and a host of other environmental injuries threaten the survival of the runs just at the time when the means are at hand to restore them to their historic strength.

Although scientists remain unsure how the miracle of the salmon cycle is performed, they are committed to a simple theory which remains unproved: more fish spawning should automatically produce more fish for harvest. Fishing times and the numbers of fishermen are reduced to conserve the runs, and prices are reduced to conserve processor revenues. But as long as fishing pressure is believed to be the root cause of declines in salmon stocks, there can be no basis for curbing the activities of polluters. Also, the development of new salmon-rearing technology, especially fish farming, raises the prospect that salmon habitat may soon not be needed—or wanted—at all.

Today, the argument over conservation continues, but with a new twist. The canners, who once stood at the centre of political and economic power in the province, now are bit players who count on farmed salmon to make up their losses to pollution and habitat destruction. Much more powerful interests now seek to exploit the habitat of the salmon for hydroelectric power, oil, transportation corridors and a host of other developments.

Salmon has become for British Columbians what a canary was for underground miners. The death of a salmon run marks the advance of destructive economic development as surely as the canary indicated the presence of poison gas. Despite the overwhelming evidence that salmon runs are in crisis because of environmental destruction, today's corporate conservationists are again raising the cry of overfishing. This time, the economists and biologists reviewing the issue have concluded that the salmon runs are threatened not by habitat loss but by the very public ownership which has, until now, assured their survival.

Fisheries managers, corporate presidents and prestigious economists damn the "tragedy of the commons" they swear has led to this crisis. Because fish in the sea are not assigned to a particular property owner, they are subject to the rule of capture, wrote Peter Pearse, the most recent author of a royal commission report on the salmon fisheries. The inevitable result is overfishing, followed by economic crisis and stock depletion. Pearse and many others, who studiously ignore the role of the processors and minimize the importance of environmental destruction, have concluded that salmon must be the property of a few if they are to survive at all. They urge a system of economic quantification of salmon habitat so that it may be traded and sold like any other commodity. Then the silent hand of the marketplace will put wild salmon in their appropriate place in the economic order of things. Under this kind of private ownership, the average fisher, whether sport, commercial or Indian, would become a poacher.

Not only do today's so-called saviours of the salmon seek to eliminate curbs on profit from the salmonid ecosystem, they also seem prepared to eliminate the resource itself wherever it stands in the way of any other economic activity. As tomorrow's private salmon owners weigh fish profits against profits from hydroelectric power, offshore oil or clearcut logging, wild stocks will be sacrificed. The fish consumer will be served by artificially produced salmon, which themselves pose a threat to the genetic diversity of our remaining wild runs.

The introduction of salmon farming on the B.C. coast has unleashed a contemporary enclosure movement. Public waters are being fenced off for private fish production, often under the control of foreign-controlled corporations which have fled stricter regulation in places like Norway. The potential for employment and food production from finfish aquaculture has been undermined by an unregulated explosion of salmon farms which threaten the coastal environment and the integrity of existing wild stocks. Salmon farming also relies on a protein equation which is an environmental absurdity. Vast stocks of low quality pelagic fish which could be used for human food are harvested, reduced to fish meal and transported, in some cases around the globe. These stocks often are overexploited and taken from the waters of countries where starvation is the lot of much of the population. The meal is fed to salmon which, if released to the wild, could have consumed protein as plankton and returned for harvest themselves. The farm-raised salmon then are reared, with the help of antibiotics, pesticides and other necessities of agricultural production, to market size and sold to consumers as a healthful product. It is hard to imagine food production more contrary to the concept of sustainable development or global responsibility.

Canadians have a choice: to protect and enhance wild salmon runs or to surrender them to the tender mercies of short-term profit takers. It is a dilemma as old as the salmon industry itself, but unless action is taken soon, it will finally be resolved at the salmon's expense.

PART ONE

FOR GREED OF GOLD

I BELIEVE NO PERSON OR PERSONS HAVE A JUST RIGHT TO WASTE THE RESOURCES OF ANY COUNTRY, WHETHER THEY BE FISHERMEN OR CANNERS. WE OWE SOMETHING TO THE COMING GENERATIONS AND OUR DUTY IS TO HAND DOWN TO THEM THE RESOURCES OF THE COUNTRY IN A PROPER STATE, NOT A HISTORY WHICH WILL TELL THEM THAT THE PEOPLE OF THIS AGE EXPLOITED AND WASTED THE FOOD SUPPLY—NATURE'S GIFT TO MANKIND—FOR GREED OF GOLD.

—FRANK ROGERS,

President of the
B.C. Fishermen's Union,
12 April 1901

STAGGERING ABUNDANCE

NO ONE KNOWS EXACTLY HOW MANY SALMON RETURN AN-nually to British Columbia's rivers. There are fewer now than there were a century ago, but still they number in the tens of millions, sufficient in many years to provide one for every Canadian and yet leave enough to perpetuate the runs.

Each year they return from the distant reaches of the Pacific, navigating over thousands of kilometres of ocean and stream to the exact spot at which they were spawned two, three four or five years before. From the banks of the rivers, their numbers seem inexhaustible. The huge dark forms of chinook and the mottled greens and purples of spawning chum salmon blend with the colours of the river bottoms, a sharp contrast to the red schools of sockeye, which thrash in the water in crimson reefs to lay the seeds of a new generation in the gravel.

The native people, who built their economy and culture on salmon, knew that the survival of the runs was not guaranteed. Conservation of the salmon was a responsibility of leadership in native society. Through a complex and varying system of fishing rights, native groups shared and husbanded the salmon harvest. Whole communities would move hundreds of kilometres to harvest salmon during the summer, and the fish was traded into the continent's interior. Failure of a run meant catastrophe.

According to the oral records of the Nklapx'm people of the Thompson River, as recorded by James Teit, salmon were introduced to the Interior by Coyote, the most powerful of the ancients. In that era, the salmon were prevented from ascending the Fraser by dams built at the mouth by the people of the coast. Transforming himself into a piece of wood, Coyote floated downstream until stopped by a dam owned by two old women. Thinking the wood suitable for a dish, they took Coyote home and used him to serve food, but fish placed on the new dish disappeared so quickly that they threw it in the fire in despair.

To their amazement, the cries of an infant issued from the fire. The women pulled out Coyote and reared him, although he was disobedient and troublesome. These women had four wooden boxes in their house and they forbade the child to remove the lids. Their chief food was salmon, a new fish to Coyote. He saw the river full of fish below the dam.

One day while the women were away, Coyote decided to break the dam and lead the salmon to his people in the Interior:

"Accordingly he rushed down and broke the dam, then went to the house and opened the four boxes. From one issued smoke; from another, wasps; from the other two salmon-flies and beetles. He then ran along the bank of the river ahead of the salmon while the smoke, the wasps and the flies also followed up the salmon. The people saw the great smoke and wondered what it was. Some of the salmon went up the Thompson, but the majority turned northward, going up the Fraser River."

The Nklapx'm elders of Lytton recall that Coyote "ordained that henceforth salmon should ascend into the interior each year; and the broken dams he transformed into rocks, which at the present day form canyons on the Fraser and Columbia rivers. To this day, the smoke, flies, wasps and the up-river summer winds are associated with the arrival of the salmon."

Today, the Fraser remains the world's pre-eminent salmon river, producing as much fish in most seasons as all the rest of British Columbia's salmon streams combined. Rising in the Rocky Mountains, it drains an area of 238,000 square kilometres, running first northwest through the wide valleys of the Rocky Mountain Trench to Prince George. Here it turns south, gathering in the waters of the Nechako, the Chilcotin, the Quesnel, the Thompson and a host of smaller tributaries as it drives through the bedrock of the Interior Plateau on its way to the Pacific Ocean. In the 20 million years that geologists estimate that the Fraser has followed this 1100-kilometre route, it has gouged a canyon up to 600 metres deep in the plateau, discharging the sediment it produces into a wide valley before pouring into the ocean through a sprawling estuary. Every element of this system supports a phase of the salmon's life cycle.

The cycle begins and ends in the cold gravel of a thousand streams scattered from the Fraser's mouth to the narrow mountain valleys in the distant reaches of the river system. As the glaciers retreated at the end of the last Ice Age, the new streams were invaded from the sea by salmon, which seem to have evolved during millions of years in the prehistoric oceans. Fossil beds in Oregon have yielded the bones of a giant salmon 190 centimetres long, equipped with 100 toothless rakers on each gill arch to sift the sea for plankton and two huge breeding teeth that recall the fangs of a modern chum salmon. Alongside these bones were the fossilized remains of a fish almost identical to today's coho, suggesting that salmon evolved from marine fish which gradually adapted to a fresh-water environment. As long as 10,000 years ago, native people along the Fraser harvested these runs.

Five species of salmon are found in North America. The largest is the chinook or spring salmon, commonly running between 14 and 18 kilograms, which usually spawns in river systems. Its fry hatch and run directly to sea, returning four or five years later to spawn. Long, thick-bodied and with a broad, square tail, chinook are believed to remain relatively close to shore, within Canada's 200-mile (370-kilometre) limit, during their life at sea.

More adventurous are the chum salmon, which spawn in streams and rivers, run directly to sea and migrate hundreds of kilometres into the Pacific. Silvery and sleek while at sea for three years, chums grow to between 3.5 and 4.5 kilograms. They undergo bizarre transformations as they prepare to spawn. Their jaws grow and hook, sprouting large curled teeth, and their skin grows dark and mottled, breaking out in splotches of purple and black. Fishermen call them dog salmon.

Chums share much of their range with coho, which prefer streams close to salt water for spawning. Ranging between 2.7 and 5.4 kilograms, coho have a simple life cycle, running to sea about a year after they hatch and returning after three years in the ocean.

Sockeye salmon, which weigh up to 4 kilograms as adults, have the most complex life cycle. Spawned in streams, they feed in a freshwater lake for one to three years before migrating to sea. In their three years in the Pacific, sockeye run as far as the extreme reaches of the Aleutians. Once they turn for home and reach fresh water, their scales seem to become almost transparent, revealing the deep red flesh beneath.

Smallest and most numerous of the salmon are the pinks. After emerging from the gravel, juvenile pinks run straight to sea, returning after two years to spawn. Most weigh only 2 kilograms but some run as high as 4.5 kilograms. Their uniform size and great abundance made them a mainstay of the canning industry. They change colour and deform as they prepare for spawning. The males develop a long twisted snout and sharp protruding hump, the reason fishermen almost invariably call them "humpies."

Through millennia of evolution and adaptation, salmon have developed the ability to exploit the advantages of habitats as diverse as the icy gravel of an inland stream and the deep offshore currents of the North Pacific. How salmon navigate over thousands of kilometres and return to spawn within a couple of metres of their birthplace is a mystery. Migration is triggered by unknown cues that direct millions of fish scattered over wide areas to begin the homeward journey. In four to ten weeks, salmon may cover 3000 kilometres, swimming 30 to 50 kilometres a day for days at a stretch. Following the stars or perhaps oriented by the electromagnetic fields generated by currents and winds, they move directly to their destination.

As the runs near land, they encounter the faint traces of fresh water flowing out into the Pacific from the rivers and streams of the Pacific Northwest coast. Following these clues and seeking out water temperatures at which they are most comfortable, they move inshore, approaching the Fraser from the north by rounding Vancouver Island to travel down Johnstone Strait, or from the southeast from the Strait of Juan de Fuca. Although runs may delay briefly just offshore to allow rains to raise water levels, the spawning migration is a journey that ends at the exact spot where the salmon emerged from the gravel. As the salmon near the spawning beds, they literally smell out their birthplaces, driving upstream at astonishing rates of speed that can reach 80 and even 145 kilometres a day.

So precise is their timing that any obstruction or delay at this point can exhaust their now meagre physical reserves. Although capable of leaping up falls and pushing through rapids, salmon can be defeated by a river obstruction or by water even a few degrees warmer than usual. If all goes well, they reach the spawning beds with several days to spare, schooling up in the deeper pools to wait until spawning is imminent. When ready, the females move onto the spawning beds, select a spot in the gravel and, twisting onto their sides, violently beat their tails on the bottom to dig a shallow depression. The males swim back and forth across the stream, eventually pairing off with the females in a mating sequence that will last several hours. Finally, quivering side by side in the "redd" or nest the female has excavated, the two salmon simultaneously release eggs and sperm. In a moment the bright orange eggs are swept by the milky cloud of milt and then settle in the nest. The female quickly moves a short distance upstream and begins a new nest, burying the previous one in the process. During the spawning period, which may last ten days, a sockeye female may deposit 500 to 1,000 eggs in each of several nests.

At last the salmon's journey ends. Spawned salmon soon seem more dead than alive, lying listlessly in the shallows with heaving gills and gaping mouths. Wounds suffered while spawning lie open to the water, tails are white and torn. Caught by the current, the spawners drift downstream to die on the beach, where they are picked over by birds and bears and then rot. As more salmon push onto the gravel, the carcasses of their predecessors, already whitening with decay, sink into the stream, returning essential nutrients to the system that produced them.

From the thousands of eggs deposited by each pair of spawners—2,000 for pink salmon, up to 3,000 for sockeye—a new generation will rise. During the winter, the eggs, washed by the icy waters of the stream and entombed as much as 46 centimetres below the surface of the gravel bed, slowly transform. Within the egg's membrane grow the heart, eyes, head and body of a salmon, attached to a yolk on which it will feed until it emerges from the gravel. Once out of the egg, the salmon is called an alevin. Any dramatic change in temperature or water level during this period, whether due to hydro dam operations or natural causes, can destroy millions of alevins. Under natural conditions, only 10 to 20 per cent of fertilized eggs produce alevins, which survive to become fry, the name for the juvenile fish that emerge as the alevins absorb their yolk sacs and move up from the gravel to the stream. The tiny alevins, guided by the stream flow and gravity, can worm their way through the gravel for long distances around obstructions to reach the stream above. Accumulations of silt, however, washed down from logging operations or landslides, can be fatal to the alevins, imprisoning them below the stream's floor. Once free, they rise to the surface, gulp enough air to stabilize their swim bladders and then begin to migrate and change into fry.

The salmon's migration to sea is no less remarkable than the journey that will bring them back. For pink salmon, this journey involves a steady drift downstream to the estuary where the fry feed and become smolts, acclimatizing to salt water, before joining a school of juvenile salmon more than 36 kilometres wide and 1800 kilometres long swirling north along the coast and into the Gulf of Alaska. Chinook, coho and chum follow similar patterns, although their fry spend longer in the home stream before moving seaward.

Sockeye follow a different pattern, always spawning in river systems that include a lake. As sockeye alevins wriggle from the gravel, they unerringly turn toward the lake, those in tributaries of the lake drifting downstream and those in outlet streams swimming against the current. Hugging the river banks, they move quickly into the lake's open water, forming schools and feeding near shore. Only after a year has passed will they run downstream to sea.

Many smolts fall prey to a host of predators. Herbicides, temperature changes, the presence of heavy metals, or infestation by bacterial or viral pathogens can fatally disrupt the migration patterns of smolts, which rely on a combination of temperature, light and hormonal cues to begin their passage to the ocean. Navigating by the sun and oriented on cloudy days by the earth's magnetic field, they leave the lakes and swim to the sea.

One Canadian scientist estimated that 50 per cent of fertilized eggs die without hatching. About 75 per cent of alevins die during emergence from the gravel, lost to predators or other natural causes. Fully 97 per cent of fry also die a quick death. Thus, a spawn of 500 male and 500 female salmon, in which each female has 4,000 eggs, may produce almost two million eggs, of which only 7,000 will become smolts to run to sea.

Of the fry that emerge from the gravel, only about three per cent will return as adults, but these fish are enough to support a harvest and still reseed the spawning grounds for another generation.

With the arrival of the fur traders, a silent, desperate battle began. Salmon soon became more valuable than the furs and gold which had attracted the traders in the first place. The salmon cycle, which had run uninterrupted for thousands of years, was altered forever. The native people, who had harvested the runs for millennia, were swept aside. The struggle to exploit and then to control the wealth of the fishery began in earnest, and ultimately, the survival of many stocks was put in doubt.

The cycles of dearth and plenty were not obvious to the first Europeans on the coast, who witnessed the salmon return to the region's rivers in staggering abundance. To the earliest explorers and fur traders, salmon seemed as commonplace and as easy to obtain as fresh water or clean air. Finding their fishing skills inadequate, they relied on the native Indians for ample supplies of cheap salmon, sometimes simply taking what provident communities had stored. Often even this was not enough. Hudson's Bay Company traders seeking to establish permanent posts in the Interior found to their dismay that the Fraser's northernmost runs often failed. Sockeye available in barter from native people fishing on the Skeena was essential to the traders' survival.

In less than a hundred years the salmon harvest was transformed from the traditional activity of scores of native Indian communities, trading among each other, into a highly mechanized industry distributing millions of fish to industrial workers on the other side of the globe.

One generation of native Indian fishermen was the indispensable guarantor of the fur trader's survival. The next was forced to defend—sometimes by force—the salmon spawning beds and their right to harvest the runs as they had for centuries; people whose fathers and mothers could recall the arrival of the first Europeans spent the summers gillnetting or toiling in canneries. The third generation found its fishing rights denied and its right to work in the new salmon industry put in question.

From the beginning, native communities were alarmed by the European newcomers who pressed into their territory from three sides in the quest for furs. Russian merchants were moving down the coast from the northwest by 1741, having established lengthy overland routes across Siberia to the markets of eastern Europe. Spanish and English expeditions probed the coast from the south during the following thirty years and, in 1793, Alexander Mackenzie canoed and walked overland from the continent's interior to the coast at Bella Coola in his search for a safe and easy route to the Pacific.

A well-educated Scot with tremendous physical courage and a strong sympathy for the voyageurs and native people he worked with, Mackenzie combined the entrepreneurial drive of a fur trader with the intellectual curiosity of a scientist. Mackenzie began his journey in the spring. He soon was able to drop his canoe into a tributary of what was to be named the Fraser River. He continued south and then west, overland to the sea, marvelling at the salmon traps and weirs he saw as he went. Once among the tribes of the coast, Mackenzie's group was able to cache its supplies of pemmican and survive on the abundant stocks of salmon.

"Salmon is so abundant in this river that these people have a constant and plentiful supply of that excellent fish," he wrote. The milky, glacier-fed waters of the Bella Coola river were crossed by an elaborate fishing weir. He could see an embankment of timber "for the purpose of placing their fishing machines," the conical wooden fish traps which were dropped into gaps in the barricade. Below the traps, fishermen supplemented the catch with dipnets.

The native people had a well-developed system of fishing rights and management. On the coast, these systems were elaborated into complex property rights exercised by chiefs according to standards established over generations. In the Interior, where fisheries were usually river-based and the runs were almost always intercepted by many groups, fishing rights appear to have been more community-oriented. Such differences however, could not obscure the fundamental importance of salmon to the culture, politics and economy of native nations.

Mackenzie was struck by the care with which the people handled the salmon. Before one chief's lodge he observed "four heaps of salmon, each of which consisted of between three and four hundred fish. Sixteen women were employed in cleaning and preparing them. They first separate the head from the body, the former of which they boil; they then cut the latter down the back on each side of the bone, leaving one third of the fish adhering to it, and afterwards take out the guts. The bone is roasted for immediate use and the other parts are dressed in the same manner, but with more attention, for future provision. While they are before the fire, troughs are placed under them to receive the oil. The roes are also carefully preserved and form a favourite article of their food."

As the expedition made its way back from the Pacific, each man bearing 9 kilograms of fish acquired from the people of the coast, Mackenzie was gratified to find his caches of food and trade goods virtually undisturbed. The canoe, left in a shelter by the Fraser, was untouched, but a careful inventory revealed the disappearance of a handful of unimportant articles. To force their return, Mackenzie used an extraordinary threat:

"I told those who remained near us, without any appearance of anger, that their relations who were gone had no idea of the mischief that would result to them from taking our property. I gravely added that the salmon, which was not only their favourite food but absolutely necessary to their existence, came from the sea which belonged to us white men; and that as, at the entrance to the river, we could prevent those fish from coming up it, we possessed the power to starve them and their children. To avert our anger, therefore, they must return all the articles that had been stolen from us. This finesse succeeded. Messengers were dispatched to order the restoration of every thing that had been taken. We purchased several large salmon from them and enjoyed a delicious meal." Those who followed in Mackenzie's footsteps would make good on his threat.

By the end of the eighteenth century, the fur traders of the North West Company were determined to find some route from the Pacific coast to the Interior to reduce their dependence on the lengthy and costly canoe supply lines from the eastern seaboard. Simon Fraser was directed to find out whether or not the river Mackenzie had followed was the Columbia.

Fraser, while forcing his way down the Fraser River to the Pacific, first observed the enormous salmon industry of the native people over an entire river system. Physically powerful, Fraser was a stubborn, arrogant man whose deep contempt for the voyageurs and native people was as strong as Mackenzie's sympathy.

In 1806 he crossed the Pacific divide and followed the McGregor River to the Fraser and then the Nechako. On 26 July 1806, he reached Stuart Lake. The salmon runs were late, and the Carrier people, who were near starvation themselves, could not supply him with salmon. When the Stuart sockeye run finally appeared on 20 September, it was too late for Fraser to pursue exploration of the river.

It was not until 1808, after a year of consolidating the new posts at Fort Fraser and Fort George, that Fraser was ready to pursue his quest for the Columbia. With two native guides, he pushed off from Fort St. James with two other traders and nineteen voyageurs on 22 May. Jules Quesnel, a trader with Fraser, was to write later that "we could never have crossed (the mountains) if the natives, who received us well, had not helped us." Fraser relied on native people for food every step of the way. Although he had acquired some salmon before leaving, he also took caches of fish he found along the route.

Fraser's expedition was a hellish experience. The voyageurs' moccasins were torn to ribbons in a day of portaging, and the surging spring waters of the river—which he hoped was the Columbia but was actually the Fraser—constantly overturned and destroyed the canoes. On 2 July, Simon Fraser finally gazed out on the Strait of Georgia and then turned his canoes toward the community of Musqueam. Most of the inhabitants retreated at his approach, then gathered behind him, threatening him with clubs. Holding their pursuers back at musket point, the explorers turned and fled back upstream.

Everywhere along the river the native people they saw were engaged in an intensive salmon harvest. By now Fraser's group had penetrated back into the heart of the river fishery, past the dipnet fisheries of the lower canyon and through the rapids that had so terrified them a few weeks before. On 29 July, he wrote, native people gave him "plenty of salmon, which they take in abundance by means of barriers." At noon on 6 August 1808, Fraser's party pulled their canoes ashore at Fort George. As far as the North West Company was concerned, the trip had been a failure. The Fraser River provided no practical access to the Pacific.

Despite their hospitality, the native people upriver had misgivings about the white strangers. "Some Indians thought they were just people from a far country and of a different race," as James Teit later recorded, "for they had heard vague rumours of the strange people with guns, who, it was expected, might find their way to this country some time; but very many people thought they were beings spoken of in their tales of the mythological period, who had taken a notion to travel again over the earth; and they often wondered what object they had in view and what results would follow. They believed their appearance forboded some great change or events of prime importance to the Indians, but in what way they did not know."

In 1852, native man drinking from the Thompson River noticed a glint of light on the gravel riverbed—a nugget of solid gold. When it was offered for sale at Kamloops, the native people were startled at the sensation it caused and the high price it brought. According to Governor James Douglas, "the whole tribe forthwith began to collect the glittering metal."

The news must have been especially exciting to Douglas because of the mediocre profits then flowing from the Hudson's Bay Company's fur trade in British Columbia. In an effort to reduce the staggering cost of supplying its posts by the long overland route from the Great Lakes, the Company constructed a new post in 1827 at Fort Langley, about 50 kilometres upstream from the mouth of the Fraser. Here the Company believed it could supply Interior forts with trade goods delivered around Cape Horn by vessels supporting other posts on the Columbia River. Soon Fort Langley was well established, but the continuing burden of a trade war with American interlopers forced the HBC to consider new ventures. An obvious answer was at hand—the salmon business. After a faltering start, Fort Langley traders built up an important salt salmon market, buying tens of thousands of fish annually from native harvesters. Native women cleaned, cured and packed the catch, which then was shipped in barrels to Hawaii, a transfer point for ships trading both to Asia and to South America. By 1847, profits from salmon exceeded those from the fur trade, but the Hawaiian market was limited and chances to expand the fishery were few. News of gold, then, was good news indeed.

There is little doubt the native peoples of the province had long been aware of the presence of gold on their territories, but they had little use for it until the arrival of the traders created a market. As long as the Europeans respected native ownership of the mineral resources of the territory, the Indians were happy to oblige. When whites tried to steal the gold, they were expelled.

For the next four years, Douglas received reports of gold from all over the territory, particularly along the Columbia watersheds where prospectors were probing the river bars for deposits like the ones which had prompted the California rush of 1848. He excitedly transmitted the news to the Colonial Office in London, but was compelled to report that American miners had been denied access to the gold by "the threatening attitude of the native tribes," who would allow digging only by retired traders who respected their rights and traditions.

American gold-diggers were expelled from the territory north of what is now Hope by the Couteaux tribes, who demanded not only recognition of their title to the land but also protection of their salmon resources.

The Thompson tribes had "openly expressed a determination," Douglas wrote, "to resist all attempts at working gold in any of the streams flowing into Thompson's River, both from a desire to monopolize the precious metal for their own benefit, and from a well-founded impression that the shoals of salmon which annually ascend those rivers and furnish the principal food of the inhabitants will be driven off, and prevented from making their annual migrations from the sea."

However, more forerunners of the coming gold rush had penetrated to the upper Fraser as early as 1856. By the spring of 1858, news of the Couteaux mines had reached San Francisco, where the newspapers were trumpeting the discovery of "a second California or Australia." Steamboat owners were offering quick passage to Victoria, and as Douglas carefully penned his warning reports to London, he took steps "to facilitate by every possible means the transport of passengers and goods to the furthest navigable point on Fraser's River" with a view to controlling "the whole trade of the gold regions."

On 25 April 1858, the steamer *Commodore* dropped anchor in Victoria and 450 American miners swarmed ashore, doubling the white population of Vancouver Island in one day. By August, 30,000 whites had rushed through

Victoria on the way to the Fraser River. Fort Langley exploded in a frenzy of trading activity. Blankets, tinware, mining tools and food poured through the trading room in return for bags of gold dust and American coins. Confident the miners would be clamouring for provisions during the winter, the Hudson's Bay Company ordered its traders to acquire as many dried salmon as the native people would sell. The gold was being taken without compensation; salmon, however, the traders still felt prepared to pay for. Without it, many miners would have starved.

On the lower Fraser, the native groups at first seemed undisturbed by the plague that settled on them. At Yale a ramshackle growth of clapboard and log hotels, bars and huts began to spread along the riverbank. The native people quickly put their packing and canoeing skills to use ferrying miners and their supplies up to the bars. More and more native people turned their hands to mining, selling the gold for a daily wage of three to four dollars. At Hill's Bar, on the Fraser, Douglas found eighty native people and thirty whites working side by side in late May. But within a few weeks the arrogance of the miners and their mistreatment of native women provoked growing outrage among the Indians. In mid-June, Douglas learned that native groups had gathered under arms at Hill's Bar and "threatened to make a clean sweep of the whole body of miners assembled there."

Mid-August brought a new report of conflict, this time with lives lost on each side. The clash occurred at a native fishing camp at Rancherie, near Boston Bar. Ten native people died, the story went, one a chief. Two whites, one a woman from Hill's Bar, were casualties on the miners' side. The exact cause of the confrontation will never be known, but more than seventy years later, George Hope, a native leader of the region, said the spark that ignited the conflict was the murder of a native man and his wife who had been selling salmon to the miners. The miners murdered the man, then raped his wife and killed her as well. A black miner took the news to the native people, who went to the miners seeking justice. In the exchange of gunfire that followed, the Indians were massacred.

In Yale there was indignation at the native people's actions, despite the one-sided outcome of the clash. More than 2,000 Indians had assembled above Yale, the Victoria *Gazette* reported, "evidently for no friendly purpose." The reason for the gathering, however, was obvious. It was the height of the fishing season, and the native groups of the territory had reached the river to find it crawling with miners cutting trees, diverting streams, digging trenches through the gravel spawning beds and destroying their traditional fishing sites. With water levels declining in the summer, miners were abandoning their little gravel rockers for larger machines. Trenches several kilometres long were under construction to drain lakes and ponds into sluices and down to the river bed. The gravel of the rich spawning beds was being pushed through the sluices and dumped aside.

News of the Boston Bar fray produced hysteria in Yale. Within hours, four companies of vigilantes totalling five hundred armed men were pushing north to deal with the "redskins" once and for all. At their head was Capt. H. M. Snyder.

At the site of the 14 August clash, Snyder found three native fish camps destroyed. "A great quantity of salmon was also destroyed by this party," the *Gazette* reported. The true number of native casualties, he now believed, was thirty-one, including five chiefs. "The Indians say that the whites are almost constantly insulting their wives and injuring them in various ways," Snyder wrote, adding with heavy understatement that "the burning of the rancheries and killing of the Indians [was] uncalled for."

On 21 August, Snyder met near what is now Lytton with Chief Spinkum and six lesser chiefs, who gathered with three hundred other native people to discuss a settlement. The terms of the settlement were not recorded, but the chiefs "appeared highly pleased" and ordered salmon served to the vigilantes. Perhaps the chiefs were relieved to have avoided one of the bloody wars that was resulting in the extermination of tribes in Oregon and Washington. Confronted by the hurricane of the gold rush, Chief Spinkum had little alternative but to accept Snyder's ultimatum.

Much has been written about Douglas's concern for the native people, but the record suggests that he did nothing to safeguard them against the massacre and destruction that he knew would follow the gold finds. It is hard to imagine the crushing impact this revolution must have had on the people of the Fraser. In a matter of months, their territory had been overrun. The invaders debated various options in the newspapers, weighing the advantages and ethics of concentration camps over extermination.

One more or less enlightened observer wrote to the *Gazette* on 26 August to suggest that it would be wise to determine the cause of native hostility before setting out to exterminate them. "One of these would seem to be the interference of mining labour with the salmon fisheries and other occupations by which the savages have hitherto subsisted." Perhaps native people should be offered food rations, the miner thought, or "located on a reservation—the only alternative for extermination."

News of the miners' depredations had penetrated to England, where the Aborigines Protection Society was pressuring Edward Bulwer-Lytton, the colonial secretary, to pursue negotiations so that "the Native title should be recognized in British Columbia, and that some reasonable adjustment of their claims should be made by the British Government. . . . Nothing short of justice in rendering payment for that which it may be necessary for us to acquire and laws framed and administered in the spirit of justice and equality, can really avail." This view found no sympathy in British Columbia.

The native question now was a low priority. It was not that he did not care about the native people, Douglas told Colonial Secretary Edward Bulwer-Lytton: "I will, hereafter, when time permits, endeavor to arrange some plan by which their interests will be permanently guarded and the race rescued from destruction." Some months later he proposed a reserve system. Lytton agreed, provided the reserves were laid out "so as to avoid checking at any future date the progress of the white colonists."

The consequences of the miners' terror campaign were devastating for the tribes in the area. On his trip to the forks, Snyder had been impressed by the sight of "the men engaged in fishing and drying salmon and the women in drying and gathering berries, making nets, baskets, etc." Now, he reported, all the people fishing near the canyon had been forced to move downriver to escape harassment.

Winter was hard that year. The Fraser froze over on two occasions, and miners left the country by the thousands. By 1859, the rush had moved north, and the canyon became quiet once more. The native fishery that year was a good one, and according to the Victoria *Colonist*, admiring miners noted how the native people "catch quantities of fish in excess of that required for their own use, which they trade off to the Hudson's Bay Co. for blankets and other necessities." In Victoria, citizens were gratified to find native people selling fresh salmon for between 12½ and 25 cents each. As the gold boom began to bust, interest stirred in this last resource under native control.

Would it not be better, the *Colonist* asked, to exploit this "imperishable productive resource" rather than the quickly exhausted minerals of the Fraser? "Here salmon can be taken in unimaginable quantity. They can be cured and barrelled at a cost trifling in comparison with the price they will command in foreign markets.

"Tens of thousands might engage annually in our salmon fisheries and consequently create thrifty homesteads and smiling firesides where, since the dawn of creation, naught has disturbed the shore but the untutored Indian. . . . No country ever had better or more valuable salmon fisheries, nor more easily developed, than ours."

THE RISE OF THE CANNERS

FROM THE TURMOIL OF THE GOLD RUSH ROSE A NEW CLASS OF entrepreneurs who made the rapacious frenzy of the mining claims into the business ethic of the province. Vast resources were expropriated, exploited and exported, but none were despoiled with such wild abandon as the salmon. The men who fastened on the salmon to make their millions awed even themselves with their colossal harvests, concluding within ten years of the first commercial catch that only government subsidy and a legislated monopoly could sustain them in the lush profits to which they had become accustomed.

Those eager to tap the wealth of the salmon runs faced two problems: how to find large markets and how to preserve the fish long enough to reach them. By the time the gold rush had exhausted itself on the banks of the upper Fraser River, Britain's salmon streams were dying. With an obedience to the laws of the marketplace that was as automatic as it was destructive, the owners of the rivers sold them for canals, power development and industrial sewers. The British salmon fisheries collapsed under the hammer blows of the Industrial Revolution and the uncontrolled poaching of a hungry population, which saw no reason to limit its catch of a resource the lords were destroying. To the entrepreneur who could link the Fraser's salmon with the ready-made markets of industrial Britain would go untold profits. The key was canning, which offered the prospect of preserving salmon indefinitely and more palatably than drying or salting. Thus, the Industrial Revolution provided both the market for the Fraser's fish and the technology by which it could be processed.

The man who did the most to unlock the Fraser's riches was Alexander Ewen, a tall, imposing Scot who arrived in the province in 1864 in response to a request from a former miner named Alexander Annandale. Annandale wanted to invest his goldfield profits in a new venture, and he hired Ewen, son of a veteran fish station manager in Scotland, to operate a saltery at New Westminster. The first season was a failure, due to Annandale's insistence on the use of trapnets. Ewen, frustrated by the low production of the trapnets and unwilling to rely on the slow harvest of native dipnets, forced a switch to gillnets, the long, floating nets that snare fish by the gills. He was soon on his own—Annandale dropped out after the first year—but Ewen shipped his production to the Hudson's Bay Company's markets in Hawaii. By 1871, he had acquired new partners for a more ambitious project—salmon canning.

Salmon canning technology was already fifty years old. It had been attempted in Ireland just after the turn of the century. In 1839, the first salmon canned in North America were processed in New Brunswick. In the west, Sacramento River salmon was being canned for export by 1864 and, in 1867, James Syme successfully canned B.C. salmon in Annandale's former saltery. He canned during the 1867 and 1868 seasons, but an economic recession and lack of capital made it impossible for him to continue. Continuous canning did not begin on the Fraser until 1871, when Ewen launched his cannery and Capt. Edward Stamp also went into production. Both used sheet tin imported all the way from Britain to make their cans.

Ewen's partners in his new venture were Alexander Loggie, a New Brunswick lobster canner and fisherman; James Wise, a commercial fisherman, and David S. Hennessy, another Maritimes canner. They hired master canner James Knowles to reopen Syme's cannery at Annieville, on the south bank of the Fraser just west of New Westminster. In 1871, their first season, the new partners produced 300 cases for export to the United Kingdom and salted 4,000 barrels. Each case held 100 one-pound (454-gram) cans, shorter and wider than today's version. After 1871, only 48 one-pound cans were placed in a case, and a 48-pound (21.8-kilogram) case became the industry standard.

Stamp did even better, using buildings at the Royal Engineers camp at Sapperton, near New Westminster. He relied on the skills of an expert tinsmith, John Sullivan Deas, an American black. When Stamp died in 1872, Deas took over the business, moved it down the river to Deas Island and quickly built it up until his pack exceeded Ewen's.

The Fraser canners shipped their product to the hungry workers of Britain. Even after transportation halfway around the world, canned salmon could be sold in Britain for half the cost of fresh meat. Workers would pool their pennies to buy a one-pound can for lunch, opening it at the shop to assure themselves of good quality. "It is not uncommon to see a laborer buy a tin of salmon for his dinner and eat it out of the tin," the New Westminster *Columbian* told its readers in 1882. By the end of the century, canned salmon had become so basic to the British diet that it formed part of the army ration.

Although Ewen soon assumed the air of a dignified industrial patriarch, the pioneer canner was avaricious, erratic and stubborn. Ultimately successful in real estate, gas and railway investments, Ewen was a die-hard Liberal and a notorious drinker. He boasted to canner Henry Doyle that in his youth he "frequently drank often and steadily for 48 hours at a stretch without eating or sleeping and was as sober at the end of that time as when I began." His peers considered him "a crazy fool" and a "curse to the business" because of his willingness to bid up the price of fish to corner the market. Yet it was his self-confidence and drive, reflected in contempt for the views of other people, that made him the central figure of the first generation of canners.

Both Ewen and Deas had special skills that made it easy for them to achieve early success, but profits flowed so readily from the canning industry that it attracted speculators like vultures to a fresh carcass. They included men like E. A. Wadhams, a merchant from New York state, who had renewed his fortune in the Cariboo gold fields. Wadhams invested in the industry as early as 1873, although he did not build his famous cannery on Rivers Inlet until 1887.

The prodigious drinking feats of Marshall English, a canner who established himself at New Westminster in 1877, inspired awe in his competitors. English, a Virginian with a background in farming, milling and mining, used his links with British capital to build what was then the largest cannery on the river. He was a hedonist, Doyle wrote later, "unable to refrain from having a good time while the money lasted," and was an infamous drinker who would excuse himself while walking with friends, throw up in the ditch and then "resume the conversation without showing any discomfort."

Another pioneer was T. E. Ladner, who established his first cannery at what became known at Ladner's Landing on the south bank of the Fraser near its mouth. A Cornwall farmer, Ladner made a small fortune for himself as a teamster in the Cariboo. He was almost as wide as he was tall, packing between 104 and 113 kilograms on his 165-centimetre frame, which he topped with a saucer-shaped hat. A life-long Conservative, he despised Ewen's willingness to compete for fish on the grounds, preferring more dignified preseason price fixing. Ladner's partners in the Delta Canning Co. formed in 1878 included J. A. Laidlaw, a Scot who made his money working an abandoned claim in the Cariboo, and Don Chisholm, another veteran of the gold rush.

A relative latecomer was J. H. Todd, who made a fortune selling notions to the miners. Todd, who was notoriously grasping, built his first cannery on the Fraser in 1882. He once attempted to pay two native people a hardtack biscuit each for the arduous task of paddling him upriver to New Westminster. "He was keen and hard, giving nothing away," recalled a contemporary, "and seized every opportunity to advance himself at the expense of others." It was a fitting description of the entire canner fraternity.

In the ten years following Ewen and Deas's first packs, new canneries were established almost every year. In 1876, Inverness cannery rose on the Skeena. At the end of the decade, the province boasted eleven canneries, including ten on the Fraser. The pack on the Fraser rose from a few hundred cases in 1870 to 42,155 in 1880 and 142,516 a year later. A new gold rush had begun.

The workers in this new venture were assembled from wherever the canners could find able-bodied men and women. The canning industry became a kingdom of sweat in which thousands of workers toiled round the clock to feed the bank accounts of a dozen businessmen. To supply their markets, the canners required ever-larger volumes of fish. An enormous fleet of gillnetters was launched on the Fraser, whose silt-laden waters made the nets all but invisible to salmon. Setting their net before high-water slack, two fishermen in a skiff would work across the current, one rowing while the other paid out the net behind. Until the 1880s, nets were hand-made by native women from costly imported flax twine. At $130 to $150 each, they formed the most expensive part of the gear. Until 1888, when the length of the net was set at 150 fathoms (274 metres), both length and depth were unregulated.

The first gillnets were set from canoes, but fishermen soon developed flat-bottomed gillnetting skiffs, which were mass produced in small yards along the river. In the 1880s, skiffs cost as little as $31. Up to 6 metres long and double-ended, they were built more stoutly if required to work near the mouth of the river. By the end of the century, when the fleet moved into the rougher waters of the Strait of Georgia, a 9-metre, round-bottomed, carvel hull, gaff-rigged skiff had evolved capable of packing up to 2250 kilograms of fish. It was patterned on the Columbia River fishing boats.

The majority of early gillnet fishermen were native people, hired on a daily basis to fish on cannery boats. They often took their wives as boat pullers, the name for the person who handled the oars. Initially, wages were $1 a day for the boat puller and $2.25 for the fisherman, but fishermen saw their wages rise as high as $2.50 by the 1890s. It was little enough considering the arduous work and hazardous conditions.

Walter Wicks, a Skeena fisherman who worked the skiffs a generation after the industry began, recalled: "Operation of the boat was simple but back-breaking work. As my partner cast the net over the stern, I pulled the boat ahead until 200 fathoms was stretched out over the water. Once the net was cast we drifted lazily down river with the tide, with the oars stern-first toward the net as the net man hauled in. There was no cabin on the boat, but we had a small tent we could rig up for protection—although it left our legs exposed to the rain. A cut-down five gallon coal oil can answered for a wood cook stove."

Managing a gillnet from a skiff was "no light matter," reported one 1893 observer, "when it is remembered that a salmon net is 300 yards long and that the work of hauling the net includes the killing of each salmon by striking it a sharp blow on the head with a stick. This sort of work all through the long night-watches, added to the discomfort and cramping in the small boat, full deserves the amount paid for it, especially as the unsuccessful nights, when but a dozen or less fish are taken, have to be reckoned with the successful nights, when the nets are hauled in as soon as floated out."

Fishermen worked twelve hours in these conditions, then returned to the camp or cannery while another crew took a shift. As increasing numbers of fishermen built their own boats, payment by piece rates began. Each cannery painted its fleet a distinctive colour to help the cannery tug find its skiffs and to detect fishermen selling to a different canner. Fishermen delivered their catch to large 9-metre scows either at the camp or on the fishing grounds. Once the scows were brimful of salmon, they were towed to the cannery.

When fish were running, canners would put fishermen "on limits," restricting the number of fish the cannery would take from each skiff to avoid an overflow. Although the goal was to pack the fish within twenty-four hours of catching them, fish often waited forty-eight hours and more without cleaning or refrigeration. Much as it pained them to do so, the canners would sometimes have to order catches reduced. On one occasion in the early 1890s, two fishermen in a single skiff landed 1,100 fish in one night, according to Ladner's son. "The cannery crew could not handle all the fish available, even when they worked 15 to 18 hours a day, stopping only for meals. Furthermore, after four days the crew reached the limit of endurance and the cannery reached the limit of its economic operation. The pressure had to be eased." After five months of this the season was ended and the fishermen dispersed, taking whatever cash was left after their cannery store purchases had been deducted.

By 1893, fishermen of all races worked the boats. There were Scandinavians, Greeks, Italians, English, French and increasing numbers of Japanese, but a large number still were native people, whose grandparents might have fled the vigilantes on the Fraser in 1858. "Two sounds I have never forgotten," wrote the younger Ladner, "are the seal's cry at night and the song of the Indian inducing fish to swim into his net. The cry of the seal closely resembled that of a dreaming infant; the Indian's song was a composition of his own—a tune of a few bars, sometimes with improvised words. On a quiet moonlit night, with the stillness so absolute as to be heard, the cry of the seal or the song of the Indian broke through with a suddenness both weird and startling."

The canners treated those who harvested and processed the salmon with no more respect than they did the fish. All early canneries were wooden, single-storey buildings built alongside a dock for landing fish and then shipping the pack. Photos taken inside the earliest Fraser River canneries show large, open buildings, with transmission shafts mounted on the overhead beams. Steam engines turned these shafts, powering long belts to run the machinery. The orderly looking scenes recorded by photographers do not convey the living hell a cannery must have been for crews who worked around the clock in the peak season. Since the amount of fish that could be canned was limited only by the supply of cans and the physical stamina of the shore crew, processing plant workers were driven with a ferocity normally reserved for animals.

At first the entire canning process was manual. Using crews of Chinese workers hired through a labour contractor, the canner would build up an inventory of cans laboriously constructed from sheet tin, each can cut, rolled and soldered by hand. In Ewen's first cannery, fish were butchered by Chinese men, then washed and cut into pieces by crews of native women. More women would fill the cans and then turn the product over to Chinese workers who soldered on the tops, boiled them in tanks, vented them, sealed the vent holes, cooled them and then lacquered them to prevent rust. By 1877, steam retorts had come into general use for cooking. They took larger loads than the tanks and cooked at higher temperatures.

Because of the competing demands of railroad construction, mining, logging and a host of other jobs, canners often faced labour shortages. To overcome them, they resorted to mechanization as often as possible. For the workers, this meant toiling under two whips—the pressure of fish piling up on the dock and the pace set by the machines displacing them from the assembly line. To minimize their labour problems, the canners relied on contractors who agreed to provide workers for a given rate per case of salmon. The contractor was paid an advance and received his final settlement on completion of the pack. The workers were hired on piece rates. After the contractor had deducted housing, food costs, his profit and various other charges at the end of the season, he paid the remainder to the crew, who often ended a season of back-breaking labour deeper in debt than when they had begun.

A brutal pace was forced on all the crews, particularly the butcher workers who beheaded the fish to begin the canning process. "It is not unusual for a Chinaman to clean as many as a thousand fish a day," reported one early observer of the industry, and fillers, the workers who stuffed the salmon into the cans, handled 1,200 to 1,400 cans in a ten-hour shift. By the late 1870s, the first soldering machines were provoking resistance among Chinese workers whose jobs were eliminated. In 1881 canners introduced gang knives, circular blades mounted side by side, which cut the fish into steaks. Thanks to innovations like these, canners increased productivity fourfold between 1877 and 1883 from 240 cases per day with a 130- to 150-person crew to 1,000 cases with a crew of 120 to 140. Ten years later the average crew had been cut to 84, but production remained constant.

Ewen later told a royal commission inquiring into the issue of Chinese labour that "but for cheap labour I do not think there would be so many canneries in existence. . . . More than three-quarters of the inside work is done by Chinese [but] the cost of their labour is less than the other quarter of whites."

Henry Bell-Irving, one of the new generation of canners who gained prominence in 1891, told commissioners that the Chinese "won't strike when you have a big pile of fish on your dock. They are less trouble and less expense than whites. They are content with rough accommodation at the canneries... I look upon them as steam engines or any other machine, the introduction of which deprives men of some particular employment but in the long run, it enormously increases employment."

Native women were equally indispensable to the fortunes of the first canners. An awestruck *Mainland Guardian* reporter toured Marshall English's cannery at Brownsville, opposite New Westminster, in August 1877, and noted the sheds where nearly fifty workers, "mostly Indians," trimmed and cleaned the fish. The dock crews slit the bellies and gutted the fish, then moved the catch to washing tables where native women slimed each one, scraping and scrubbing the interior cavity until it was clean. From the sheds, the fish were moved by handcart to the gang knives. The other inside workers were all Chinese, and "it was wonderful to see the dexterity with which the rows of celestials filled each can to a nicety." A less starry-eyed observer wrote that the Chinese butcher worked "like a machine, without haste and without rest." The 250 Chinese and 50 white and native workers at English and Co. produced 450 cases or 21,600 one-pound (454-gram) tins a day from landings of about 5,000 fish.

"An inspector watched the slimers continually," Ladner's son recorded. "If he saw any sloppy work, he reported it to one of the foremen. Indian women were dealt with by the white foreman and Chinese by the China foreman. Chinese resented a reprimand from a white man unless he had acquired popularity from customary civility toward them. The foremen spoke to the workers concerning any poor practice. If they did not improve, they were put on lower-paid jobs." Chinese workers wore a number and a bookkeeper traced their activities throughout the day.

During their hours off, the Chinese workers were herded into the China house, usually a two-storey building filled with three-tiered bunks. No mattresses were provided; beds were 30-centimetre-wide boards. A small open area served as a dining hall, heated by a wood stove. Cooking facilities usually were limited to a long brick fireplace under a lean-to outside.

When the season was finished, however, the Chinese crews were expelled by the contractors from even these hovels and moved back to Chinatowns in Victoria, Vancouver and New Westminster, where dozens of men were confined to tiny airless rooms and typhoid bred in the open sewers. Unless they could find other jobs, they existed in subhuman conditions waiting for the next salmon season. Until then, the contractor provided sufficient rice for two meals a day. Oolichans, a few greens and whatever could be scavenged rounded out the diet. Scurvy, tuberculosis and other diseases ravaged the shore crews and many succumbed to malnutrition. It must have seemed a bitter irony to face starvation during the winter after seeing thousands of salmon wasted daily during the summer. "Mere words cannot portray a realistic picture of their condition while unemployed," Ladner's son conceded, adding paternalistically that "all the Chinese were fatalistic and patiently submitted to whatever might be their lot, even unto death from malnutrition."

Resistance from the Chinese crews was spontaneous and disorganized. Denied any citizenship rights, isolated by racism and locked in an economic prison of debt and starvation, there was little they could do to challenge the canners, but they never accepted their lot. When new machinery threatened their jobs, they struck, and when a foreman's pressure became unendurable, they brought him into line.

Working alongside the Chinese but in a different world were the native people, who were hired both for fishing and processing. Thousands of native people were drawn into cannery labour, as they were into mining, lumbering and every other industrial activity in the growing B.C. economy. Cannery work, however, was available for the whole family, and entire communities canoed from as far as the Queen Charlotte Islands to work in the Fraser canneries. Canners usually retained native crews through a village boss, but people often changed employers. Unlike the Chinese, they had homes and food to return to if they decided to quit. Native fishermen were paid wages, and their wives and children were employed on piece rates.

Native village boss Charles Nowell later described the hiring system that had its roots in the earliest days of the industry: "I was given authority by the manager to promise the Indians what I would do for them if they came to that cannery. I used to know beforehand what the price of the sockeye would be and I would tell them that I'd give them gumboots free or some rain coats or extra money so that I'd get the good fishermen for this cannery."

Native crews often sought to pit one canner against another before committing their labour. The cannery season allowed close and constant contact among native groups that lived hundreds of kilometres apart, and this close co-operation contributed to united economic and political action.

The first groups to arrive at the Fraser canneries each season were the Chewasin and Musqueam, who lived close by. Later arrivals were from Comox, Chemainus, Cape Mudge, and finally the Skeena, the Nass and the Queen Charlotte Islands. As the canoes grounded on the beach, people would establish their credit at the cannery store and set up camp. "Tents and huts are erected in an incredibly short space of time, a few yards from the river brink," wrote journalist H. H. Gowen, "beds and bedding are passed from the women in the boats to the men on the shore; fires are lighted in such dangerous proximity to the walls of the tents that the absence of a great conflagration is a daily miracle and before many hours there is the Indian encampment as though it had existed for months, with fires burning and dogs barking and fowls cackling and an ancient fish-like smell asserting its supremacy."

Like the Chinese, the native workers wore numbers for bookkeeping purposes. To the gratification of the canners, they even built their own shelter, fashioning houses from split cedar, matting and the odd scrap of tinplate from the cannery. They lived and ate much as they did at home, harvesting salmon, sturgeon, clams, cockles and oolichan.

Around these camps rose towns to pick the pockets of those lucky enough to earn some wages in the canneries. Days off in New Westminster were dominated by the dances, gambling and picnics of the cannery crews; and Steveston, which grew up at the mouth of the Fraser, was a hive of bars, gambling joints and whorehouses that roared into life with the arrival of the salmon and subsided into a rural village at season's end.

Profits from this vast system of exploitation were enormous, and the early canners naturally wished to keep them for themselves. Ewen and Deas treated those who came after them with the disdain that miners reserved for claim-jumpers. In 1874, Deas applied to the federal government for the exclusive right to gillnet on a key stretch of the Fraser, hoping to guarantee his supply of fish against any erosion by new competitors. He lobbied Ottawa for his monopoly until 1878, when better-connected canners ensured that he was turned down. The exchange of letters with Deas awakened Ottawa's Department of Marine and Fisheries to its new responsibilities on the Pacific seaboard. In 1874, A. C. Anderson was appointed B.C.'s first federal fisheries inspector. And in 1875 the Fisheries Act was extended to British Columbia for the first time, but no specific regulations for the province were developed until 1878.

The first restrictions on the salmon industry were mild indeed. Offal was not to be dumped in the river, and canners were to stop fishing for thirty-six hours each weekend to assure that sufficient spawners escaped the nets. The canners carried on as if nothing had happened.

Until 1876, when the canners realized that sockeye could be sold as easily in the United Kingdom as the traditional chinook (or spring) salmon, the big chinooks formed the backbone of the canning industry, as they did on the Columbia. To intercept chinook on the Fraser, many other species of salmon had to be caught as well. All these unmarketable fish were destroyed. On the Fraser, this meant that at least 10,000 sockeye died in Ewen's nets in the month of May alone during the early years of the fishery. Fishermen hunting the big chinooks simply clubbed all other salmon that hit their nets and threw them back dead into the water. Pinks and chums received this treatment for almost twenty years.

Among Anderson's first tasks was defending the canners against indignant attacks from the public over the wasteful plunder of the salmon. In December 1877, a reporter for the New Westminster *Columbian* hoped the government had made Anderson aware of the "wanton destruction of fish life of which more than one company was guilty; that he has heard that as many as 5,000 dead fish were thrown back in a single day because there were no facilities on hand for preserving them; that the salmon were followed to the salmon grounds and there captured; that nets were stretched across the river. . . . We shall be agreeably surprised if the effects of last summer's overfishing (if wholesale butchery can be called fishing) be not felt for many years."

Another writer, who signed himself "Sockeye," told the *Mainland Guardian* in August 1877 that "it has been patent to the most casual observer that in many instances during the present season there has been a reckless waste of valuable fish, a fact which has been fully attested by the presence of floating masses of putrid carcasses which have been polluting every arm of the river from the city to the Gulf. . . . Is it not monstrous that some of our canneries, not content with the plethora of fish with which they have been glutted to overflowing during the passage of the fish up to the spawning grounds, are, with a ruthless vandalism at which every feeling of humanity involuntarily re-coiled, catching them on the banks of which their spawn is deposited?

"This wholesale sacrifice under these circumstances is not only a disgrace to a civilized community but it will also, if allowed unchecked, speedily end in the final extermination of the fish." The gillnet fleet that year totalled only sixty-five boats.

Anderson's investigations confirmed that canners Finlayson and Lane had discarded as many as 3,000 fish a day. He also conceded that Ewen had re-opened the Fort Langley fish station to acquire additional fish from native harvesters, fish taken close to the spawning grounds. It might also be true, he added, that some canners, having acquired unexpected volumes of fish, canned only the belly flaps and threw the rest away. But he warned the government against accepting all public criticisms of the canners at face value. He pioneered in what was to become a fundamental duty of government fisheries officials, acting as official defender and apologist for the canners while facilitating their stampede for profits.

Even the canners soon became worried by the destruction. Despite steadily increasing effort, pack totals fluctuated, probably at this point a reflection of natural changes in abundance rather than of fishing pressure. Fearful of a decline in stocks but determined to avoid any reduction in the harvest, the canners raised a cry for artificial production. "Build hatcheries," they told Anderson, "and we'll pay part of the cost." Later generations of canners would always offer the same solution when confronted with the consequence of their greed. Subsequent cannery kings would draw the line, however, at any financial contribution to the cost of rectifying their mistakes unless they gained ownership of the fish produced.

News of the canners' pleas reached Samuel Wilmot, dominion superintendent of fish culture, who had begun his career as an amateur fisheries biologist in Ontario. Wilmot had proved the feasibility of fertilizing salmon eggs in trays and incubating them until they hatched. The federal government considered that Wilmot had "established beyond all question the entire feasibility of reproducing unlimited quantities of any species of fish which it is at all desirable to multiply beyond the natural facilities afford by our streams and lakes."

When Anderson appealed for a hatchery in his first report, Wilmot agreed that a hatchery would help, but he warned that "a policy for the preservation and protection of fish by setting aside close seasons for the natural reproduction should be most stringently enforced." The Bon Accord hatchery, managed by Thomas Mowat, was established opposite New Westminster and finally went into production in 1884, incubating 5.5 million eggs. Other facilities followed, but the canners came to rue the day they had encouraged Wilmot's interest in their affairs.

Conservation was all very well, but the canners fought tooth and nail against any measures that might increase the number of spawners at the expense of the pack. They had agreed to the thirty-six-hour weekly closure imposed in 1878 because it avoided Sunday labour, but in 1881 they successfully argued for its elimination "to ease strain on the pack" of low sockeye returns. Even in 1884, when a carryover from the previous year was "pressing on the market like a load on a dyspeptic's stomach," fisheries guardians were forced to admit that "a great deal of imperfect fish has no doubt been put up through the hurried and imperfect packing during the last part of the season" as the canners greedily harvested every available sockeye.

Labour shortages during that period prompted the canners to rely even more heavily on the harvest of native fishers up river. Quality was poor, and Anderson feared the practice was an abuse of the "Indian privilege," first legislated in 1877, to take fish for personal food use only, but he did not intervene.

Generally, government officials looked upon the canners with a benevolent eye. The public was assured that the canners were honourable men who assiduously upheld the regulations. Fishery guardian John Buie reported in 1888 that he "found the cannery men willing to comply with all the requirements of the Fisheries Act and when any of their boats were found trespassing I am satisfied it is without their knowledge or consent." On the other hand, it was exceedingly difficult to know what was really going on. Buie and his partner were the sole representatives of the government on more than 110 kilometres of fishing grounds. They patrolled in a pair of rowboats and their fawning praise for those who had appointed them stemmed from the knowledge that those who crossed swords with the canners confronted the most powerful men in British Columbia.

Behind the canners stood a small group of Victoria merchants at the heart of the province's political and economic power. Made enormously wealthy by the gold rush and the subsequent economic expansion, these commission merchants provided the canners with raw materials, financing and access to markets. Although capable of building a cannery and organizing production, the original canners lacked the capital to finance the long period between the acquisition of tin, labour and fish through to the final sale in Britain up to eighteen months later. They relied for additional capital on the commission merchants, both in San Francisco and Victoria, who did very well for themselves in the process. Canner Henry Doyle noted that the agents "made a profit on what supplies they furnished to canners; on transportation charges on the ships they chartered; and they were paid a net 2½ per cent brokerage fee of what the pack sold for if sent abroad or five per cent on Canadian sales."

The magnitude of the profits produced by the industry can be seen from the experience of investors who financed the Gulf of Georgia cannery in Steveston in 1889. The cannery was built on credit of $4,000 advanced by an agent that year. They packed 13,716 cases of sockeye in their first season, paid all debts and sold the cannery to Anglo British Columbia Packing for $35,000. During the same period, the commission agency of Finlay, Durham and Brodie bought four canneries, operated them for a season, bought a fifth cannery and declared a 50 per cent profit on the year's operations.

By 1881, American commission agents controlled 30 per cent of the Canadian canning industry. Evans, Coleman and Evans of San Francisco, the American arm of a British group, financed a number of firms, but R. P. Rithet, British Columbia's great finance capitalist, and Robert A. Ward, another Victoria commission agent with a brother managing the Bank of B.C., advanced from offering credit to canners to investing directly. Rithet linked up with Ladner's Delta Canning, while Ward, originally a Rithet employee, moved into agency work for Ewen's canneries and ultimately to the presidency of the first B.C. canners' association.

As the financial assets of the canners multiplied, their demands for protection from the cold winds of reduced profits grew louder. In 1888, the Victoria Board of Trade recommended the introduction of a licence scheme to limit the fishing effort on the Fraser. The canners' gambit was not a new one. Licences for fishermen had been issued since 1877, primarily to the canners who owned the bulk of the fleet. In 1882, after a fluctuation in profits, the Victoria Board of Trade had proposed that licensing be put under the control of a board of "the vested interests, to be run for their own protection."

Fearful that public concern about overfishing, offal and waste of fish would force the government's hand, the canners met in September 1888 with cabinet minister Mackenzie Bowell. The canners were anxious to "protect the rivers from overfishing," the board's Robert Ward, himself a canner, told Bowell. Was it possible, Ward inquired, to limit the number of canneries? The canners' proposal was far-reaching. Not only should the numbers of canneries be limited, they said, but only 500 gillnetters should be licensed for the Fraser. These licences were to be issued to the canners on an equal basis, 40 boats per cannery. Only 40 would be reserved for independent fishermen.

Unfortunately, Bowell replied, a control on the number of canneries would be restraint of trade. Instead, he suggested, the department could regulate "the number of fishing boats on the river." Restraint of capital would be unconscionable, but restraint of labour simply made good sense. As Henry Doyle commented later, "the canners, having sufficient for their own requirements, wanted the total of [gillnet licences] so limited that no newcomer could engage in the salmon canning business." Thus was conservation prostituted to the service of profit.

To maintain and advance their efforts, the canners decided in December 1888 to form the B.C. Fisheries Association. Its aim was simple: to preserve the profits of the industry. As if in answer to the canners' prayers, the salmon stepped in where Tory politicians were temporarily unable to assist. The runs that year set a record, and some canners ran out of cans.

A remarkable 1889 photo of the pioneer cannerymen shows Ewen seated at the centre of a small group on a cannery store boardwalk, his legs crossed casually and his hands folded in his lap. On his left are E. A. Wadhams and D. J. Munn, one of Ewen's partners in the 1880s. On Ewen's right are Marshall English and Ben Young, sometimes called "The Salmon King." Ranged behind are T. E. Ladner, J. A. Laidlaw and some lesser canners who never played a prominent role. J. H. Todd, the perennial outsider, is not present.

For nearly a generation, the canners and their backers mined the salmon resources unfettered by any regulation or public control. The only power great enough to curb them emerged from the industry itself. To their annoyance, the canners learned that the workers who made the industry's wheels go round not only had different ideas on how the salmon should be harvested but also possessed the political clout to make their interest felt. The ten men on the boardwalk were meeting to devise some means of retaining control of the resource on which their fortunes were built.

3

THE REVOLT OF THE

FREE FISHERMEN

ON 24 MAY 1889, A FEW DOZEN FISHERMEN CROWDED INTO a small New Westminster meeting room to debate what was, for them, a life or death issue. Just weeks before, the Tory government of Sir John A. Macdonald had announced sweeping changes to the fisheries regulations, ostensibly designed to assure the conservation of salmon runs. Licences, which formerly had been issued freely, now would be limited to only 450 for the entire Fraser River, and all but 100 of these were to be issued to canners. The regulations threatened disaster for more than two hundred men who made their living fishing almost year-round. If the new rules were allowed to stand, more than a hundred of these "free fishermen" would be forced to work under the canners' thumb or quit fishing.

The men who met in New Westminster that evening were determined to confront the canners. From their small gathering grew a movement that within four years would force fundamental changes in the management of the industry. The struggle over who should control the wealth of the salmon had been joined.

Small cities now stood at New Westminster and Vancouver as well as Victoria, cities capable of absorbing substantial quantities of fresh salmon. Even more important was the rail connection with the east. Refrigerated cars could carry frozen spring salmon to the restaurant tables of Montreal and New York within ten days of the harvest. To feed these new markets, a new kind of fisherman had developed, a man with his own boat whose season began with the arrival of the spring salmon and ended when the snow flew. By the end of the 1880s, between a hundred and two hundred fishermen earned their living in this manner, selling to fresh fish dealers in the spring and fall, and delivering to the canneries when the sockeye ran.

For the first time, the canners saw part of the fishery move outside their control. The independent fishermen wanted secure sales contracts and demanded improved prices. When fish were bountiful, the canneries could flood their floors with the production of their own boats. But when fish were scarce, the production of the independent boats was crucial. The existence of the "free fishermen" created the first competitive price pressures among canners, who were used to paying only the absolute minimum cost for fishing labour to acquire raw product.

As new canneries rose along the river, the economic and political power of these independent fishermen began to grow. They had the vote and they used it. More importantly, they were vitally concerned not just with this year's profit but with the future of the industry. When the Tories imposed the new regulations to "conserve" the fish, the fishermen took action.

The new regulations reflected both the lobbying of the canners and growing public anger at the canners' pillaging of the runs. The many farmers who now worked small plots along the Fraser were outraged by the annual flood of putrid salmon offal that filled the river's sloughs and back-eddies. Blame for a typhus outbreak in 1887 was laid at the canners' door, but their political power seemed impregnable. Public concern about overharvesting was also brushed aside. One fisherman warned in the *Columbian* early in 1889 that the legislated canners' monopoly threatened to produce "an aristocracy equal to the codfish aristocracy of Boston."

The canners had tried to quell the public's anger by urging "conservation measures" to limit the numbers of independent fishermen. The effect of such restrictions would be to assure the catch to those canners who held fishing licences. But the Macdonald government, influenced by the clamour for stronger protection of the run, had included some other new rules in the legislative package. Particularly shocking for the canners was the decision to enforce long-standing controls on the dumping of offal and a new regulation restricting gillnets to only one-third of the river's width.

Even more obnoxious to the canners was the government's decision to extend the old thirty-six-hour weekly closure—the only absolutely effective conservation measure—to forty-eight hours. "This weekly closed time is unnecessarily long," declared the canners, who believed such an extension would threaten the foundations of society. "It conduces to laziness, gambling and drunkenness, diminishes the profits of all parties, etc., etc."

Although the new regulations threatened a loss of some fish to canners, they implied a direct loss of livelihood for fishermen. The 24 May meeting marked their first serious effort to fight back. Fishermen James Wise and J. E. Lord led the discussion. Employment was a fundamental concern, they said, but conservation came first. They threw down the gauntlet to canners and fisheries officials who claimed to be vitally concerned about conservation. Let the government completely close fishing seaward of Ladner's Landing, the meeting agreed, and begin "better regulating the time and place for fishing."

As they compared their experiences on the issuance of new licences, the fishermen became even more outraged. Fisheries inspector Thomas Mowat had already disposed of all but 7 of the independent licenses, issuing 44 to early season fishermen, 12 to freezer companies and 37 to native bands. This left only about 10 fishermen out in the cold, he said. The fishermen knew otherwise. Almost 100 had been thrown out of the industry by Mowat's back-door dealings, and their protests reached Ottawa. The government, sensitive to the political winds, directed Mowat to issue an additional 50 licences. Organization had produced its first victory for fishermen.

Appalled at the uproar, the Tories then retreated further. The regulations were suspended for one year. In 1890, the limit of 500 boats was implemented, with 150 reserved for fishermen and 350 allocated among canners. New canneries were to receive licences based on their working capacity as determined by the inspector of fisheries. Last, but not least, the doughty Samuel Wilmot, Canada's foremost fish culturalist, was dispatched to hold a one-man royal commission of inquiry into the entire issue of licence limitation. The fishermen's protest had saved at least 50 jobs. Now they were asking a more basic question. Why should the canners have any licences at all? The canners, for their part, had been adjusting their strategy as well. Realizing their dream of a private preserve on the Fraser was not to be, they devised a new means to ensure a continued control of the catch.

The canners' campaign had begun months before in the quiet board room of the Victoria Board of Trade, where men like R. P. Rithet and Robert Ward considered their options. Despite the increased effort of the past ten years, the pack on the Fraser had declined. There had been 734 gillnets licensed for the Fraser in 1886 and 935 in 1887, yet the pack stubbornly had failed to increase. Early in the decade, eleven canneries had shared in the 199,000-case bonanza provided by the runs of 1882. An economic depression and poor runs had pushed the industry down to six canneries and only 38,437 cases just two years later. By 1886, the number of canneries had once again begun to climb, but the pack failed to keep pace.

Eleven operations shared 99,177 cases in 1886, and by 1889 there were sixteen canneries ready to work. From Sacramento, where uncontrolled gold mining had stripped the spawning beds, came news of catastrophic declines. Even the mighty Columbia showed signs of strain under the relentless assault of gillnets, traps and fish wheels. The canners had a gnawing fear that they were slaughtering the goose that was laying their golden eggs, but their fears were coloured by a record pack of 303,875 cases in 1889.

Wary of the new political clout of the fishermen, the canners used the moratorium on new regulations to amend their position. Conservation of fish seemed less urgent. Let fishermen have all the licences they wished, the canners' association said, but preserve a guaranteed share for the canners. It was a cunning move. A limited group of independent fishermen would have economic power when runs were weak. But if their numbers were unlimited, they would compete to undercut each other. As an added bonus, they provided their own boats and nets. Never again, the canners calculated, would fishermen be able to hold them to ransom.

Into this boiling pot of intrigue stepped Wilmot, with all the strengths and weaknesses of a man who has seen his personal obsession with the artificial rearing of fish turn into a building block of government policy. Hailed as the father of artificial propagation for his hatchery experiments with Atlantic salmon in Lake Ontario, Wilmot knew nothing of fishing and surprisingly little about Pacific salmon. He believed, for example, that all Pacific salmon were of a single species, like the Atlantic runs, and often erroneously suggested that Pacific salmon, like their Atlantic counterparts, could spawn several times. He arrived in New Westminster at the peak of the 1890 sockeye runs, the second boom year in a row for the canners. He owed the canners nothing, however, and his unvarnished account of the slaughter on the Fraser was a public relations catastrophe for them.

Seventeen canneries were at work between New Westminster and Steveston that year, handling up to 150,000 fish a day. "The extraordinary quantities of salmon that were being caught . . . would be quite beyond the conception of anyone unless he had been an eye-witness to the prodigious numbers that were delivered at and pass through these canneries daily," Wilmot wrote in his report. He was also astonished by "the wholesale and wanton waste that is going on in throwing away as offal such a vast quantity of rich, wholesome fish, food which ought and might be made use of profitably for human food."

A coloured diagram included in his report showed how little of a sockeye was canned: everything forward of the belly and rear of the vent was discarded, thrown away with the guts through a hole in floor to pollute the river. When times were tight and runs poor, the canners would extract 2 to 2.3 kilograms from a 3.2 to 3.6 kilogram fish, Wilmot said, but when runs peaked they were satisfied with only 1.8.

"The question arises," Wilmot continued, "why should such a sacrifice of fish food be allowed to gratify the avarice of the packers and the fastidious taste of the wealthier class of consumers?" In 1889, he calculated, the year after the canners had declared a crisis of "overfishing," the destruction of fish fit for canning was equivalent to 277,489 sockeye of a total catch of about 2.9 million, or almost 10 per cent of the landings.

Wilmot further inflamed the canners by ridiculing their regulatory proposals. To increase the number of cannery licences would "simply mean that the department would be aiding the avaricious fishermen to destroy in a greater degree the reduced stock of salmon entering the river," he told the minister. He recommended a 500-boat limit, an annual closed time, a ban on dumping of offal and a limit on the number of canneries. He did not recommend the issuance of cannery licences.

The Wilmot report satisfied no one. It underlined the problems of the industry but ignored the fundamental economic problem of who should control the sale of raw fish. The canners put enormous pressure on fisheries minister Charles Hibbert Tupper to ditch Wilmot's report altogether. The aggravated Tupper, under siege by enraged canners and fishermen, ordered Wilmot to perform his task once more, this time as a full royal commission with the assistance of two other commissioners with links to the canners. Wilmot also was directed to hold public hearings in fishing communities.

Wilmot's hearings of 1892 gave voice for the first time to the independent fishermen challenging the canners' rule over the resource. They demanded open entry to the fishery for "bona fide fishermen," those with a real connection and commitment to the industry. Against the canners' monopoly, they counterpoised a licensing system based on true conservation and protection of employment. Access to the fish would be open to all who qualified, and conservation would be assured by closures and gear restrictions.

The fishermen told a tale of staggering abuse of the resource and scandalous manipulation of the licensing system. Dummy canneries had been erected to obtain extra licences, they revealed, and fisheries officers had collaborated in a racket that forced fishermen to pay large sums for the right to fish. Significantly, the first witness to testify was Ewen's former partner, James Wise, who told the commission that "when the free people on the banks of the Fraser could not catch a fish at their own doors, why we might as well be in Russia or Ireland or some other country of that description. There is nothing in another other part of Canada or the states where a monopoly is given to the few like here."

William Costigan had attempted to obtain an independent licence from Mowat and been refused, but learned it could be purchased in a tavern for $50. A fisherman on one of Ewen's cannery boats testified that the industry patriarch contracted to pay his fishermen 50 per cent of the price of the fish, generating 10 cents a fish for the fisherman when sockeye were worth 20 cents. On a season's catch of 3,400 fish, then, Ewen received effective rent of $340 for a boat and licence "not worth $100."

Even the base price was fixed, fishermen charged. "The canners every year meet and have an understanding and they bind themselves not to give over a certain price for the fish," said George Holliday. "Of course, they have command of the river, seeing they have almost all the licences." John Stevens, a native of Greece resident in New Westminster since 1882, demanded "justice for the fishermen. The last three years the canneries have had control and fishermen have had no rights at all." (Stevens's grandson, Homer, would make a similar case seventy-five years later as president of the United Fishermen and Allied Workers Union.)

The fishermen, white and native, demanded unlimited entry and abolition of cannery licences. To maintain the cannery monopoly, the native fishermen said, would force them into work that paid only $1.50 a day.

The canners declined to answer the fishermen's charges. They had become arrogant after two years of unprecedented profits produced by unexpectedly bountiful runs. Mowat had reported in 1891 that "the canners have reaped a rich harvest during the past four years. If their own statements in this respect can be relied on, each cannery made from $15,000 to $75,000 per season; "still, with all their advantages they do not appear satisfied because the regulations framed by the department did not allow them to fish just as they wished, regardless of future results."

The canners found it difficult to maintain the pretence that they were interested in conservation, but Wilmot, stung by the abuse he had received for his first report, pressed the canners on the issue. Under questioning, D. J. Munn conceded that Wilmot was right—up to one-third of the fish was thrown away. The previous year, he acknowledged, one canner had used a dummy cannery to acquire licences that produced $20,000 worth of fish. The fraudulent cannery had cost only $5,000 to build. Canner Peter Birrell said he favoured an annual winter closed season "because there is no fish to be had" at that time. "Very generous," Wilmot commented dryly. Ladner said flatly that he believed it "impossible to overfish the river," a sentiment shared by Ewen, who now declared there never had been a scarcity of fish. Munn, one of Ewen's partners, complained that any requirement to dispose properly of salmon offal would be "tantamount to forcing us off the river." Marshall English opposed proper control of offal because of stories he had heard that salmon bred in the waste. Wilmot dismissed him as a fool.

In stark contrast was the testimony of Charlie Caplin, chief of the Musqueam, who testified through an interpreter that "the nets are too long and it stops the salmon from going up and has a tendency to kill them all. . . . It will destroy the salmon in time."

On 14 March, Wilmot concluded his second tour of the industry with a river cruise on the steamer *Robert Dunsmuir.* In a quick meeting in a stateroom,

Wilmot hashed out his recommendations with his fellow commissioners, whose sympathies for the canners were reflected in Wilmot's report. Regulations for disposal of offal, closed time and so on were quickly decided along the lines the canners proposed. Conservation was not discussed. All agreed that there should be no limit on the number of licences and that canneries should be guaranteed at least 20 "tied" licences each. (The government later raised this number to 25.) "I don't see what the fishermen have to do with it," said David Higgins, a member of the commission, who was editor of the Victoria *Colonist*. "They are like trade associations everywhere. They have no sympathy with capital at all, while capital feeds them." As a sop to fishermen, the commissioners agreed to limit licences to "bona fide" fishermen only, a term they never clearly defined.

It was a pyrrhic victory for the fishermen. For the big years, the canners retained their core fleet of contract boats. In lean years, unlimited numbers of "independent" fishermen would bid against each other to sell their catch. The canners had not achieved the absolute ownership they sought in 1888, but they won something almost as good. As the cost of harvesting fish rose, they hurried to turn the burden over to fishermen. Wage rates gave way to piece rates, and cannery boats gave way to "independent fishermen" working under contract. Even more boats were built by canners for rental to fishermen who acquired their own licences.

The implementation of Wilmot's report sparked a new rush for fish, this time through the expansion of the fleet. In 1892, the number of licences jumped from 500 to 721. Cannery licences increased from 350 to 417, and individual licences from 150 to 304. In 1893, canneries owned 909 of the 1,174 boats working on the river.

The fleet's growth, which was to be even more dramatic by the turn of the century, responded to a basic economic law. Profit could no longer be assured by expansion of production, because the size of the run was fixed by biological factors. Individual canners' packs could only be increased by greater competition for existing stocks. This required more boats for more intensive fishing. But the increased capital investment eroded profit. The canners, therefore, shifted the burden of boat ownership over to fishermen in a process that continued for the next ninety years.

As long as the canners controlled the market for the raw fish, fishermen were welcome to the freedom to provide their own boats. Fundamentally, however, their economic relationship to the canners was unchanged from the days when they were paid wages to fish cannery boats.

With the power of the fishermen apparently curbed, the canners turned to the other side of the question—too many canneries. By the spring of 1891, a round of mergers and consolidation was well under way. Individual canneries were merged into larger organizations, often with coastwide operations. J. H. Todd held two plants under his command, the Ewen group had five, and Victoria Canning, which united Ladner and Rithet, controlled the production of several more. Rithet, Ewen, Todd and B.C. Canning, a British company, controlled the Fraser with the exception of the plants owned by Anglo–British Columbia Packing; ABC, as it was called, was the creation of Henry Bell-Irving.

It was Bell-Irving who had the foresight and determination to make the fishermen's charge of monopoly come true with a corporate coup. Ewen had won his pre-eminence because of his skills as a "practical canner." Bell-Irving moved to the front ranks because of his understanding of finance capital. A British engineer and merchant who had emigrated to B.C. to work on the CPR, Bell-Irving was a tireless financier and corporate organizer. After settling in Vancouver, he parlayed his inheritance into a considerable fortune by riding the real estate boom and investing in a grocery business that built up a healthy import and export trade.

His introduction to the fishing industry came when he organized the first direct shipment of canned salmon around the Horn on the steamer *Titania,* which had been about to return empty after delivering rails from England. Struck by the opportunity to make a profit, he began to research the industry. As a broker with United Kingdom backers, he was perfectly situated to assemble the industry's largest combine. In November 1890, he began acquiring options to purchase individual canneries. His proposed company was to include Marshall English's operations, B.C. Packing and Wadhams's plants, as well as Garry Point and North Pacific on the Skeena. He estimated he needed $410,000 in capital.

In 1891, Bell-Irving formed Anglo–British Columbia Packing and began to acquire assets. First he wisely obtained a commitment from the deputy minister of fisheries that no increase would be allowed in Fraser licences, effectively eliminating the prospect of new canneries. He retained Tory MP Gordon Corbould as his lawyer to cement his political ties. He then acquired options on nine canneries and sold them to ABC for $330,000, retaining for his personal profit the lucrative and less risky commission sales business. Two more plants came later. By 1893, the new combine was complete. It included two Skeena canneries and six canneries which accounted for 70 per cent of the Fraser production, making ABC the largest sockeye producer in the world.

On 1 July 1893, Bell-Irving was able to host competitors like Munn, Todd, Ewen and English at a meeting in his office to establish labour rates and prices. They agreed fishermen paid wages would be given $2.25 a day. Independent fishermen would be paid 6 cents a fish if offal regulations were enforced, 7 cents if they were not. In 1892, the price had been 10 cents a fish.

This new ability to cut prices resulted not only from the canners' own strength but from growing divisions among fishermen, divisions based on race.

The warnings of a river monopoly had come true. Confronted by a united group of canners, fishermen had to organize as well. As open entry caused the number of independent fishermen to soar, the size of the cannery fleet tumbled. In 1893, the canners had controlled 909 of 1,174 gillnetters registered on the Fraser. By 1899, they owned only 460 of the 2,722 boats licensed, and in 1900 their fleet fell to 450 out of 3,683 working the run. Many of the new fishermen were Japanese immigrants. From a handful of boats in 1893, the Japanese fleet rose to 452 vessels in 1896 and a staggering 1,655 in 1897.

The fishermen quickly understood what Ladner had grasped in 1893, that unlimited access to the fishery doomed fishermen to a cutthroat struggle among themselves—unless they organized to present a common front to the canners. On 20 May 1893 they formed the Fraser River Fishermen's Protective and Benevolent Association. A key plank in their program was elimination of the Japanese fishermen, but there were more legitimate demands as well: a tax on imports of fish from American traps, elimination of cannery licences and a ban on American fishermen on the Fraser. Their goal was also to maintain sockeye prices and to win an increase for wage-earning fishermen from $2.25 to $3 a day. The contract fishermen, as the "free fishermen" now were called, elected Alex Anderson as their first president.

The movement to trade unionism was spreading throughout the Pacific Northwest, fanned by a long depression and by the harsh attacks on wages and working conditions launched by the growing combines and trusts spawned by America's exploding capitalist economy. Fraser River fishermen were well aware of the experience of the Columbia River fishermen, many of whom fished in American waters off the mouth of the Fraser. The struggle to unionize the Columbia had begun in 1877, and strikes that year and in 1885 had been broken only after violent confrontations. The Columbia River Fishermen's Protective Union, formed in 1880, had struck successfully in 1890 to raise the price of chinook salmon from $1 to $1.25, but victory had come only after pitched battles with firearms. By 1893, the Columbia River men were again organizing to challenge the Astoria canners, who were undercutting the fishermen with the production of traps and fish wheels.

In British Columbia, the unionization drive was sweeping the marine industries. Deep-sea sailors, sealers and fishermen confronted the same bosses. Rithet, for example, who bankrolled Ladner, had interests in sealing and Hawaiian sugar. He shared shipping investments with Robert Dunsmuir, Vancouver Island's iron-heeled coal magnate, who in turn had links with Robert Ward, a prominent canner and sealing schooner owner. Given the similar skills required in deep-sea shipping, sealing and fishing, it was not surprising

that the call to union organization struck a responsive chord in all three industries. In the fishing industry alone, more than 1,600 fishermen and boat pullers had responded to the union drive by the time the FRFPBA was formed. In
the entire maritime industry, between 3,000 and 4,000 workers had organized, an impressive total considering the province's entire non-native population stood at less than 100,000.

The new fishermen's union faced a formidable challenge. The hundreds of
new licences issued since the end of limited entry had gone largely to new immigrants, including several hundred Japanese fishermen. Although the white
fishermen who helped organize the new association made an easy alliance with
the native fishermen, they disdained an offer of unity from the Japanese fleet.
In fact, they made oriental exclusion a key policy of their union, a concession
to the racism then endemic in the labour movement. But division on ethnic
lines was an evil they could ill afford. Once the canners became aware of its existence, they were able to exploit it with devastating effect.

With the main runs not due until mid-July, the canners and the fishermen
manoeuvred for an advantage. The union's demands were studiously ignored.
Ladner expected the unlimited licensing scheme to save the canners. He was so
confident that he had urged a fixed price of 6 cents, not 7 cents as proposed by
Bell-Irving. On 7 July, Ladner gloated at the prospect of even steeper cuts.
Prices were cut to as low as 4 cents.

Bell-Irving heard from English on 11 July that "the Fisherman Union is
playing the devil," and he promptly took steps to organize strikebreakers. "I
called on Mr. Kito, Japanese consul," he wrote in his diary, "and asked him to
find out where I could lay my hands on a number of men on short notice." Six
days later, Kito brought good news. He said he could "furnish 130 fishermen
at short notice—three days—and 200 more if required, little longer notice."
Bell-Irving then sat down to draft an advertisement offering a $50 reward for
information leading to the arrest of anyone participating in "any combination
or conspiracy to raise the rate of wages."

On 13 July, Birrell, Ewen, Ladner, English and Bell-Irving met to develop
their strategy. "Decided to ignore fishermen's association and maintain same
prices," Bell-Irving recorded. The strike began the next day, but the canners
took heart from a telegram sent by J. H. Turner, the provincial finance minister, a veteran of the gold rush and a frequent financier for the mining and canning czars of the province. Turner vowed to "back us up all he can re strikers."

The fishermen, having recruited as many as 100 native gillnetters to their
ranks, voted to strike. They tied up on 14 July for ten long days, fighting
scabs, police and virulent attacks in the press, which termed the strikers "Columbia River men, Italians and other foreigners . . . the riff-raff of all nations." To break the native fishermen, the canners advanced their wages 10

per cent, then sent in the Indian agents in an effort to force them back to work. Most held firm, as did several hundred Japanese fishermen and boat pullers. The whites could not make the same claim. The canners hired scabs, and slowly the strength ebbed from the strike.

The canners withstood the union's main demands but were forced to hold the sockeye price at 7 cents and to increase wage rates. Far from disintegrating, the union affiliated with provincial labour bodies and fielded 300 marchers for the 1893 Labour Day parade. The experience chastened the canners, whose easy contempt for the union was replaced by fear.

The 1893 strike established trade unionism in the fishing industry. From the FRFPBA to the union of today there is an almost unbroken line. A new voice, albeit a faltering one, had joined the debate over the future of the salmon resource. Although the fishermen were divided along race lines and lacked any links with the shore workforce, their strike proved that the canners' combine could be resisted.

For the time being, however, the canners reigned supreme. When public protest against the dumping of offal continued in 1894, fisheries inspector John McNab, who had replaced Mowat in 1891, hired W. M. Galbraith to investigate enforcement of the existing regulations. Galbraith's report, which was suppressed and remains buried in fisheries department files, stated that in two months of investigation he had "never seen a fishing boat properly marked on the Fraser River." As far as offal was concerned, "none of the fishery regulations had been enforced." The Fraser was the canners' gold mine and their sewer.

To contend with the wholesale poaching organized by the canners, the department would need at least five steamers with bulletproof pilot houses, five rifles each and net guards on the props, Galbraith said. In reality there was a single fisheries guardian with two helpers for the entire period from 1 March to 31 October. They had a single launch in July and August only.

The flamboyant Marshall English managed seven canneries, Galbraith learned. Despite repeated convictions for violations of regulations and notwithstanding cancellation of all 40 licences for Phoenix and Britannia canneries, English fished his entire fleet all season. Bell-Irving was licensed for 33 boats at Steveston but fished 74. The fine for fishing 70 boats in one case had been only $5.

Moreover, Galbraith learned, McNab himself had advised the canners of an undercover detective in their midst. In fact, McNab had instructed Galbraith to ignore cases of illegally marked boats. When Galbraith proved overzealous, McNab dismissed him.

In his report, which finally wound up on the desk of James Gaudin, master of the Department of Marine and Fisheries vessel *Quadra*, Galbraith told of the testimony of a fisheries guardian named Green, based in Ladner: "Mr. Green informed me that it was never intended that the regulations should be enforced as I enforced them, that no man could afford to do it, for if he did he would make an enemy of every man on the river and be driven out of the country."

No one with any integrity who came close to the canners could stand their greed for long. Charles Hibbert Tupper, who laboured hard for the canners as federal fisheries minister from 1888 to 1894, told a friend in 1894 that "the more I have striven to meet their [the canners'] views, the more savage have been their attacks upon my department and myself." The department had yielded to the canners repeatedly, Tupper complained, but still they were not satisfied, rejecting even a twelve-hour extension in the closed time.

"Poor Mr. Ladner's factories put up 864,000 one-pound cans in 1892 and only 2,760,682 in 1893," snorted Tupper. "Mr. Ladner had three canneries before I began annoying him, but in 1890 he undertook a fourth. This one packed 180,000 one-pound cans in 1892 and 862,400 in 1893. Mr. Ladner has a short memory when he seeks to place upon me his real grievances, which are that fish do not retain their remunerative price."

So the cycles of salmon continued, the three off-years building up to the fourth-year tidal wave of sockeye that spelled the big years: years of nets sunk from the weight of fish, canneries overwhelmed, scowloads of salmon left to rot in the sun, and Fraser River banks alive with maggots erupting from the ankle-deep offal of millions of slaughtered fish. More boats were launched, more nets were set, more efficient machines roared in the canneries, more hatcheries were built, more fish were harvested, canned and sold, but still the industry was failing by the one yardstick that mattered—fish did not retain their remunerative price.

The flood of fish produced an industry wracked by failure. Profits and wages declined. To their fleets of gillnetters, the canners added traps, then purse seines, then more gillnetters. More investors crowded to the trough, adding more canneries, yet more fishing gear and more bankers to satisfy. The canners' incessant efforts to raise their profits were forestalled time and again by the independent fishermen, whose growing numbers and political clout offered a source of supply for new canners and a political counterbalance to the canners' Ottawa and Victoria connections. It was the fishermen who offered real conservation measures when the canners sought only to increase the catch, and it was the fishermen whose political power twice denied efforts to return the sockeye to the tight control of a monied elite. The battle was joined almost as soon as the 1893 strike was resolved.

Chastened by the struggles of 1893, the canners sought by whatever means available to restore their control over harvesting and to reduce the cost of fish.

With the economic advantages of new canning technology temporarily exhausted, the canners looked instead to new and cheaper harvesting technology, particularly salmon traps. Highly productive, based on exclusive leases and operated with small crews, traps offered fertile possibilities for profit, political jobbery, monopoly and strikebreaking.

Trap technology was relatively simple. A barricade, often over 900 metres long, was attached to piles driven into near-shore waters. This long lead— sometimes a pair of leads designed to funnel fish to the trap—intercepted the salmon and drew them into shore. Once at the open end of the leads, the salmon swam into the heart, a holding area from which there was no escape. This heart opened into a still smaller enclosure called the pot, from which the salmon could be brailed or dipnetted directly into scows for the trip to the cannery. If desired, the heart could be closed off and the salmon diverted back to their migration.

Despite the initial high capital costs, well-located traps were tantamount to a guaranteed share of the run. Where traps were operated, no fish escaped. Unlike gillnets, which permitted the passage of small fish, traps harvested everything moving along the shore, a marine equivalent of clearcut logging.

Salmon traps exploited the industry's growing knowledge of the route of the sockeye on their return voyage to the Fraser's mouth. In their homeward migration from the Strait of Juan de Fuca to the mouth of the Fraser, the sockeye runs swing to the south side of the deep channel between Vancouver Island and the Olympic Peninsula, threading their way through the San Juan Islands and spilling into Puget Sound. In 1885, an American entrepreneur established a trap at Point Roberts, the tiny chip of U.S. territory which dangles from Canada into Boundary Bay from the 49th paralel at the very mouth of the Fraser. The salmon runs, following the shore in their search for the river mouth, could be guided by long barriers into the heart of the traps and harvested at the owners' leisure.

According to Doyle, E. A. Wadhams and Daniel Drysdale were the true pioneers of the trap fishery at Point Roberts, investing the proceeds from the sale of their B.C. assets to ABC Packing. By doing so, they undermined both the conservation of the runs and the profitability of the Fraser canneries, but they proved that capital knows no borders, particularly in the salmon industry. Both were making good money by 1893, when Drysdale had a net return for the season of $75,000, a huge sum for that era. He sold out the same year to the Alaska Packers' Association (APA) for $300,000, a sum that the APA later claimed to have recouped in the profits of three years' operation.

For the owner, a trap was a licence to print money, but for the public it became a symbol of corporate control of the salmon resource, particularly in this period of growing public outrage at the depredations of monopolies and trusts.

The debate over traps revolved around several themes elaborated with greater effect almost a century later by salmon farmers. The canners appealed to government to disregard the unemployment and monopoly control which could result from traps. This new technology was essential to remain competitive, they argued, and to maintain a place in world markets by reducing the cost of raw material. They listed the ostensible conservation benefits, conjuring up images of canners who took only what they required, releasing the surplus to spawn and ending the dreadful waste of daily limits in the gillnet fishery. Finally, they said, these traps were necessary to ensure that Canada received a fair share of a Fraser catch increasingly harvested in U.S. waters.

The Canadian canners' demands might have prevailed if enough trap locations had been available for all. But only a few dozen lucrative locations were available in Canadian waters because the runs tended to hug the American side of the Strait of Juan de Fuca. The political weight of fishermen played a decisive role as well. Against the pleas of the trap owners, the fishermen argued in favour of public ownership of the resource. They offered alternative conservation measures, if that was what the canners wanted, which protected jobs and the salmon. They exposed the catastrophic destruction of fish runs by traps which ran night and day, regardless of market demand or cannery capacity. They urged the use of less destructive technology, including purse seines and deeper gillnets, to meet the competitive challenge of American traps.

Samuel Wilmot counselled against issuing trap leases for sites along the south shore of Vancouver Island, warning the minister that they were "of such magnitude and so grasping in their character as to cause serious caution and consideration. It would appear to be most impolitic and suicidal for the general public in relation to the salmon wealth in B.C. to favour these applications." Charles Hibbert Tupper concurred, but he was motivated more by concern for the interests of canners located on the Fraser than he was for the public interest. Those canners who relied on gillnets, he feared, would be wiped out. As a result of his ban, some Fraser canners, notably Bell-Irving, established their own trap operations at Point Roberts. Friends of the government found that the ban on traps was flexible. By 1896, Point Roberts and Boundary Bay were studded with twenty-one traps, including two in Canadian territory. Rithet and Bell-Irving were granted the two leases for the Canadian waters of Boundary Bay by Liberal fisheries minister Louis Davies to "place them on a more even footing with their neighbours across the line," but bids for leases farther seaward were rejected out of concern "for the general welfare of the salmon industry and the protection of the fish."

To placate canners who were denied the right to establish their own traps, the Canadian Boundary Bay leases were declared to be "experimental" only. The leases were a constant irritant to fishermen and to Bell-Irving's competitors, but his clout in Ottawa was so great that a brief audience with Sir Wilfrid Laurier and Louis Davies in 1897 secured their renewal. This political patronage infuriated the public and became a potent symbol of the graft and corruption which attended exclusive fisheries licences. These "experimental permits" were continued even after Davies declared a general ban on traps in B.C. waters in 1900.

The secure position of Fraser canners was further reinforced by tariffs and export controls, which compelled fishermen to deliver within the province, while assuring canners access to fish produced by U.S.-based traps.

In the big years, the traps drove the price of fish down sharply. In 1900, the cost of sockeye from Puget Sound traps was 2.5 cents a fish at a time when American gillnetters were paid 12.5 cents. The catching capacity of some traps grossly exceeded processing capacity. One operation took as many as 70,000 fish in a single day.

"It was a sight never to be forgotten when the winchnet tumbled its load after load of magnificent silver fish full of life and energy onto the deck of a scow," a friend told Davies in 1901. "Now and again there would be a huge spring salmon of say 50 or 60 pounds weight, but nearly all were sockeye, averaging 6 or 7 pounds." The Alaska Packers' Association plants at Blaine, Washington, handled the production of traps capable of landing 125,000 fish a day. "The catch of one good American trap, which takes at most six men to look after it, is equivalent to 150 Fraser River boats employing 300 men." Yet there was no fear of depletion, the canners swore, so long as the government kept building hatcheries.

While Canadians struggled over control of the industry, an increasing share of the runs was being taken by Americans. By the turn of the century, one canner estimated that 60 per cent of the Fraser River run was taken in traps. The Puget Sound fishing machines swallowed enormous volumes of fish, hundreds of thousands of which died in the traps because the canneries were glutted. American canners turned a blind eye to the dreadful waste, reasoning that a fish they killed could not be canned and marketed by Canadian competitors.

The hungry Canadian canners responded in the only way they knew how, with hundreds of new boats to scour the river for every available fish. Despite the increased competition, prices fell as fishermen undercut each other. B.C. gillnetters, hoping their daily catch limits would be dropped or unenforced, often overfished and added to the slaughter. In many cases, Canadian canners were unable to handle the domestic gillnet catch because they had imported trap fish from Puget Sound.

As the fish traps chewed away at the runs, the length of the sockeye season began to decline. "In former years, salmon used to enter the Fraser River in separate and distinct runs," Henry Doyle told fisheries minister Louis

Prefontaine in 1903. "Sometimes two, sometimes four or five runs would occur in one season from July 1 to August 25. . . . With the advent of trap fishing, however, all this was changed. The numerous obstacles encountered [by the salmon] checked the progress of the early runs until they were joined by the later ones and thus today our catches are all made in practically ten days' time." Far from delaying the early runs, the traps were destroying them, leaving only the largest ones with enough strength to survive the onslaught. This biological fact, however, was disregarded by most in the industry.

By 1901, almost 10 per cent of the B.C. pack was made up of fish purchased from U.S. traps. The pressure on the runs was compounded by the growing American commitment to purse seines, which mopped up fish missed by the traps. From a single American trap in 1885, the number grew to 21 by 1896 and 120 by 1899, most of which operated all season. The frenzied expansion of fishing effort produced the paradox of downward pressure on fish prices paid to fishermen at the same time that canners' costs in B.C. were rising. The decline in prices paid to fishermen was not enough to make up for the costs of cannery expansion and a host of other factors. The industry spiralled down into deeper crisis.

The increase in fishing effort was matched by an increase in the number of canneries, from fifteen in 1887 to forty-seven in 1899. The canners found it difficult to process all the fish available, but as their numbers expanded they greedily bid against each other for a secure supply. Fishing effort doubled and then tripled the 1893 level by the end of the decade, but the average catch per boat fell so sharply that price increases could not make up the lost income. Canners were in a similar squeeze. The bidding war drove up the cost of raw fish while the price of canned salmon dropped. The result: fishermen's earnings crashed because of low catches, and canner's costs skyrocketed because of competition for the catch.

The fishermen's initial efforts to control access to the fishery met with some success. Laurier's government accepted their proposals to restrict licences to British subjects resident in Canada but balked at demands to eliminate cannery licences. Determined to counter the fishermen's growing political strength, the canners organized a new united front. The B.C. Salmon Packers Association, later called the Fraser River Canners Association, was created in 1898. Only three canneries were not represented. The new effort quickly bore fruit. Although they saw the cannery licences reduced to ten per plant, the canners were able to defeat the rule restricting licences to bona fide fishermen. The result was more licences than ever in 1899.

Fishermen responded with a reorganization of their own. Abandoning the moribund Fraser River Fishermen's Protective and Benevolent Association, New Westminster fishermen formed the B.C. Fishermen's Union in 1899.

4

COME BACK WITH

YOUR GOLDEN CLOTHES

I believe the working of the people in unison is the meaning of assimilation.

—HOZUMI YONEMURA,
*Japanese Fishermen's Association,
in testimony to the Duff Commission,
14 August 1922*

BY 1900, A WAVE OF ANTI-ORIENTAL SENTIMENT WAS SWEEP-
ing the province, fuelled by the arrival of several thousand new Asian immigrants, many actually destined for the United States. A deep well of racism
had been developing in B.C. society for some time.

The first Japanese to immigrate to British Columbia became a fisherman.
Manzo Nagano jumped ship in New Westminster in 1877 at the age of nineteen and soon found work gillnetting on the Fraser with an Italian partner. He
was the first of a wave of immigrants from the poverty-stricken and heavily
populated southern prefectures of Japan.

Between 1887 and 1900, the total number of Japanese immigrants to B.C.
was fewer than 5,000, of which about 2,000 worked in the fishing industry.
The conditions of their arrival, however, and the industries in which they
found work magnified their impact. Many had left Japan with the firm intention of returning when their fortunes were made. This dream of an early and
wealthy return was epitomized by the common farewell which families to gave
their emigrant men: "Come back with your golden clothes."

"The only things they brought with them were hope, ambition and good
health with a natural aptitude for work," wrote Japanese-Canadian researcher
Regenda Sumida who met some of these pioneers. "The only welcome they received was from the capitalists, who desired all the labour they could get out
of them. They encountered unexpected opposition from the labouring classes
and a great deal of contempt from the middle classes." Most spoke no English
whatsoever, and added to their sense of isolation "was the feeling of loneliness
and nostalgia which arose from the strange customs, the strange food, the
strange environment and the strange language."

Not surprisingly, the Japanese congregated where work and community support were available. Steveston, then a hamlet on the banks of the Fraser dominated by a string of canneries, quickly became a centre for the Japanese in the province.

Life for the immigrant men was arduous and lonely, even in the tiny Japanese world they created in Steveston. There as elsewhere, the labour contractor or house boss offered the only quick and certain prospect of employment. An honest one could make an immigrant's life much easier, but the boss's own livelihood depended on how much fish he could compel his men to produce. "The boss controlled 20 or 30 boats," Asamatsu Murakami, a veteran of this system, told Daphne Marlatt decades later, "and a Japanese boss talked to the cannery about lending or buying nets and gear for the fishermen. The boss was responsible, very responsible for them. If a fisherman got into debt, the boss had to pay it off. So he had to be careful to eliminate bad habits like drinking, otherwise he lost money. None of the men had wives then, they were all single. And as there were no women, they'd get wild. Just a few drinks and they'd start a fight. I saw a lot of fights. Some men killed each other, some were put in jail."

The Japanese were condemned by their white counterparts for their low standard of living, but they had no choice. On their meagre earnings they were supporting themselves, repaying the debts incurred to labour contractors and sending precious dollars home to those who had financed their trips. The boss charged for everything—food, clothes, even for handling their mail. In the words of Ken Adachi, whose chronicle of the Japanese Canadians remains the pre-eminent history of these people, "the immigrant was a chattel."

Once the salmon season was over, money was scarce in the bunkhouses used by the Japanese fishermen. Some became expert boat-builders, recovering driftwood from the Fraser to cut their planks. Others cut cordwood for the canneries, cleared land or produced shingles on contract. Some explored new fisheries disregarded by the white majority, trolling off the west coast of Vancouver Island or seining chum salmon for the salted salmon markets of Hokkaido. A salt herring business was established, and a handful of the immigrants, the resilient Manzo Nagano among them, accumulated modest wealth. Most lived for the salmon season, though, with the bang of the Marine and Fisheries gun at Garry Point setting off a roar of cedar corks going over the sides of 1,000 gillnetters.

The licensing requirements established in the fishing industry in 1892 limited the fishery to British subjects. But a Japanese immigrant resident for three years in Canada could apply for a naturalization certificate, which opened the door to a fishing licence. These naturalization papers became, in effect, a job ticket, and the subject of endless controversy when evidence emerged that they were passed from hand to hand or even sold to fishermen who could not obtain them legitimately. There were frequent accusations that federal officials issued the papers on a wholesale basis to undermine union organization in the fishing industry, a charge heatedly denied by the department.

Standing behind the labour contractors and over the entire Japanese community was the consul, whose role as guardian and overseer was a reflection of the special trading relationship created between Great Britain and Japan by the Anglo-Japanese Treaty of 1894. That treaty, which prohibited each side from discriminating against the nationals of the other, originally exempted Canada from its provisions, a fact which enabled Canada to deny Japanese the vote in 1895.

The legislation that stripped Asians, natives and East Indians of the right to vote was strongly supported by the labour movement, even though it removed from Japanese fishermen the single most important tool white fishermen had used to secure some emancipation from the canners. The consequences of the law were far-reaching, because many professions, even hand-logging, were open only to those with the right to vote.

Convinced that Asian workers could not be organized, labour supported laws like the Alien Labour Act, passed by B.C. in 1897 and later disallowed by Ottawa, which would have banned Asian labour on any construction work conducted under provincial jurisdiction.

Despite the profound divisions that existed between Japanese and their white and native counterparts, tenuous bonds of solidarity were created by the experience of life in the industry. Although Bell-Irving could call on the Japanese consul during the 1893 strike to simplify the task of finding scabs, several hundred Japanese fishermen stood by the whites until the bitter end of the same dispute. In the midst of the 1900 strike, when a sudden storm threatened to destroy boats pulled up along the dikes, white and Japanese fishermen worked side by side to avert disaster. Yet, it is easy to imagine the fear and confusion the threat of a strike must have created in recent immigrants whose chief source of information was labour contractors or the all-powerful consul.

The Japanese, many still expecting to return home, were products of the profound changes reshaping their homeland. Their philosophy lay in the future. A Japanese fishermen would work hard "for future peace or security," Rintaro Hayashi, a prominent leader of the Japanese fishermen of a later generation, told Daphne Marlatt. "He sacrifices his present for that so he accepts having a hard life." This philosophy was reinforced by the Japanese fishermen's complete dependence on the canners. Since they lived year-round in cannery housing and were dependent on their cannery account for food, fishing gear and even a licence, "they could not protest against whatever price the cannery might announce."

5

AT LIBERTY TO FISH AS FORMERLY

Once
All *the land was theirs*
And now a little space
Of their vast inheritance
Had been picked out for them
By the white men
But even on this spot
They were not FREE
To fish and hunt
After their ancient manner
Because of white men's law!

—ARNIE, *"God and the Millionaires,"*
newspaper clipping, possibly the
Seattle Times, *May* 1920

BY MID-JUNE 1900, STEVESTON'S POPULATION ALREADY
was swelling from its winter level of 400 to 500 to its summer peak of almost
6,000. The China houses were full, their crews working round the clock to
prepare cans for the coming season. Along the waterfront, Japanese and white
fishermen were preparing their nets and readying their boats. At Scottish Canadian cannery, which lay at the very mouth of the Fraser River, all was in
readiness. Hundreds of cords of firewood lay stacked behind the cannery to fire
the boilers. Heaps of charcoal for the stoves of Chinese and Japanese workers
were piled behind the bunkhouses. Tanks of lye had been prepared for cleaning gear, and hundreds of kilograms of rice and other food had been stored for
the summer. In the can loft, thousands of hand-made one-pound (454-gram)
tins rose in ranks almost to the ceiling. Soon the salmon would start running,
but anxious eyes watched the Strait of Georgia for the signs of the workers
whose labour would be critical to the season's success—the native men and
women who were travelling to the canneries from a score of coastal villages.

Ed DeBeck, who later became the province's superintendent of brokers and
clerk of the legislature, was one of the white shore crew who paced the docks
that spring waiting for the arrival of the native workers. Finally a lookout
spotted sails to the north. "Here they came on a flood tide," he wrote many
years later, "bowling along ahead of a westerly wind, great canoes 50 feet and

over, spread to an eight-foot beam, each with four sails wing on wing. Some came all the way from the Skeena, but most were Kwakiutl." The shore crew counted twenty-four canoes in the flotilla, twelve large ones and an equal number of 40-footers (12 metres), all packed with men, women, children and dogs. Half of the fleet passed the cannery and continued upriver, but a dozen of the canoes turned toward the cannery dock. "In the last few hundred yards, sails were lowered and they started singing Indian songs until they got to five or six yards from the wharf. With a final shout, a sudden silence. Dead silence for about a minute. Then the biggest chief stood up and, with speaking staff in hand, made a short speech. A sudden stop, a barked order and then all hell broke loose, every paddle clawing water to sidle the canoe up to the wharf." The children poured ashore first, desperate to stretch their legs after a day and a night afloat. The canoes had made the run from Cape Mudge to the Sand Heads in twenty-four hours, the paddlers told the shore crew, a total distance of 210 kilometres. With favourable winds, the entire passage from Prince Rupert or the Queen Charlottes might last less than two weeks.

In 1900, native fishermen on the Fraser stood at a turning point in their people's history. Before that date, native labour and skills had made the industry possible. After that date, native men and women had to struggle to retain any place in the wealth-producing machine they had helped to create.

Only about 420 native people then had licences of any type for the commercial salmon fishery on the Fraser. Twice as many whites were licensed, and three times as many Japanese. By contrast, in 1880, more than 600 native people had gillnet licences, twice the number fished by whites, and no Japanese had set a net. Still earlier, in the days of the Hudson's Bay Company salt salmon trade, literally thousands of native people had participated in the harvest, working according to their own system of fishing rights and privileges.

The assault on native rights, both aboriginal fishing rights and the right to equal opportunity for employment, had begun in earnest with the first conservation crisis of the 1870s. It gathered momentum as the chaotic expansion of the industry reached its first limits in 1900. As always in the fishing industry, the argument was cloaked in the rhetoric of conservation, and as always, it was really about money. The native people had fish, and others wanted it. Since the others were the most powerful members of white society, they got it.

The early canning industry had offered native people an economic windfall. Participation in the fishery and in cannery labour fitted in with a seasonal round that included work in other fields as well as their traditional fisheries in August and September. The canners not only provided the gear, they also paid for the fish, often using connections to important chiefs to secure their labour supply. There was no interference with the traditional fishery, and where native people could find a market, they did.

Problems did arise, however, when the canners' wanton destruction of fish provoked public outrage and Ottawa extended its fisheries jurisdiction to British Columbia in 1875. For Ottawa's agents in the province, the resolution of conflicts between Canada's fishing laws and the rights claimed by native people was the most difficult and delicate issue they faced. They sought a pragmatic solution which recognized both.

The conservation battles began in earnest in 1876, when Finlay, Durham and Brodie managed to put up a pack of 4,122 cases of one-pound (454-gram) cans in their 1876 season, enough to reap a $24,800 revenue but equivalent to only about 90 000 kilograms of fish. This harvest, miniscule by modern standards, provoked a storm of controversy in the communities along the Fraser. Public opinion was divided, with some convinced that the stocks were inexhaustible and others that they were on the brink of collapse. The canners sought a middle course, suggesting that runs were good but that any problems could be traced to the fishing activities of the native people. The appointment of A. C. Anderson as the province's first federal fisheries overseer and the extension of the federal Fisheries Act to the province were designed to calm the fears of the alarmists. Although the canners could count on Anderson to heap scorn on those who predicted doom if the industry expanded, they could not compel him to agree that the native fishery posed a threat to anyone, least of all the fish.

Anderson had come by his opinions through a lifetime of experience on the coast, first as an employee of the Hudson's Bay Company and later as a member of the first commission charged with establishing native reserves. In his second report, published in 1878, Anderson heatedly defended the canners from "the most palpable exaggerations and misstatements," among which was the claim that one company was "even pursuing the fish to their spawning grounds and molesting them there." This company, in fact, was Ewen and Wise, which had reopened the Fort Langley buying station "with a view of obtaining, from a wider area, a sufficiency of fish to meet their requirements." This harvest undoubtedly was taken in native fisheries, which Anderson defended even more energetically than he did the canners.

Protection of aboriginal fishing rights was a cornerstone of Anderson's policy. He wrote to the minister in Ottawa, "The exercise of these rights, unfettered by wanton or ignorant interference, is to many of the tribes an object of prime importance; and as a matter of expediency alone, omitting entirely the higher consideration of the moral claim, their protection demands the earnest care of the Government." In his capacity as a member of the Indian claims commission, Anderson attempted to ensure whenever possible that hereditary rights to various fishing spots were protected. He urged Ottawa to pass legislation declaring that the Fisheries Act "as modified to suit the exigencies of this Province, shall not be deemed to apply to the Indians working to supply their own wants in their accustomed way."

Anderson enclosed the views of Indian superintendent I. W. Powell, who warned that the expansion of the canning industry "excites much talk among the Indians of white people monopolizing their favourite fishing grounds. . . . Stringent regulations to prevent the destruction of spawning grounds, and to provide for the proper protection of Indians in the possession of certain fishing places—considering themselves as they do, the sole owners of all such localities—should be made."

The policy proposed by Anderson and Powell was pragmatic and realistic. They assumed that native people would continue their aboriginal fisheries as before, selling the fish as necessary for personal subsistence, but would substitute participation in the canning industry for the commercial and trading aspect of their traditional harvests. The policy seemed workable and common sense. It failed because it relied on good faith on the part of the national government.

There were four main reasons for the immediate collapse of Anderson's proposals. First of all, it was to be implemented unilaterally, in the absence of any comprehensive negotiated settlement of rights, particularly as to land. As a result, aboriginal fishing rights existed at the sufferance of officials in Ottawa, not because of any acknowledged legal obligation. Secondly, the policy relied on a distinction between subsistence and commercial fishing which seemed obvious to whites but which seemed absurd and contrived to native people. Thirdly, it assumed that traditional fishing spots would be identified and their associated rights confirmed. Such fishing spots were identified in many cases, but tribal groups never were granted exclusive rights of any sort. In cases where the rights were granted by reserve commissions, they were later repudiated. And finally, the promise of jobs was immediately betrayed. It never had much relevance to Interior bands far removed from the canneries of the coast, but even coastal peoples soon found themselves marginal workers in an industry they had helped to found. Within a generation, they found their existing rights under assault and their access to the new industry reduced and then nearly eliminated.

The attack began almost before the ink was dry on Anderson's memorandum. Although both Anderson and Powell had received strong backing from Ottawa in their efforts to see reserves enlarged and fishing sites protected, provincial politicians were blocking their efforts at every turn. In 1876, while Anderson was supervising the extension of the Fisheries Act to B.C., the provincial government simply evaded the land question. Later, however, British Columbia denied the existence of aboriginal rights.

The expansion and development of the canning industry forced Anderson to clarify his policy on traditional fisheries almost as soon as he developed it. By 1878, conflicts between white and native fishermen were occurring coastwide. In August of that year, Anderson was "duly authorized to suspend the application [of the Fisheries Act] in regard to the Indians of fishery regulations." Up to that time, Anderson had ordered his officials to leave native fishers strictly alone "save in cases of obvious abuse, while fishing for their own use in their accustomed way." At the same time, he ruled, where native people were "fishing with white men and with modern appliances, the Indians so fishing should be considered as coming in all respects under the general law."

From an administrator's point of view, Anderson's distinction was simple common sense. When native people fished as native people, using traditional locations and gear, they would not be restricted. (Even their right to trade and sell the catch was taken for granted.) When they fished as workers, however, delivering to the canners, they would be compelled to submit to the same restrictions everyone faced in that fishery.

Early in 1879, Anderson forwarded to fisheries minister James Pope a copy of a provincial publication which summarized all the relevant documents concerning the land question. "I would willingly quiet the alarm of those zealous agitators . . . who contend that the untrammelled exercise of the aboriginal fishing rights must necessarily cause the ruin of the fisheries," he wrote. "These objectors are oblivious of the fact that, up at least to the advent of the white man, the fisheries through the Province were admittedly unimpaired." The release of the provincial documents, including the Douglas treaties, had convinced Anderson of something else: "In my opinion, the exercise of the aboriginal fishing rights cannot legally be interfered with." Quoting Douglas's pledge to allow native fisheries to carry on "as formerly," Anderson urged the government "that the Indians of this Province be formally exempted, by Order in Council, from the application of the general fishery law. In this way their position will be publicly understood; and the risk will be avoided that, in some remote part of this wide region, some over-zealous official may, through ignorance, be tempted to misapply the intention of the law as at present authorized, and thus originate troubles which it will be more easy to excite than to allay." Despite Anderson's prescient warnings, Ottawa declined to act.

By the autumn of the next year, Anderson felt compelled to intervene when canners began the large-scale purchases of fish caught in the native fishery far above tidewater at New Westminster, the limit of legal operation of the gill-netters. Such commerce opened "a wide field of abuse," he warned, but the abuse was by canners seeking to evade the closed time, not by native people. The earliest instances of enforcement of the ban on sale were always where cannery competition was the harshest, especially on the reaches of the Fraser fished by Sto:lo communities between New Westminster and Yale.

A year later, Anderson advocated, with the canners' support, the creation of a system of licences "whereby effective control of the salmon fisheries may be maintained." His estimation of the importance of aboriginal fishing rights had changed as he trimmed his sails to the political realities. After years of insisting on the importance and moral necessity of acknowledging such fishing rights, he now portrayed them as a legally meaningless way of securing the native people's co-operation. Native fishing stations should still be secured, he argued, especially at locations "on which they are largely dependent for subsistence." From a commercial point of view, these locations were largely worthless, he said, but "to the Indians themselves the confirmation of a prescriptive and to them a valuable right is not therefore the less pleasing." Rights that Anderson had once advocated as a moral imperative were now to be freely granted where the "principles they conferred are nugatory"—entirely worthless.

As a result, the federal government pursued a policy that was completely contradictory. On the lower Fraser, generally the area downstream from Hope, direct sale of fish taken in native harvests was suppressed. It continued unhindered on the upper Fraser, on the Nass and parts of the Skeena. In locations such as Alert Bay, where seine leases were granted on native fishing spots, both sides were assured that their rights were unimpaired and the employment of native workers on the drag seines usually resolved the potential conflict.

The pressure for action against the native people intensified in 1888 when the pack declined. The downturn sent a chill through the industry. In Ottawa, where the collapse of the fabled runs of the Sacramento and Columbia was well known, it seemed time for firmer measures. The government amended the Fisheries Act to spell out for the first time some conservation measures to protect the salmon fishery. "Fishing by means of nets or other apparatus without leases or licences from the Minister of Marine and Fisheries is prohibited in all waters of the Province of British Columbia," the amendment began, "provided always that Indians shall, at all times, have liberty to fish for the purpose of providing food for themselves but not for sale, barter or traffic, by any means other than with drift nets or spearing."

From an administrative point of view, the law seemed straightforward. If the canners were to be controlled, they had to be denied access to fish taken during closed periods. From a native point of view, however, the law contradicted reality. As historian Reuben Ware has noted, "in the traditional social systems of the Indians in British Columbia, there was no distinction between 'food fishing' and commercial fishing. . . . The same techniques were used and the same social practices took place during both 'food fishing' and commercial fishing." Native chiefs, sensitive to any encroachment on their rights, not only rejected limits on their right to trade and sell their catch but also categorically refused to accept any licensing system.

Many canners on the coast had quietly accepted this state of affairs. On the Nimpkish, a twenty-one-year lease granted to a Mr. Hudson by the colonial government was not recognized by the Kwakiutl, but they willingly sold their catch to the "lease-holder" and both parties co-existed happily. Similar arrangements prevailed at Lowe Inlet, where the local canner simply hired the native people to harvest his catch and life went on.

This calm atmosphere was shattered, however, when Ottawa's fisheries guardians set out in their skiffs to collect licence fees. On the Nass, where two canneries were flourishing, guardian John McNab wrote that "the chief very gravely informed me that I had done wrong in collecting money for fishing on the Nass without having asked permission from him, that the river belonged to him and his people, that it was right that white men should buy licences, but that he and his people should receive the money, that they were entitled to have it all." The Nisga'a chief, evidently a reasonable man, offered to let McNab keep half of his fees for his troubles and let him off with a warning. It was the same on the Skeena, where people at Hazelton defied the regulations and sold their production to the canners, who welcomed it eagerly.

The Nass remained a hotpoint for several years, with threats of gunplay in 1889, but the fears of depletion that had provoked the first efforts at licensing soon gave way to euphoria at the news the runs were recovering. This improvement the authorities had no doubt was due to Samuel Wilmot's hatcheries. On 1 June 1892, licences were extended without limit to bona fide fishermen who were British subjects. Any resident settler was granted the unrestricted right to fish for personal use.

While the regulations seemed to equalize the rights of native and non-native fishers, they in fact confirmed the secondary status of native people. Denied the vote, denied the right to pre-empt land and rejected in their efforts to achieve a comprehensive land claims settlement, they lacked the political clout to resist the coming restructuring of the industry.

The canners had always been careful to ensure that proposals for licence limitation were tailored to sustain the dependency of native fishers. They argued for retention of their attached cannery licences on the basis that such licences ensured native participation in the industry. This understanding of aboriginal rights became a constant theme of the canners for more than a century. When Wilmot toured the river in 1891, canner D. J. Munn urged retention of cannery licences because "our Indian labour must be given employment. They are the best kind of labour we can get. They come and bring their families with them and these latter—their women and children—find employment inside the cannery." Alexander Ewen declared it was "impossible to put up a large quantity of fish . . . unless you have Indian labour."

The cut in attached cannery licences that accompanied the regulation changes in 1892 fell very heavily on native fishers, who united with their white counterparts to demand an entirely open fishery that ended canner control. Chiefs who testified at Wilmot's inquiry not only insisted on full access to the commercial fishery but deplored its impact on the runs. Charlie Caplin, chief of the Musqueam, who testified the same day as Munn, protested the government's refusal to grant independent licences to native fishers, which left them subject to the wage-cutting of the canners. "He grumbles also about the depth of the nets; he thinks they are killing salmon too fast down at the mouth of the river," his interpreter told Wilmot. "Ask him if the salmon are scarcer or more numerous than years ago," Wilmot said. "He says they are nothing now to when he was a boy," the interpreter replied.

The local Indian agent testified that of 3,500 to 4,000 native people who normally participated in the Fraser fishery, either as fishermen or boat pullers, only forty obtained licences in the first limitation. After earning $600 to $1,000 as fishermen, those expelled were now reduced to wages of $1.50 a day in the cannery, the agent told Wilmot, an indication of why the canners were so enthusiastic about that aspect of the new policy. Wilmot's subsequent report did nothing to ease the shortage; native fishermen, most of whom lived elsewhere on the coast, remained dependent on the canners, who very quickly began to replace them with Japanese fishermen subject to even harsher controls.

The Fraser native groups found themselves fighting a rearguard action to retain their right to fish at all. In 1894, the government had introduced food-fishing permits, which native people were supposed to possess to fish for personal consumption. Non-natives did not require a recreational or food-fishing permit at this time. Despite intense protest, this new restriction was imposed on the lower Fraser to control the time, location and quantity of native fishing. The pressure was greatest where settlement and urban development were most advanced.

A poignant but typical case was that of the Coquitlam band, whose reserve adjoined the Coquitlam River. In 1899, Chief Johnny learned of two threats—a dam and a proposal by local sport-fishing interests to create a private reserve on the river. "If our fishing is stopped, we can't live," he wrote in an appeal to the minister of fisheries. "We are all loyal subjects of the Queen and would like to be given a chance to live honestly and comfortably and if the creek is taken from us it will be very hard for us. It is like a man taking the food out of our cupboard. The creek is our storehouse." In desperation, he sought compensation of $3,000 a year for his band of thirty. No reply is recorded in the department's files.

It was the same on the Cowichan, where a battle over the native use of fishing weirs began in the early 1880s and was fought out for more than a generation. Leading the onslaught on the Cowichan were sport fishermen who wanted the native harvest eliminated. Although native rights were curtailed and then largely eliminated in order to conserve the salmon running to the Cowichan, exclusive purse seine leases were granted in 1907 to friends of the government and logging began in the headwaters during the same period.

The 1895 protest of the Cowichan people could serve as a summary of all that would come. "We claim that the fish is our property," the people wrote to Ottawa. "We own it by natural right and therefore we consider as unjust all Government Regulations depriving us totally or partly of that right. Our history proves that we do not destroy the fish. On the other hand, it is evident that the white population does destroy it. The protective regulations then should embrace the white people only, not the Indians. We do take fish for our own daily use, to have a living, and we make use of all the fish we take; the white population on the contrary, takes fish mostly for pleasure's sake and usually destroys the small fish by throwing it away."

One native response to these pressures was trade unionism. Throughout the bitter struggles around licensing, native and white commercial fishermen made easy alliances in which the white fishermen often acknowledged the native people's broader concerns for aboriginal fisheries.

6

THE GREAT STRIKES

ON ANY NORMAL SUMMER SUNDAY AT THE TURN OF THE CEN-
tury, more than 3,700 gillnets hit the water as the salmon fleet went to work
on the Fraser. On 8 July 1900, however, only a handful of the gillnet skiffs
had left the dock. As they set their gear, they quickly were surrounded by
other boats bearing a large number 25 on their sails and were driven back to
shore. This intensive picketing soon established the authority of the new B.C.
Fishermen's Union over the river. From now on, union pickets told the scabs,
there would be no fishing until canners promised sockeye prices of 25 cents a
fish. The canners' nightmare of a fishery closed by strike action had come to
pass.

The 1900 strike and the equally hard-fought struggle of 1901 marked the
eruption of open warfare over control of the fishing industry. It seemed that no
amount of salmon could break the economic prison the industry had built for
itself. Caught between rising costs and declining revenues, canners and fishermen confronted each other in a desperate test of strength.

During the seven short years since the first Fraser strike, the industry had
been transformed. The rapacious chaos of the industry's first generation had
been replaced by a much more sophisticated and automated exploitation of the
resource, backed by finance capitalists in distant money markets like London
and Toronto, a change that was reflected throughout North American industry. The same deep currents influenced the labour force. In 1893, a handful of
"independent fishermen" had confronted an informal alliance of "practical
canners." By 1900, fishermen's illusions of independence were long gone. The
thousands of fishermen who tied up that year believed themselves to be "bona

fide fishermen," full-time workers who relied on the industry for their livelihood and demanded a measure of security and justice.

Confronting them was a new breed of canners drawn from the province's growing class of industrialists, men like Henry Bell-Irving, whose ability to match old country money with frontier investment opportunities made him more concerned about next year's dividends than with the next generation's supply of sockeye. Although Bell-Irving organized and led the canners against the fishermen, the struggle produced two new corporate leaders, Henry Doyle and William Barker, a pair of Americans who helped build B.C.'s biggest canning company.

If Bell-Irving, Doyle, Barker and their shadowy bankers epitomized the corporate side of the industry, Frank Rogers, Will MacClain and Charles Durham represented the new currents among the workers. Of the three, Rogers was a longshoreman, MacClain a machinist and Durham the only fisherman, but what they lacked in fishing experience they more than made up in their ability to express the aspirations of fishermen and to weld together the organization that would work towards those goals. Rogers, in particular, had a vision of the fish as the common resource of working people.

Both active in the socialist movements of the day, Rogers and MacClain were at the centre of an explosion of industrial union organization that was sweeping the province. It was indicative of Rogers's insight and principles that he steadfastly opposed exclusion of Asians from the fishing industry and the union, although that demand was a cornerstone of labour council and labour party programs in that period. A magnetic speaker, slender, fair and mustachioed, Rogers was a scourge of B.C.'s ruling class until felled by a strikebreaker's bullet in the back in 1903.

In April 1900, when news trickled north that Puget Sound canners would pay 28 cents a fish for sockeye, B.C. fishermen were outraged to learn that their canners proposed to offer only 20 cents, a 5-cent cut from the 1899 level. Even that figure was later reduced. The battle line was drawn. Both canners and fishermen well knew that prices that year would determine how much fishermen could expect in the massive big year fishery due in 1901.

The creation of the B.C. Fishermen's Union ignited organizing throughout the Fraser Valley and as far afield as the Skeena. Within a few months, locals of the union had been established in Vancouver, New Westminster, Steveston, Ladner, Eburne, Port Simpson and Canoe Pass. All were affiliated to the Vancouver Trades and Labour Council and the national Trades and Labour Congress. A key figure in the early organizational drive was customs officer J. H. Watson, a Vancouver Labour Council executive member and a prominent Liberal, who espoused the Asiatic exclusion policy then prevalent in the labour movement. But leadership quickly passed to others who rejected division on race lines. Alliances were forged with the Japanese fishermen. Native Indian fishermen were enrolled in the new union's locals on the basis of full equality, usually according to tribal group. These new alliances, however, proved hard to maintain.

The native workers who listened carefully to their chief's invocation at the Scottish Canadian dock in 1900 were in for a very difficult summer, in large part because of the regulatory changes which were ending their role in the industry. It was clear that only one group in society now had an inalienable right to fish, and that was the canners. Those actually doing the fishing, in this case, were the canners' Japanese workers, whose economic dependency on the canneries was absolute. Their numbers had risen from a few hundred in 1893 to several thousand by 1900, almost entirely at the expense of native fishers. The number of licences held by natives fell from 850 in 1896 to 423 in 1900, a period in which the number of Japanese licences rose from 782 to 1,804.

"They regarded fishing as their inherent and aboriginal right and reacted violently to any encroachment on it," wrote Percy Gladstone, the historian whose work has done the most to highlight the role of native people in the commercial fishing industry. "Their hostility, directly largely against the Japanese, led them to align themselves solidly with the white fishermen and was the major reason for the role of Indians in unionism." This hostility was not initially racist, although that was its result. The Grand Lodge of the new fishermen's union included native locals in Port Simpson, Cowichan and other communities which relied on the Fraser for employment in the industry.

It is important to note that white fishermen largely understood and supported the native standpoint. As early as 1893, when organizers had sought native support for the Fraser River Fishermen's Protective and Benevolent Association, aboriginal fishing rights had been acknowledged. During the formative days of that union, an organizer who signed himself only "E. R." reported on his activities to the *Coast Seamen's Journal* of San Francisco. He wrote that "the white fishermen, seeing that their organization without the Indians, who have the primary right to fish, would hardly be in a position to cope with the cannery men, are trying to get the Indians to join." Throughout the 1890s, white fishermen always supported native demands for access to fishing licences, and both native people and whites shared hostility to the Japanese.

When the union's demands for negotiations were ignored, fishermen set 8 July as the deadline for the strike. Both sides dug in to await the confrontation. The strikers had to overcome a decade of deep-seated racial animosities in the fleet to consolidate their organization. When the deadline arrived, fishermen were united as never before. On that first day of the strike, they poured from the docks and netfloats into a meadow for "a monster meeting such as had never been seen in the history of Steveston." Chief Kelly of the Tsimshian reminded the white fishermen of their collapse in 1893 and pleaded with them not to betray the native fishermen again. Addressing the crowd from atop a stack of cordwood, Rogers vowed that "force will not be used unless it is necessary, but no fish will be sold below the price set by the union." The Japanese had promised their support to the strike, Rogers said, but heavy picketing must continue. The fishermen then marched from cannery to cannery, addressing Japanese fishermen at each float through interpreters. Picket boats were dispatched from Mission to the Strait of Georgia and, notwithstanding Rogers's promise, the handful of scabs they discovered "were handled so that the fishing industry did not interest them for the rest of the season."

Under Bell-Irving's direction, the canners adamantly refused to talk. With the fish not yet running, they hoped the strike would exhaust itself. But union organization and picketing were formidable. Strike kitchens in Steveston, supplied by fish caught under permit and by donations from small businessmen, fed hundreds of workers a day, particularly the hard-pressed Japanese fishermen whose supplies had been cut off by the canners the moment they joined the strike.

After seven days, the canners were forced to alter their position. Through E. F. Bremner, of the federal Department of Labour, they offered to hold the price of 20 cents and reduce it to 15 cents only if the run was heavy, taking all fish caught without imposing boat limits. The proposal was soundly defeated in votes by the Japanese and by union members. By the end of the second week of the strike, the strikers' demands had been modified. They sought only a fixed price for the season of 20 cents, the right of independent fishermen to deliver to any cannery, and equal boat limits for cannery and independent fishermen if limits were imposed. The canners countered with only 15 cents across the board.

For two weeks, the canneries sat silent. Individual canners threatened to close for the season, arguing the impossibility of earning a profit at 25 cents a fish. By 22 July, the canners' mood had changed from resignation to menacing anger as the peak of the run approached. The canners were "indignant at the lack of protection" offered to strikebreakers, reported the Victoria *Colonist*, which issued an editorial broadside demanding government intervention. A telegram on 21 July from canner W. A. Duncan to the federal fisheries minister reflected the changed mood: "For 14 days a system of intimidation has existed on Fraser River. Agitators and others openly interfere with such as venture out, throwing their fish overboard and threatening them with firearms. Absolute contempt exists for all authority." He demanded government action, but Ottawa quickly passed the appeal to Victoria. To the canners' outrage, the provincial authorities resisted the call to arms. One canner told the *Colonist,* "We expect bloodshed before the strike is over."

A mass meeting of the strikers the next day showed they were in no mood to settle. In an open field by the Steveston Opera House, more than 1,500 gathered to hear addresses from Rogers and MacClain. Then fishermen were separated from the crowd and asked to vote for the price they would settle for—20 cents, 22 cents or 25 cents. As hundreds watched from the sidelines, the men marched up, marked ballots and placed them in the chairman's hat. "Among the loitering crowds at one side," a reporter for the Vancouver *World* wrote on 22 July, "was a collection of what appeared to be half the Indian population of British Columbia. They sat in the grass in the sun and talked among themselves. Their women were dressed in all the gaudy colours of the rainbow. There were all nationalities ranging between the Indians and the whites—from a Mexican with hair hanging down his back to Chileans and Kanakas." The Kanakas were descendants of Hawaiian immigrants.

As the strike moved into its third week, Bell-Irving organized a provocation to break the impasse. Loading nonunion fishermen into two skiffs, he surrounded them with armed special police in cannery tugs and sent them out to fish. Determined picketing soon drove the strikebreakers to shore, where they were treated to a dockside lecture by Rogers. The only confrontation had been verbal, but Bell-Irving had the excuse he needed to call for military assistance. Rogers was arrested and charged with intimidation.

With Rogers shackled, bundled into a coach and headed for a Vancouver jail cell, Bell-Irving next moved against the Japanese fishermen, who were held in thrall by cannery managers who controlled their naturalization papers. A Japanese account of the 1900 strike prepared almost a generation later recalls the desperate situation of Japanese fishermen whose food "was provided by the canneries and paid for at the end of the season." The consul advised the fishermen to set their nets under the protection of armed cannery guards, but the Japanese fleet remained solidly behind the strike for almost two weeks.

The canners arranged for payment of $1,500 to a man named Oki, the Japanese union's vice-president and a labour contractor for the Lighthouse Cannery. The Japanese fishermen gathered 3,000 strong in Steveston the day of Rogers's arrest to debate the strike. The meeting was dominated by false reports that settlement was imminent. Ultimately, the leaders of Gyosha Dantai, the Steveston Fishermen's Association, organized a mass return to work. They never regretted it. "Our decision to start fishing for 20 cents resulted in our victory and the development of Steveston as the residence of our people," Dantai's official history concluded, but the strikebreaking of 1900 and 1901 confirmed a racial split in the industry which laid the basis for the eventual destruction of the Steveston Japanese community altogether.

Now Bell-Irving implemented the third part of his strategy, convening three justices of the peace in Steveston to call out the militia. The three, who included a cannery manager, a cannery foreman and an ex-cannery manager, issued the required orders. In Vancouver, militia commander Lieut.-Col. T. E. Worsnop was awakened by a courier and warned to be ready for the call to arms. In the early morning hours of 24 July, trumpeters raced through the streets of the city blaring their horns. About 200 of Vancouver's business class, members of the 6th Duke of Connaught's Own Rifles under the direction of Worsnop and cannery shareholder C. Gardiner-Johnson, responded and gathered on the Union Steamship dock at dawn, where the vessels *Rithet* and *Comox* were waiting with steam up to move the troops to Steveston. Amid the jeers and catcalls of Vancouver workers attracted by the trumpets, the men were issued with ball cartridges and marched on board. The night cruise to Steveston was uneventful.

As the sun rose over Steveston, the town was buzzing. On the field beside the Gulf of Georgia cannery, the militia paraded and presented arms under the bemused gaze of hundreds of strikers, who mockingly dubbed them "the Sockeye Fusiliers." Because the summer sun made their pillbox hats unendurably hot, the militiamen had been issued floppy straw hats as a substitute. To give the brims a military air, the soldiers cut stars from canning tin and pinned up one side. Behind the militia, massed on the docks, were hundreds of Japanese fishermen readying their boats. Protected by armed cannery guards, the fleet set out, its sails "like a large and beautiful crowd of butterflies."

Suddenly a ripple ran through the crowd. Rogers, released on bail, had arrived back in Steveston. Standing on a packing crate, he addressed a huge crowd at a spontaneous meeting a few blocks to the east, blaming the continuing strike on a power play by Bell-Irving. A motion to hold to the 25-cent demand was passed amid stormy applause, and the strikers marched more than a thousand strong on Malcolm and Windsor, where Bell-Irving himself was encamped with the troops. The marchers swirled around the little band like the tide, an endless stream of men and women of all races laughing, cheering, jeering and regaling the militia with ironic choruses of "Soldiers of the Queen." A shaken Bell-Irving implored Worsnop to read the Riot Act. The colonel prudently refused, "although the great, seeming never-ending string of strikers appeared to be closing around the handful of men." The order to seize arms was issued and, for a few moments, it seemed the canners' threat of bloodshed would become a reality. Then the tension eased and the buoyant strikers dispersed.

Several hundred Japanese fishermen hung up their nets, declaring that they had been tricked into believing the settlement was industry-wide. The white fishermen repeated their determination to fight on, inspired by the continued support among pro-union Japanese and by the fact that eight canneries had no Japanese fishermen to provide raw product.

Now the native fishermen and their families proved decisive. Without an agreement, the chiefs declared, they would head home, taking the cannery crews with them. The steadfast support of the native women was a source of union strength neither union nor canners had counted on. Unable to break the strike with the nonunion Japanese fleet alone, Bell-Irving had to sue for peace. Negotiations resumed, and by 30 July Rogers was able to recommend acceptance of a flat season-long price of 19 cents. Fishing began the next day.

Although the goal of 25 cents a fish was not achieved, the final agreement marked a defeat for the canners and victory for the fishermen. For the first time, the canners had been forced to concede a share of their economic wealth to their employees. Unlike the dispute of 1893, which had involved a relatively small group of fishermen in the struggle, the 1900 strike mobilized shoreworkers, fishermen of all races and the general public in the fight against the canners. Partly for that reason it marked a milestone in B.C. labour history.

United in a common cause, fishermen could exercise some control over their destiny. But this fundamental lesson, so clearly grasped by Rogers, was missed by many of his fellow workers. Although Bell-Irving's manipulation of ethnic divisions failed to break the 1900 strike, he understood the importance of this technique better than the average fisherman. Despite Rogers's efforts, fishermen blamed the Japanese for their weakness, rather than the licensing and immigration policies which made the Japanese easy prey for strikebreaking canners.

As the massive big year run of 1901 approached, the canners again moved to cut prices, offering to pay 12½ cents to 27 July, when the runs would peak, and then 10 cents a fish for the balance of the season. The fishermen again demanded a fixed price throughout the season—this time, 15 cents. After an initial skirmish on the Skeena, where native picketers drove back about 300 Japanese strikebreakers, battle was joined on the Fraser.

In 1901, the canners deployed more than armed police in their struggle with the fishermen. In May, provincial Attorney-General D. M. Eberts introduced a bill to take provincial control of fisheries and to allow the creation of trap leases to be sold at auction. Rogers denounced the bill as a move to give canners control of the resource, but price negotiations soon dominated the fishermen's agenda. At an enormous meeting at Chilliwack on 7 June, native people from the Skeena to the Fraser met and voted unanimously to reject the canners' offer. Thirty-three chiefs vowed they would "not go to the canneries until the offer to fish for 15 cents is accepted," a decision which denied the canners both fishermen and cannery labour.

Although the labour movement and public opinion favoured exclusion of Asian immigrants, the B.C. Fishermen's Union restricted its demands to control of the naturalization papers fraud. A Vancouver mass meeting during the 1901 strike was dominated by the issue of Japanese immigration because native and white fishermen believed the wholesale release of naturalization papers was designed to build up a captive force of scab fishermen. Union president Ernest Burns told the meeting that laws in Canada were made for the protection of property, not humanity. "The idea of ill-treating Japs and scabs was foolish," he said. "A scab was one who of necessity had to work for wages that others would not work for. The two should combine if there was to be success." Such idealism cut little ice with the strikers.

Rogers and Charles Durham were named to head the strike committee, and Rogers immediately attempted to forge a new alliance with the Japanese. It was not forthcoming. By 17 June, talks with the canners were deadlocked, despite the union's reduction of its demand to 12½ cents throughout the season. The canners had agreed to 12½ cents, but only until 3 August, the day they expected the heavy runs to arrive. Their position, warned Rogers, meant a "strike was now inevitable."

The reasons for the canners' intransigence soon became obvious. The fishermen learned of plans to import trap fish to B.C.'s canneries for 15 cents a fish. This high price was an indication of how much the canners wished to break the union. A Japanese contractor named Oikano, claiming to represent 2,000 Japanese fishermen, said his men would fish for 10 cents provided there was no limit on deliveries. By 20 June, the Japanese Fishermen's Association had accepted the canners' offer of 12½ cents and a 250-fish daily limit after 3 August. Two days later the canners announced a unilateral reduction in the number of boats from 4,000 to 3,108. Fishermen were in a turbulent mood on 26 June as they gathered for a mass meeting in Vancouver's Market Hall.

Even if the fishermen's demands were accepted in total, one fisherman told the crowd, the canners were good for $2 profit per case. They expected to sell for $4 a case. Packing costs were $1 a case. "Throw off one dollar a case," he suggested, "for leeway in the shape of fast horses, wine and sleepless nights, which all businessmen had, especially when they possess a good cheque book, and that would leave them a profit of $20,000 on a capital stock of $20,000."

Chief Jimmy Harry's arithmetic was more straightforward. "At one time the Indians owned the whole country, river and everything," he declared. "No trouble then and no strike." Now his people would insist on 12½ cents because last year they had worked for 18 cents and still gone home in debt. Rogers appealed "to the labouring men of Vancouver not to go fishing before a settlement." The strike deadline was set for 30 June at midnight.

As the strike began, the Japanese fleet largely remained tied up in support, proof that Rogers's efforts had not been entirely wasted. Bell-Irving and his cronies concentrated their fire on this weak point in the fishermen's front, counting on the labour contractors, who were deeply in debt with preseason advances, to drive their workers onto the grounds.

Two crews that did try to fish on 7 July were beaten senseless. The next night, the vanguard of the sockeye run was in the river. At least a hundred skiffs left the docks, escorted by twenty-six armed patrol boats. As crowds watched from shore, the union pickets, each with a large U on the sail, manoeuvred through the fleet. Within a few days, the number of strikebreakers had swelled to several hundred, each landing 200 fish a night. Rogers told reporters that he had learned of cash advances from the canners to Japanese fishermen to purchase rifles and revolvers. A statement, signed by Rogers, said "the fishermen consider this arming of the Japanese as a step which means civil war and will ask all white men and Indians to govern themselves accordingly." Pickets now would be armed, Rogers warned, and settlement would only come with agreement on fixed minimum prices, unlimited deliveries, preference for union men and no employment of Japanese until all union men were employed.

Picketing became intense. Every boat fishing was boarded. Weapons were thrown overboard, nets cut to pieces, and strikebreakers put ashore while their boats were set adrift.

As the first week of the strike came to an end, the weather worsened and the winds turned to blow from the east, warning of a summer gale ready to pound the waters of the Strait of Georgia. On 10 July, just before the storm hit, gunfire erupted off Point Grey and six union fishermen—an Englishman, an Austrian, a German, a black West Indian and two Filipinos or Chileans—were arrested for intimidation. Police seized four shotguns and a revolver.

As the storm blew itself out, the papers reported sensational news. Between six and fourteen Japanese had been marooned by strikers on Bowen Island. They were rescued by the steamer *Defiant* and returned to Vancouver, where they implicated Rogers in their abduction. Rogers and union man Joe Desplanes were charged along with the six men arrested on 10 July with eight counts of intimidation.

This time there was no bail for Rogers. From his cell in New Westminster, where he was locked up for twenty-one hours a day, he urged no reprisals for his arrest. On 19 July, the fishermen ended their strike on the canner's terms of 12½ cents for the first quarter of the pack and 10 cents for the remainder. The fleet sailed.

On 30 July, the run hit in earnest. Daily gillnet catches rose to 300, then

400 and finally 700. The Puget Sound traps groaned with fish, and on 9 August the canners finally imposed a limit of 200 fish per boat. Cannery crews soon fell behind, and the newspapers reported appalling waste as thousands of salmon were thrown away.

With the run surging past, the Chinese workers could assert their authority. At the Gulf of Georgia cannery, a foreman was surrounded by his crew and agreed at knifepoint to rehire two contract workers he had fired for sloppy work. A few weeks later another crew in New Westminster threw down their knives in protest against the brutal pace set by an iron butcher and automated canner. In a third strike, the *Province* reported on 4 September that Chinese crews halted for a time the installation of a fish-packing machine which "takes the place easily of about 30 Chinese." The machine "worked so fast that it took the Chinese all their time to keep up with it and they had to hustle. Finally they threw down their knives and stated that either the machine must go or they would walk out of the factory. The machine was shut down." On 4 October the *World* reported that a foreman had to draw his gun to subdue a crew that threatened him with knives. He "warned the foreman of the Celestial gang that he would shoot the first man who disputed his authority."

By 12 August the river was polluted with the carcasses of hundreds of thousands of fish and the offal from several million more. Fish were so thick, both dead and alive, that the *World* claimed that the "big and powerful steamer *Surrey* has more difficulty in pushing her way through the mass of salmon using the river than she had in the ice floes of last winter." In Vancouver, the stench of rotting salmon carried by the tides onto English Bay beaches disturbed the West End gentry. When the sockeye finally were past, the Fraser pack stood at 873,600 cases. The Puget Sound traps had claimed a staggering total of 1.1 million cases.

That fall, Rogers and his colleagues came to trial in Vancouver, where he admitted picketing on the grounds that night in July but denied all the other allegations of the Japanese fishermen. The jury acquitted them, provoking prosecutor W. J. Bowser to complain the crown "could not get a fair trial" in such a union town. A new trial in New Westminster resulted in a hung jury, and Rogers went free.

With the big run behind them, the fishermen's bargaining power declined. In 1902, the canners were able to impose a sliding scale of prices on the fishermen without resistance. A brief strike protested cuts in the price of spring salmon, but the B.C. Fishermen's Union could recommend only that locals "be guided by temporary arrangements and their own judgement" on sockeye prices. On 15 July, Durham concluded an agreement based on a sliding scale of prices ranging from 11 cents to a high of 20 cents if the pack was fewer than 200,000 cases. The canners also promised priority to union men and native people, and to deduct and remit union dues. The union men accepted the sliding scale amid recriminations and charges of a sellout.

After the battles of 1900 and 1901, the B.C. Fishermen's Union was exhausted and internally divided. Charles Durham remained in the leadership, but Rogers was replaced by Joseph Watson, a Liberal party activist for whom anti-orientalism was an article of faith. Union leaders refused to wait for the Japanese to come to a better agreement because they were "remembering how they have dealt with us during the two preceding years." The union's treatment of its native allies was equally tawdry. A union spokesman tried to explain away native opposition to the settlement with the comment that native people "as a rule are not quite capable of seeing through the intricacies involved." White fishermen in Steveston condemned the leadership and, in a sharp reversal of the previous summer, two native fishermen were stopped from setting their nets by a boatload of Japanese pickets with drawn revolvers. For three days, the Japanese held out for a fixed price until pressure from the consul compelled them to submit to the sliding scale. The lesson should have been obvious—when divided three ways, the fishermen were helpless.

Now absorbed in the battle against trap privileges, the white fishermen were little concerned with the prospect of a Japanese takeover of the industry or even a minimum price. Native fishermen, however, were less complacent, as they found their jobs taken by recent arrivals who were proving adept at gillnetting. A hand-scrawled letter from Chief James David arrived in Ottawa in 1901, addressed only to Sovereign Queen Victoria. "An Indian do appeal to you for assistance to do the best you can to keep the Japanese from fishing in the province of British Columbia. Help us Indians along to keep the Japanese away from us." A civil servant wrote "no action" across the letter and filed it away. It soon was followed by a petition from Chief Harry Squamish, Chief Tom Mission, Chief Joe Capilano and the elders of the bands of False Creek, Musqueam, New Westminster, Point Roberts and Katzie appealing for government aid to achieve "a settled price during the season," as well as action against the Japanese who "work for such little pay that we have no chance to make a living."

The year 1902 was a gloomy one of poor catches and death on the grounds. A bitter southeaster caught the fleet at sea late in July, sinking seven boats and drowning ten fishermen. At season's end, with all bargaining power long gone, fishermen went to court to fight an attempt by the canners to inflate the pack size to avoid paying higher prices. Their lawsuit was dismissed.

As long as the canners could supply their plants with fish, any strike could be broken. The fishermen had shown the potential of united action but had been overcome by factors far beyond their control. With the threat of a fishermen's organization eliminated, the canners convened a special meeting in New

Westminster. Their goal, according to the *News-Advertiser,* was an arrangement "whereby the number of canneries will be decreased." The time for cutthroat competition was over.

Into this tangle of corporate interests and corrupt politics came a 27-year-old American businessman named Henry Doyle. With an acute sense of timing and a disregard for traditional ways of doing things, Doyle cut through the chaos of the canning sector to create the B.C. Packers' Association, a corporation that would come to dominate the industry.

Son of a New York twine merchant, Doyle became interested in the salmon fishery when his father received a 1,000-pound (454-kilogram) order from San Francisco. The twine was for gillnet, Doyle was told, and he set out to learn everything he could about an industry which was to make his fortune. As sales to the West Coast expanded, the Doyles found themselves perfectly situated to follow the industry's economic advances and retreats.

Doyle's genius lay in understanding that the problem was too many canneries, not insufficient fish. The number of fish was adequate, even too high, but the cost of harvest had driven the cost of catching the fish higher at a time when markets were swamped. Between 1890 and 1900 the cost of raw fish per case of salmon had risen 168 per cent while world market prices had declined 25 per cent. The huge increase in the number of fishermen meant this money was dissipated in an enormous fleet, but the growing strength of the union suggested the cost of fish would stabilize, if not rise. The cost of this fleet was a burden in itself. In 1881, the capital cost of boats and nets accounted for only 25 per cent of the industry's investment, but by 1905, the figure was 50 per cent.

Despite the success of Bell-Irving's combine and the example of Alaska Packers', the B.C. canners refused to merge, pinning their hopes instead on traps and price-fixing. The enormous run of 1901 shattered these illusions with a pack of 1.1 million cases in the United States and 928,000 in Canada. The total Pacific seaboard pack from California to Alaska of 5 million cases was double existing market demand and quality was poor.

Fisheries officials reported that B.C. canners had paid but 10⅝ cents a fish in 1901, only to be undercut by their American competitors, "the consequences being that while the present prices in London and Liverpool markets would leave a profit to the Puget Sound canners, the B.C. pack could not be sold except at a loss."

The long-awaited crisis was at hand. As the 1901 season drew to a close, Doyle learned that many canneries were teetering on the brink of receivership. He secured letters of introduction to the general managers of the largest banks in Toronto and Montreal and caught the eastbound train. His proposal was simple. He would acquire options to buy all available canneries and to merge them into a single organization. Less than two weeks later he was back in Vancouver with the agreement of the banks to pursue amalgamation. His financial backer was Aemilius Jarvis, a Bay Street stock promoter. Doyle went to work.

In sixty days of hectic activity he interviewed almost every canner on the coast. His offer was straightforward. He would purchase their assets on condition that they would promise never to re-enter the fishery. The new company would consolidate and merge canneries wherever possible. The result would be fewer fishermen and a reduced cost of fish as the new near-monopoly developed "the power to control entry of fishermen into the fishery" as well as the power to control prices.

Of all the cost-cutting advantages offered by his plan, Doyle said, "the opportunity of reducing the price of fish is most worthy of consideration." The number of boats on the Fraser he estimated at 3,000, twice the number required to harvest the catch efficiently. Doyle proposed to reduce the number of boats on the Fraser to 2,500 and to transfer 500 to 1,000 boats to northern rivers, which he believed had too few vessels.

The remaining fishermen would be grateful for their new lot in life because "by increasing their catch they could make as much money on a lower price per fish as they make today with smaller catches and higher selling prices." At the same time, the newly consolidated canneries could introduce technology to drastically lower labour costs. By 1900, automatic equipment to cook and wipe the cans had eliminated crews of fifteen to twenty workers at each of those stages of production. Two men on a soldering machine could do the work of twenty-five manual solderers. By 1900, a crew of 130 to 150 workers using modern equipment could produce 1,500 to 2,000 cases a day, double the volume possible in 1883.

The brash young Doyle made the rounds of the canners. Bell-Irving dickered and then refused to participate. Charles Todd, as stubborn and flint-hearted as his father, at first accepted and then refused, hoping the Victoria government would reward him with trap leases. Others, however, quickly signed on. The new combine's success was assured when Alexander Ewen agreed to come on board as president. The British Columbia Packers' Association was formed on 20 May 1902.

The new empire was built from thirty-four companies holding forty-two canneries coastwide, the majority on the Fraser. Doyle immediately closed seven canneries on the Fraser and two in Rivers Inlet. The first closures were followed by many more. For the hundreds of workers, particularly native people, who relied on these canneries for employment, Doyle's miracle was an economic nightmare. In the remaining canneries, new equipment ruthlessly winnowed the ranks of the survivors. The notorious "Iron Chink," so-called in derisive honour of the men it replaced, was introduced to head and gut salmon at a rate of sixty to seventy-five fish a minute with a three-man crew. Before 1900, twenty-five men could handle only 1,500 to 2,000 fish in a ten-hour day. Now a single iron butcher could keep two canning lines amply supplied with a fraction of the labour.

Fishermen faced a drastic reduction in their power. Where scores of canners had competed for their production in 1901, there now stood a handful of dominant companies capable of fixing prices around a small conference table. Through corporate concentration, the canners could acquire a control of the fleet they could only dream of achieving by legislative means.

The combination of open entry to the fishery and corporate concentration in the processing sector meant fishermen would be forestalled from becoming wage labour in the same sense as their allies in the shore plants. The increasing transfer to individual fishermen of the risk and capital investment not only saved the canners enormous amounts of money but also confirmed fishermen as individual producers, a fact that produced delusions of grandeur among those who aspired to the status of "independent businessmen." In reality, they were about as independent as tenant sharecroppers, relying on the companies both for markets and debt financing. Although the battles of 1900 and 1901 had taught fishermen a political lesson in trade union action, that unanimity soon disintegrated under the corrosive effect of racism.

The eastern bankers who backed Doyle appreciated his initiative but soon found the self-assured twenty-seven-year-old too flamboyant for their taste. By 1904 he had been purged from company management, charged with overspending. He had done his work well, however. With world market prices recovering, B.C. Packers' dominated the Fraser. William Barker, an American canner with access to trap production and long experience in the American salmon combines based in Astoria, Washington, was hired to run the company with strict attention to the bottom line. Profits rose steadily and averaged between $300,000 and $475,000 a year between 1908 and 1916.

7

THE PROHIBITION OF

THE BABINE BARRICADES

Our Heavenly Father
Put SALMON *in our rivers*
Giving us FOOD
Before the white man came
But NOW
White man millionaires
Who can afford
Better FOODS
Than our salmon
Have come to take our fish
To make a little MONEY!

—ARNIE, *"God and the Millionaires,"*
newspaper clipping, possibly the
Seattle Times, *May 1920*

THE ECONOMIC CRISIS THAT SHOOK THE FRASER SALMON IN-
dustry in 1902 sent the surviving canners on a renewed hunt for fish. With
Canadian harvests on the Fraser sharply reduced by American traps, it was obvious that any new supplies would have to come from other runs in Canadian
waters. Public opinion was sharply opposed to traps. More fish, if any were to
be had, would have to come from the existing harvest, or that part of the harvest still not being taken by the canners. The richest prize was obvious: the
enormously productive native traps and weirs of the Babine system, known to
the canners as the Babine Barricades.

The Babine Barricades had supported a substantial fish trade for centuries.
The bulk of this harvest was taken in traps and weirs near the entrance to
Babine Lake, a huge sockeye nursery at the headwaters of the Babine River.
The river, which joined the Skeena at what now is called Hazelton, was one of
the largest sockeye producers between the Fraser and Bristol Bay. Its runs
could be tapped by a handful of traps located close to its source at the lake itself.

Although B.C. native people took fish by every conceivable method, including hook, spear and net, their most important gear was traps and weirs. The construction of a large trap or weir was a major task, and the year's food supply for an entire village depended on its success. Ownership rights varied, depending on the size and location of the operation, but Hilary Stewart, who has documented early native fishing methods, found that large weirs normally were owned by an entire village.

River weirs could take many forms, but usually rested on a framework of piles driven deep into the river bed. To the pile framework were secured lattice panels made of light, straight branches bound with bark. When the fishery was over, the lattices could be removed easily. Normally, the ice and flooding of spring breakup completed the destruction of the weir.

Once in operation, the weirs forced the salmon into pens or conical traps, where they could be harvested by dipnet or spear. When the run was at its peak, these fishing stations were hives of activity as thousands of salmon were butchered and smoked. These weirs produced enough salmon to supply the needs of tribes far into the Interior.

The Babine Indians not only sat at the hub of a substantial trading network between the coast and the Interior, they also had worked in the coastal fishing industry since 1876 when commercial canning began on the Skeena. For a generation, native families had made the trip from the Charlottes and the Upper Skeena to gillnet and work in the canneries around Port Essington and the site of what later became Prince Rupert. When the canning season was over, they returned home for the traditional fishery.

Early in 1904, the Skeena canners began their campaign to eliminate the Babine Barricades. Eager to assist was John Williams, newly appointed fisheries inspector for District 2, which stretched all the way from the Fraser to the Alaska Panhandle. In his first report to Ottawa, Williams identified native barricades as the major reason for declining salmon runs.

Late in 1904, Williams was directed by Ottawa to convene a meeting of northern canners to determine their views on the question of traps in northern waters. The canners voted by a three-to-one margin to oppose commercial traps on the north coast, in part because of the difficulty of determining who should get the few good locations. Williams assured the canners that his minister intended to enforce the regulations against the native sale of fish and "more particularly at Babine Lake that no nets or barricades are constructed." In a followup letter to fisheries minister Louis Prefontaine, the canners claimed the native people would suffer no hardship through loss of their fishery, but if the barricades remained, "the canning industry on the Skeena will be destroyed." They also threatened to withdraw their support of the provincial Liberals if their request was not granted. Privately, however, they predicted the number of canneries on the Skeena would double once the native catch was added to their take.

Williams already had dispatched fisheries overseer Hans Helgesen to the Upper Skeena to investigate the barricades and to enforce a ban on trap fishing. At Babine village Helgesen found what he was looking for—two immense barricades 800 metres apart which completely bridged the river's 183-metre width. Heavy posts driven a couple of metres into the river bottom and standing 1.2 metres above the water had been strung across the river at 1.8-metre intervals. Bracing them were long, sloping poles driven deep into the bottom and attached to each post's top. Stringers linked the entire system together, and panels "beautifully made of slats woven together with bark set in front of all . . . made a magnificent fence which not a single fish could get through." Openings in the fence admitted the fish to twelve big traps or bins, periodically emptied by men who gaffed the catch into canoes for transfer to shore.

These traps were operated under the direction of Chief Atio, to whom Helgesen explained Ottawa's fishing laws, including the ban on traps, the prohibition on sale of fish and the requirement for a food fish permit. The chief was unimpressed. "He said they have had an indisputable right for all time in the past," Helgesen recalled, "that if it was taken away the old people would starve . . . and he wanted to know to what extent the government would support them, he thought it unfair to forbid them selling fish when the cannerymen sold all theirs."

Helgesen pressed on. The barricades were illegal, he told Atio, and if the Babine people did not destroy them "nothing will save them from punishment or imprisonment." Finally a number of men plunged into the icy water and began to dismantle the weirs, stopping after two hours to demand payment. After a great deal of shouting and argument, Helgesen hired six of the men to finish the job. Atio may have considered the arrangement a good one. The season was almost over and his band had been paid to perform a job they would have had to do in any case. Another chief was not so willing to bend to the regulations and demanded $600 compensation for the loss of the barricades, vowing that without such payment "the barricades would be constructed again if he had to die for it."

On the banks of the Babine, Helgesen counted at least sixteen smokehouses each 9 metres square filled with salmon. Tens of thousands more fish were drying on racks outside. More than 750,000 had been harvested in the six weeks since the fishery began, he estimated, a figure which must have elated the canners. With that many fish released for harvest, there would be ample to fuel several canneries and still leave extra to spawn. Helgesen and his partner continued their tour around the lake to the Tatchi, Tiltitcha and Fifteen-Mile rivers, destroying weirs at each location. At each of the barricades Helgesen found fish delayed by the weirs, yet every stream appeared well stocked. The possibility that the native people deliberately released sufficient fish to assure a good escapement did not occur to him. A final visit to Morricetown Canyon, on the way back to Hazelton, revealed an intensive fishery. Relying on his powers under various clauses of the Fisheries Act, Helgesen closed the canyon, a vital food source to local bands, to fishing by any means except with a dry fly.

Despite the clear gains Helgesen had achieved, his superiors were troubled by the native people's obvious intransigence. Inquiries to the Department of Indian Affairs were not encouraging. In July 1905, with the fish again running upriver, Helgesen once more boarded a steamer for the Upper Skeena, taking with him a number of gillnets donated by the canners as substitutes for the prohibited barricades. At Babine village, a large crowd gathered round to view the new fishing gear. "Everything went well until he opened the web," a fisheries department memorandum records, "when their countenances fell, as they saw it was old web." Evidently, the canners had hoped to buy off these veterans of both the commercial and traditional fishery with rotten nets. After a lengthy council with the chiefs, Helgesen vowed to bring new web every year if they would agree to abandon their barricades. The chiefs agreed. Helgesen later learned that the Babine harvest for that year was only 40,000 fish, or about 5 per cent of the previous year's catch. Nonetheless, he told Ottawa, everyone in the region had ample supplies of food.

Although no direct account of that winter on the Babine has survived in fisheries records, the hardships can be surmised. With only a small fraction of their normal catch, the Babine people had nothing to trade and insufficient food to last through the winter months. As spring breakup drove the ice off the lake and down the river, the chiefs directed their people to rebuild the weirs and to refuse Helgesen's nets. In August, Helgesen dispatched two fisheries guardians and three special constables to arrest the barricade builders and destroy their weirs.

In a letter some months later recalling the "fierce fracas" which then ensued on the Babine, Helgesen tried to recreate the tensions those men must have felt as they paddled their canoes downstream from Babine Post. As his own excitement rose, his spelling deteriorated. The fracas began, he reported, with a sad farewell at Babine Post from Chief George, who solemnly shook the fisheries guardians' hands and wished them farewell as women "sang in their most musical strain . . . to signify the last farewell and the song of death." After landing their canoe some distance upstream, the gallant band walked down to the barricade where they found what Helgesen described as "a desperate situation . . . an infuriated mob, with their sleaves rolled up, their fierce passion aroused, shaking with excitement." Undaunted, D. G. Wells plunged into the crowd to make some arrests, but after some minor blows and being "jostled about in a fearful manner," he and his men retreated to their canoe, where they spent the night listening to the triumphant yells and rifle volleys of the native people.

The next morning, 23 August, Wells again led his wary crew toward the barricades, now defended by a skirmish line of very angry women. Once again, the foolhardy Wells plunged forward, provoking a wild melee as the women dragged him and his men away from the weirs.

When word of the stand-off reached Helgesen, he panicked. Rushing to the telegraph office, he advised Victoria and Ottawa of a near-insurrection on the Babine, in which "multitudes of squaws armed with clubs" assaulted his men as they attacked the weirs. Behind the women, he wrote, were "fifty or sixty [men] in line on bank of river with clubs, all shaking with excitement frothing at the mouth looking like fiends turned loose from Hades." There was only one thing to do, he concluded: "Nothing can allay trouble but force." But Prefontaine could not get the approval of Indian Affairs for harsh action. The Babine people's fishing rights had never before been disputed, the department told him, and undoubtedly had a foundation in Canadian law.

Helgesen felt compelled to make another personal appearance at Babine, but a long meeting with the chiefs early in September proved futile. Not only did the chiefs insist on maintaining their weirs, they also refused to surrender nine men wanted by Helgesen on charges of illegal fishing. Finally, an intervention by Father Coccola, the local Roman Catholic missionary, broke the deadlock. With the priest's assistance, Chief George communicated his willingness to open the weirs from noon Saturday to 6 P.M. Sunday for a distance of 3.6 metres, a fishing closure similar to those imposed on the canners. "We wish to meet the wishes of the government," Chief George said, "but it means starvation."

Louis Brodeur, the newly appointed fisheries minister, accepted the chief's offer, and Chief George responded by directing the nine wanted men to surrender to Helgesen. Contrary to government pledges that the men would be released pending the outcome of a special conference in Ottawa, white authorities tried and convicted the men on various counts, jailing several who could not afford the fines. Despite this show of bad faith, Chief George and Chief William Tszak joined Father Coccola for the long train ride to Ottawa. On 24 October 1906, the three men joined Brodeur, Williams and Helgesen in the Ottawa office of Frank Oliver, minister responsible for Indian Affairs.

Chief George described how his people had suffered from the loss of the barricades. With the weirs, the August fishery was sufficient to meet their food supplies for a year and leave enough for sale to the Stuart Lake Indians, but nets were almost useless in the clear waters of the river. Father Coccola carefully corrected the more lurid details of Helgesen's account of the "fracas" by the riverside. It was the fisheries guardians who had demanded that the native men come out and fight, he reported, but the men, far from frothing and shaking, simply had told them that "the women are strong enough for you."

Brodeur pressed Williams and Helgesen for proof that the barricades threatened the stock. In his frustration, Williams finally became candid. "The trouble is the Indians are so lazy and idle they will not do anything at all. The reason they want barricades is because the women can go and shovel the fish out," he said. "Let them come down to the cannery and work as all other Indians do, not loaf. The Babine Indians must realize that they must work as the other Indians do, they cannot be spared." This outburst revealed a second motive for the canners' determination. They sought not only the fish taken by the Babine Barricades but the labour of the native people.

Brodeur upheld his party's promise to the canners by rejecting any compromise on the issue. In the famous Barricades Agreement of 1906, the fisheries department promised to provide every head of family with nets sufficient to provide enough food for personal use and trade. Although the Indian Affairs department had pressed for maintaining the barricades, it agreed to this arrangement because Brodeur acknowledged the right of the native people to sell their catch. For its part, the Ministry of the Interior promised to pay for the nets and seek more agricultural land for the Babine reserve. To the end, Oliver pressed for recognition of the rights of the Babine people, urging Brodeur to allow the native people to use the barricades to provide "sufficient for their food and for purposes of barter through the year" as well as compensation for any barricades removed. Brodeur's tart rejection of Oliver's proposal argued that to allow the barricades would create an impossible precedent, opening the way for traps all up and down the coast.

Helgesen continued on his crusade, destroying barricades and traps in many areas of the north coast and northern Interior. At what is now Kitwancool, where the Kitwancool River joins the Upper Skeena west of Hazelton, the chiefs prevailed on fisheries guardian Charles Durham to intercede for them in Ottawa. Durham, who four years before had led the B.C. Fishermen's Union in bargaining with the Fraser canners, told Brodeur the band's three hundred members could not possibly catch fish with a net in their small river fishery.

"The Indians further contend that during the generations for which they have lived at their village, there has been no diminution in the salmon," Durham wrote, "notwithstanding their barricades, until later years, and they attribute the recent decrease of fish consequently not to their barricades but to the excessive fishing of the canneries. When they could go down to the coast and earn sufficient at the canneries during the fishing season to enable them to buy enough provisions to keep them through the long and severe winter, they were satisfied. Now, however, a man's average earnings in the season will be only about $75 and at Git-win-cool village, a 50-pound sack of flour is worth at least $4 and other things in proportion, if at all obtainable. . . .

"The Indians claim that the barricade prohibition is a death blow to them in order to favour the Cannerymen; therefore they think that if the Government persists in enforcing this law, it ought to give the Indians who suffer by it some recompensation or palliative in the shape of either provisions or money, and take it out of the canners who are the gainers."

Durham's appeal fell on deaf ears. The Kitwancool barricades, and many others, were destroyed.

The Barricades Agreement on the Babine remains a landmark in the long struggle over aboriginal fishing rights. A full ten years after Ottawa imposed food-fishing permits on some Fraser bands, the Babine people were able to force acknowledgement of their right to fish and to sell their catch. Their moral victory was small consolation, however, because their barricades were lost.

The canners celebrated their achievement in a testimonial dinner in 1910 on the occasion of Hans Helgesen's retirement. They presented him with a gold cane, a purse of $630 and a letter of appreciation "for the active and important part you played in obtaining the permanent prohibition of the Babine Barricades."

8

THE FISH EXTERMINATED,

THE INDUSTRY DESTROYED

AT THE TURN OF THE CENTURY, THE PROVINCE'S POLITICIANS, previously absorbed in railway scandals, timber leasing and mining ventures, suddenly became sharply aware of the enormous value of the salmon fishery and indignant at Ottawa's apparent neglect. Their interest was prompted by the canners, who in 1901 submitted to the legislature a memorial that implied Ottawa was to blame for the obvious depletion of the resource. The memorial, endorsed by every major canner in the province, noted that the fishing industry was the province's second largest. The canners claimed to employ 15,000 workers and to have paid $1.25 million for the Fraser sockeye catch alone. Dominion licence revenues in 1900 amounted to $47,865, but what was Ottawa's expenditure for fish culture? A mere $2,389.

After thirty years of commercial fishing, only four hatcheries existed in the province, the canners complained, and "practically nothing has been done to clear the natural spawning beds, clearing log jams and the construction of fish ladders where necessary." These measures would be helpful but insufficient. Only by hatchery propagation, they insisted, "could the runs avoid collapse." They proposed a royalty on every case packed "to be used exclusively for the conservation of the industry." It was an offer they later would prefer to forget.

Although catch figures did not support the claim of depletion, there was a crisis both on the approaches to the Fraser, where American traps were proliferating, and on the spawning beds of the Fraser and the Thompson, where hydraulic gold mining was devastating kilometres of spawning gravel. Scores of placer mining operations in the Cariboo were ripping apart the headwaters of the Horsefly, the Quesnel and many other streams which supported millions of sockeye. In a single year, the Horsefly was reduced to a 9-metre trench for a distance of 215 metres, the mine tailings rushing downstream to pollute the rest of the river.

The industry was painfully aware of how similar mining techniques had destroyed chinook salmon runs to the Sacramento River. In California, a young biologist named John Pease Babcock claimed to be restoring the stocks with hatchery production. At the suggestion of canner R. P. Rithet, the province appointed Babcock as fisheries commissioner for B.C. His job was to uphold the province's interest in the stocks both by monitoring federal performance and by directing provincial fisheries policy.

Babcock's study of Pacific salmon had won him international acclaim, and his recruitment to B.C. reflected the canners' fear that they were headed for disaster if they failed to take action to rebuild stocks. Babcock promised great things. Hatcheries, he claimed, could make the weak years of the Fraser cycle as strong as the big years, and insure the industry against any man-made or natural disaster. The obsession with hatcheries, which dated back to the dawn of the industry, reflected a fatal arrogance. Although canners and politicians paid lip service to the need to maintain natural spawning capacity, they could not find the courage to restrict harvests or to protect salmon habitat. Confident that man could produce more fish than nature, they built hatcheries.

A Republican whose conservative bent naturally endeared him to the canners, Babcock's arrogance and inflexibility led him to an early humiliation. Although skilled in the handling of chinook, he was illiterate in the ways of the sockeye, which had never been present in California. His first B.C. project was the massive Seton Lake hatchery, where 40 million sockeye eggs were hatched and reared in a simple wooden facility some 64 metres long and 12 metres wide. To make up shortages of eggs in one locality, Babcock transferred them from elsewhere, on the mistaken theory that all sockeye were a single race. The "home stream" theory was false, he declared, because abundant sockeye had returned to the Quesnel despite the destruction of the brood year by gold miners. Despite years of effort, the Seton hatchery failed to produce an increased catch, to the delight of Babcock's detractors. Experts later agreed it may even have damaged the runs.

The selective use of catch statistics seemed to support Babcock's conviction that the runs were in serious decline. The total Fraser pack in 1901 had been a staggering 2 million cases, of which 1.1 million had been taken in Washington State. The following year saw only 633,033 cases packed, a sharp decline, but above the brood year pack of 508,101 in 1898. In 1903, the Fraser produced 372,020 cases and in 1904 the pack was a miserable 196,107 cases.

But Babcock's hatchery projects were only part of his strategy to save the industry. Aware of the outrage provoked by the slaughter at the Puget Sound traps, he proposed an audacious conservation scheme that would place restrictions on the traps. The only solution, Babcock told the legislature, would be a minimum thirty-six-hour weekly closure in Washington, a complete closure in Washington after 25 August, elimination of the fishery above the New Westminster bridge in Canada, and total American and Canadian closures from 10 July to 15 September in 1906, 1907 and 1908. The alternative to closure was ruin: "If it is not done, not only is there grave danger of the fish being exterminated, but it is almost certain that the canning industry will be destroyed."

This draconian scheme found quick favour with editorial writers, the *Colonist* hailing it as "the heroic program which has been adopted as presenting the only logical method of preserving the salmon industry." Henry Doyle was enraged. The problem was not declining runs, he cried, but expanding greed. When the pack was less than one-third of what canners had illegitimately expected, "they set up the cry of 'the run of fish is diminishing.' "

Babcock's closure call became a rallying point for canners both in Puget Sound and B.C. to exert every possible pressure north and south of the line to win legislation enforcing the closure for 1906 and 1908. (Evidently, three years in a row was too much to bear.) But conservation was not their main consideration. Bell-Irving, who was not the only B.C. canner with traps on both sides of the line, was finding depletion a profitable state of affairs. New traps on the U.S. were slaughtering the spring salmon, he told a correspondent, and the industry was learning that fewer fish could mean more money. By carrying over one-third of this 1905 pack to 1906, he calculated, the price would advance 25 per cent, but the cost of the carryover would add only about 10 per cent to his overhead.

Late in 1904, a delegation of Puget Sound canners and B.C. operators with Puget Sound interests travelled to Ottawa to press their case. If Ottawa would close the Fraser for three years, they promised, Puget Sound traps would shut as well. Louis Prefontaine, the fisheries minister, was deluged with representations. Aulay Morrison, Liberal MP for New Westminster, reminded Prefontaine where his bread was buttered. "Our friends are the fishermen," he wrote, while the canners were a "Tory organization controlled by the Packers Association." He urged rejection of the closure demand.

Prefontaine dithered, then came down firmly on both sides of the fence. An Order in Council early in 1905 proposed to close the Fraser from 10 July to 25 August 1906. Similar legislation was put before the Washington State legislature. In a rationale that would be repeated for every future closure down to the modern era, Prefontaine predicted his action would "bring to the fishermen in due course vastly increased catches and earnings. To refuse . . . would be to hasten the extermination of the fish and permanent closure of the fishery and canning industries of the Fraser River."

In what was perhaps the most desperate effort of their young organization, the New Westminster fishermen linked up with the Puget Sound Fishermen's Union to defeat the Washington State closure bill.

Angered by the growing move to trusts and cartels, the public was ready to back workingmen against combines on principle. On 13 February 1909 a Vancouver *Province* reporter likened the closure bills to an effort to "create a salmon trust in defiance of the population." The result would be a salmon cartel run by eastern capitalists, he wrote, with enormous profits "all taken from the working population of the fishing districts on the one hand and the consumers of salmon on the other."

Determined to retain the moral high ground, the fishermen advanced a program of real conservation. Ed Rosenberg, of the Puget Sound union, proposed to drop the total closure but to implement a weekly thirty-six-hour closed time every year. The canners turned him down on the grounds that such rigid restrictions would destroy the industry. Blocked by a filibuster on an unrelated railway bill, the closure legislation died on the order paper. The thirty-six-hour weekly closure did pass, but was completely ignored throughout the following season. "Fish in Vast Shoals Choke Unlifted Salmon Traps while Millions Die and Will be Waste before Utilized," shouted a headline on the 27 July *Puget Sound American.* State Governor Mead reported "flagrant violations of the thirty-six-hour law," but the corporate conservationists in cannery offices denied everything.

Prefontaine was relieved of his ordeal by a cabinet shuffle. The Order in Council was cancelled for 1906, but left in place for 1908 as an incentive to the Americans and a concession to the canners. The new minister, Louis Brodeur, took refuge in the dodge of a royal commission. To be headed by E. E. Prince, the commission was to investigate every aspect of the fishery, making recommendations for "preservation, protection and development of fishing industries." The controversy over traps and the Fraser closure were to dominate the commission's work. Of the five men assigned to work with Prince, two were sure to support a closure. They were banker Campbell Sweeny, of Vancouver, and Babcock. Richard Hall, a Victoria canner, enjoyed strong government connections, and J. C. Brown, of New Westminster, reflected the pro-fishermen sentiment of that city. G. W. Taylor, of Wellington, was an unknown quantity.

Despite its partisan beginnings, the Prince commission became a sounding board for all the problems confronting an industry that was coming of age at last. Internally, the canners faced problems of overcapitalization, despite the creation of B.C. Packers'. Forty-nine canneries were operating on the coast, and packing capacity was a whopping 58,000 cases a day. Automation had trimmed labour costs to the bone, but there was an increasing scarcity of labour. New markets, particularly for salted and frozen fish, were diverting production from the canneries to the point that prices were rising beyond what canners wished to pay even without strong union intervention. Finally there was the heart-stopping boom and bust cycle of the fishery, the seasonal fluctuations which apparently had no scientific reason apart from isolated environmental disasters. The industry did have some advantages, however. It had established markets in Japan, Australia, Chile and the United Kingdom. Higher processing standards and the shorter time between harvest and packing produced premium quality and higher prices.

During its three-year life, the commission reflected all the diverse concerns of the industry from stream obstructions to the native fishery. The fundamental issue, however, was the management of the Fraser, on which the commissioners split. Testimony before the commission became a verbal war between the fishermen on one side, and the canners, led by Bell-Irving and Barker, on the other.

The fishermen built their cases on the time-honoured principle that the salmon were the public resource of the Canadian people, not a private preserve to be enjoyed by a privileged few. Newfoundland immigrant John Kendall saw the canners as the main threat to the salmon's survival. "If we want to maintain this industry it must be taken from the hands of the canners of British Columbia and placed in the hands of people that is independent of canners and independent of the fishermen altogether. Then, instead of the fishing industry being run for the accommodation of the few, it would be run for the accommodation of the public."

The suggestion that fishing above New Westminster, conducted primarily by settlers supplementing agricultural earnings, was a threat to the resource, galled fishermen most of all. Many testified that canners towed their fleets above New Westminster when the river was closed below, a claim corroborated by U.S. observers. The three hundred fishermen and boat pullers above New Westminster were not opposed to conservation: they favoured the elimination of traps and an extended closed period each week.

One fisherman told Prince "there's a lot of fishermen that think this commission isn't here to protect the salmon, but to protect the capitalists."

In New Westminster, George Mackie of the B.C. Fishermen's Union said, "We strongly protest against the granting of what we consider public rights to private individuals." If conservation was really required, he added, cancellation of trap licences and all cannery licences would be positive first steps.

But Barker and Robert Bell-Irving counterattacked hard. Traps were essential for conservation, said Barker, because they offered the possibility of selective fishing: "It is a wonder that there are so many fish with the little protection that they have had." In a moment of rare candour, he added, "We have all tried to get as many fish as we could in any way that we could." His solution was elimination of native traps and creation of more hatcheries, although existing hatcheries had admittedly provided few obvious benefits.

Fishermen contrasted the canners' new obsession with conservation with the obscene waste of the previous fishing season. Dinsmore cannery had been so glutted by excess trap fish that an entire scow load was simply dumped in the river. "I saw the fish, one lot, laying on the floors of the cannery just a mass of maggots," testified T. Adams. An enraged Barker shouted from the audience that "Dinsmore cannery never canned a bad fish," but the canners' truthfulness on this score came in for another drubbing when J. A. Goodale testified on the quality of fish taken with Robert Draney's seine licence at Rivers Inlet. After shipment to Nanaimo for canning, fish held by the tail fell in half. "It's plenty fresh enough," replied Draney. "You can get good full weight in a tin."

The seine licences issued by Prince since 1903 had inflamed fishermen against the department and the canners. Issued for several kilometres of foreshore, each licence was controlled by a canner who extorted money from seine fishermen. Venacio Martinolich, whose family established one of the great dynasties of the B.C. seine fleet, condemned the practice of leasing seine licences. Farrell and Tregent held the seine lease for the entire east coast of Vancouver Island from Deep Bay to Comox, he testified, and leased the permit to Japanese saltery owners who then charged him for the right to fish. Two fishermen testified that fisheries officer John Williams had profited from his trafficking in seine licences, an intolerable act of graft to fishermen who were working for two months a year on the seine fishery to take home season's earnings of only $76 each.

The commissioners ran into equally stiff resistance when they met with American canners and government officials in Washington State in November 1905. When Prince declared that "the fish have been so persistently slaughtered on the way to the spawning ground that the supply is threatened," the Americans said the first concern should be propagation, not protection. Traps took only the fringes of the schools, the U.S. side suggested, but after that the wall-to-wall gillnets in the Fraser did a devastating job.

The commission's final report reflected the pressure of the fishermen's campaign. Prince and the majority recommended sharp restrictions in gillnet lengths and depths as well as increased closed times. Between Mission and Steveston, they proposed a sixty-hour closure in the off years. Outside the Fraser's mouth, however, the old thirty-six-hour closure would remain. In the big years, the entire system would close for only thirty-six hours a week. Gillnet lengths were to be held to 150 fathoms (274 metres) and depths to sixty meshes, a sharp cut from the eighty meshes then common in the river fishery. It was far from the total closure Babcock had hoped for, but it offered big dividends to the Fraser River canners and threatened the livelihood of the independent fishermen. Brown, who spoke for the New Westminster interests, dissented from the majority report because of the longer closure proposed above the New Westminster bridge.

Babcock and Sweeny did the job they were sent for, insisting in their minority report on a drastic total closure of the river in 1908, 1910, 1911 and 1912, as well as permanent total closure above the New Westminster bridge. Brushing aside the trap issue, which they deemed insoluble, they declared that overfishing was the sole cause of the decline and elimination of river fishing the only available solution. But the closure campaign was already a dead issue. The minority report was ignored.

Prince's majority report was forwarded to Brodeur in October 1906 and received widespread publication in the coastal press. New Westminster, angered by the proposal for an upriver closure, made ready to oppose it. But on 18 February, the New Westminster interests were stunned by the news that a delegation of canners had quietly slipped out of town to meet with the fisheries minister in Ottawa in a desperate final push to implement the total closure recommendation. "Canners Try to Steal March on Fishermen," the *Columbian* brayed. "Local Forces Prepare to Oppose It." Within forty-eight hours, a joint delegation of independent canners and union fishermen, headed by Henry Doyle and George Mackie, caught the next train east. The embattled Brodeur met both delegations at once on 7 March.

Doyle was not the only canner to throw in his lot with the fishermen. Although purged from the management of B.C. Packers', he was authorized to act for minority shareholders, among which he and Ewen were the leaders. Other independent canners were vitally concerned about the machinations of the bankers and the Bell-Irvings. Complete closure of the Fraser—as opposed to mesh restrictions and other measures to conserve sockeye—would devastate both the independent fishermen and the small canners who relied upon them to supply pink salmon, spring salmon, chums and coho for salt and fresh fish markets around the Pacific and as far east as Montreal and New York.

Through close ties to J. C. Brown, Doyle had kept himself informed on a daily basis of the internal wrangling among the commissioners. Doyle's presentation in a key meeting with Brodeur was devastating for the Fraser River Canners Association. He reserved his heaviest fire for Barker, who had attempted to prove the decline of the runs by showing that "canners failed to obtain all the pack prepared for." The problem lay not with the fish, Doyle countered, but with the greed of the canners. "They made preparations for more fish than past statistics would give them any right to expect and then blamed the fish instead of themselves when the results proved disappointing."

Finally, he proved that the runs actually were increasing rather than declining.

Doyle's notes of that meeting in a crowded Parliament Hill office offer a fascinating insight into the horse-trading to which fisheries management ultimately was reduced. After a day of debate, the two delegations were deadlocked. It fell to Liberal MP Ralph Smith to offer a compromise: a sixty-hour closure above New Westminster and a forty-eight-hour weekly closure below. "A most excellent suggestion," cried Barker. "It's a wonder no one has thought of it before." Deep down, he confessed, the FRCA did not like the minority recommendations it had so loudly endorsed. They now supported Prince's proposals because "it was better to suffer hardship for a short time than to kill the industry."

Mackie protested. There was no need for further restriction, he said, but if longer closures were suggested, they should be equal for all gear, above or below New Westminster. Impossible, declared Barker. If longer closures were imposed on the traps and seines, "it would mean the absolute closing down of every cannery on the Fraser River, as with any longer closed time . . . nothing but a straight loss could be expected and rather than face that the canneries would not be operated." Clearly Barker was more concerned with conservation of profit than with preservation of the stock. The meeting soon adjourned, with a perplexed Brodeur promising to consider all viewpoints.

The next day Doyle and Barker interviewed Prince, who was keen to tell his visitors of the abundant sockeye spawners he had seen in Harrison Lake the previous August. "Could those fish have moved up before the gillnet fishery began in June?" asked Mackie. "By no means," replied Prince. "The fish I saw were fish that had come up within 10 days." "Then," said Mackie, "they must have gone up during the time the nets were operating full blast. They must have got up during the fishing season in spite of the claim that the river nets prevented their doing so." A nonplussed Prince agreed that must be the case. Doyle and Mackie hurried to Smith and other MPs with the news. If the Harrison sockeye were as abundant as Prince suggested, then no further restriction was necessary.

The Order in Council passed by the government was hammered out by both sides in a meeting with Prince. The New Westminster forces agreed to the longer closure for 1907 and 1908 only in return for new hatcheries on the Babine and the Stuart, a tributary of the Fraser. Ultimately, new hatcheries also were built at Lakelse and on the Nechako. Residents upriver of New Westminster were granted special nontransferable licences for the sockeye fishery. A final victory for the fishermen was a ban on the import of raw fish. The fishermen's union would support the import of trap fish, Mackie said, provided they were in turn allowed to sell to the United States. After much debate, the canners agreed to a ban on both imports and exports.

Despite many subsequent alarms over the management of the river, the fight against the Fraser closures ended in victory for the fishermen. Aided by the split in the canners' ranks, with Doyle ably advancing the case of independent canners, the fishermen succeeded in defending the gains they had made a decade before. For white British subjects, the Fraser remained an open fishery, which was a victory considering the tenor of the times. For Japanese and native fishermen, none of whom had the right to vote, there was no political pressure which could be brought to bear. They remained locked into the canners' empire.

An intensive anti-oriental campaign culminated in 1907 in Vancouver, with wild race riots which saw much of Chinatown and Japantown sacked. These riots led to a gentlemen's agreement between Japan and Great Britain, which still handled Canada's foreign policy, that Japan would limit emigration to Canada to four hundred males a year.

Even before the gentlemen's agreement, the fisheries department was plotting to deny Japanese access to lucrative new fisheries then opening up. A decision to legalize purse-seining under licence in 1903 was accompanied by an agreement that "white men and Indians only to be permitted to participate in purse-seining and trapnet fishing, thus excluding Chinese, Japanese, etc., without the enactment of any formal restriction or prohibition by law." The zealous E. E. Prince felt the goal of the race restriction should be to eliminate as well "Greeks, Italians and other parties not being white men."

Although the gentlemen's agreement drew some of the fire from the anti-oriental movement, provincial authorities had not relaxed their drive to exclude Chinese and Japanese from the provincial economy. This obsession was linked to the province's determination to become involved in the direction of the fisheries. Provincial legislation to take over the industry was disallowed by Ottawa in 1908, but the federal authorities were compelled to co-ordinate their actions with Victoria pending the outcome of a Supreme Court reference. In 1912, this resulted in a federal policy granting unattached licences to white fishermen coastwide, regardless of the boat rating or limitation that might exist in a particular area.

9

BLOCKADE AT HELL'S GATE

IN THE SPRING OF 1912, THE FRASER RIVER BORE A CARGO of human corpses through Hell's Gate. Sometimes floating singly, sometimes in pairs, they snagged on branches or drifted in back eddies, until the current carried them away. They were railway construction workers who had been helping to drive a second track through the Fraser Canyon, and their passage was accompanied by the thunder of dynamite and falling rock. Driven at a frantic pace by foremen determined to hammer the last spike by 1915, the crews drilled and blasted relentlessly, and dozens of men were killed or maimed as the track crawled south.

Construction work on the CNOR (Canadian Northern Railway, now the Canadian National Railway) made the Fraser impassable for most salmon. Famine stalked the native people of the Fraser and Thompson rivers and the traditional salmon economy of the Interior was destroyed for three generations. The commercial fishery on the Fraser was reduced to a shell. Only now, nearly a century after the event, are the salmon runs close to recovery and the consequences of what must have been the greatest single environmental disaster in the province's history are still felt.

The catastrophe became known as the Hell's Gate slide, which implies that some act of God brought down the rock that choked the Fraser Canyon. In fact, the disaster resulted from deliberate and illegal construction techniques of the railway and should really be called a blockade. The magnitude of the disaster was covered up by officials who allowed fishing to continue even when they knew every spawner was required for the survival of the runs. When the tremendous losses finally became obvious, these same officials attempted to eliminate aboriginal fishing above the slide rather than ameliorate the slide's effects or crimp the profits of the canners. The price of building the CNOR was the destruction of the largest sockeye run the world has ever known.

By 1912, British Columbia was riding the crest of the greatest economic boom in its history. Fortunes had been made in mining and salmon canning a generation before. Now even more money could be made in real estate and railway construction. Under the Conservative government of Richard McBride, the industrialist was king and the function of government was to serve him. McBride's right-hand man was William "Billy" Bowser, a machine politician and attorney general, who never hesitated to bring force to bear against workers who interfered with the rush for profit. (Bowser was also, by coincidence, the provincial fisheries minister.) In the supercharged atmosphere of graft and corruption that marked British Columbia politics, railway construction was the newest and most lucrative gold rush, concentrated this time on mining taxpayers' pockets.

The scheme for a third railway to the Pacific, to join the Canadian Pacific Railway (CPR) on the Fraser and the Grand Trunk along the Skeena, had been hatched by railway promoters William Mackenzie and Donald Mann with the assistance of Richard McBride and veteran Tory Charles Tupper. McBride had arranged for provincial guarantees of $21,750 a kilometre and tax-free status until 1924, provided the line was completed by 1 July 1914, when he expected his lavish subsidies to bear fruit in a provincial election.

It is doubtful a new railway was required at all. The CPR had a shorter route and ample capacity, but the promoters decided to build the new line and worry about how to use it later. To compensate for the greater length of their right of way, Mackenzie and Mann required gentler curves and easier grades to achieve the high train speeds necessary to compete with the CPR. In the Fraser Canyon, the CNOR contractors had to hack the roadbed from solid rock, driving fifteen tunnels totalling 2,636 metres in a 42-kilometre stretch. Costs soared to $217,485 a kilometre and foremen seemed unable to squeeze more production from the road gangs. Rather than bear the time and cost of rock removal, the CNOR simply blew the debris into the river, in direct violation of the law.

Along the treacherous cliffs of the Fraser Canyon's east bank, where native people had hung a tracery of ladders and bridges a century before, thousands of workers blasted the benches and tunnels to carry the new track to the Pacific. Most were recent immigrants, but many were grandsons and great-grandsons of the native men and women who had met Simon Fraser. From communities at Yale, Spuzzum, Boston Bar, Kanaka Bar and Lytton, labour contractors hired construction workers and bought pack trains and fish. None of the workers was Asian, because McBride had insisted on a secret protocol to his subsidy agreements banning them from the construction work.

Between Hope and Kamloops, at least 4,000 men were concentrated in stinking clapboard camps, surviving on miserable rations and so indebted to labour contractors that many could not even afford the train fare to leave. Many workers died in blasting accidents, their bodies tumbled into the river along with the tonnes of rock the CNOR could not afford to remove. Determined to escape, some tried to walk to the coast or to Kamloops, and one ill-fated crew of sixty-four launched a raft on the Fraser flood, never to be seen alive again. One anonymous worker wrote in the 22 June 1912 issue of the *B.C. Federationist* that "men were cheaper to the contractor than timber that would have prevented the fall of rock that had caused the accident." If the railway thought so little of men, then the salmon which swarmed in the Fraser each fall must have seemed inconsequential indeed.

Sockeye fever gripped the salmon industry as it made preparations to harvest the big year run of 1913, despite disquieting signs in salmon markets. The first serious recession in many years had cut prices in Europe, forcing a number of small operators to dump inventories from their 1912 pack. But few canners were complaining. The first decade of the twentieth century had already been dubbed "the golden age of salmon canning," and it seemed the good times would never end.

During the twenty years from 1893 to 1913, more salmon were canned on the Fraser than in any similar period before or since. The off-year catches consistently produced between 400,000 and 600,000 cases, suggesting a catch of more than 5 million fish, until 1903, when they dropped significantly to between 150,000 and 300,000 cases. The big year catches stagger the imagination, exceeding one million cases in 1897, 2 million in 1901 and an unprecedented 2.4 million in that watershed year of 1913, when the run must have exceeded 30 million sockeye.

Early in the new year, editorial writers had been startled by the B.C. Packers' Association report of a $437,493 profit in 1912 "after liberal deductions for depreciation," a sure sign of progressive fiscal procedures and happy shareholders. The pack had neared one million cases that year, reported the New Westminster *Daily News,* and Pacific coast production exceeded 7 million.

Canneries that had not turned a wheel since the last big year were opened up, renovated and readied for action, some equipped to use the new sanitary can, which eliminated the need for both soldered lids and substantial numbers of Chinese contract workers. Of course, there would always be work for the Chinese, as canner Martin Monk assured a royal commission on labour. They worked fifteen to sixteen hours a day for only $3 to $4. "White men could hardly handle this work," he said, "as they might cut their hands." B.C.

Packers' William Barker gave a franker explanation in his testimony to the same inquiry: "A good white man can probably get better wages elsewhere."

Although the price of sockeye was expected to drop from 40 cents to 25 cents a fish in 1912, more than 4,000 fishermen operating more than 2,500 boats were expected to set their nets when the season opened.

In New Westminster, federal fisheries chief inspector F. H. Cunningham provided an analysis of the 1912 licences which gave an insight into the racist mentality of the times and the changing composition of the fleet. Of the 1,430 licences issued that year, 660 went to Japanese, 230 to native people and the rest to whites. After careful calculation and study, Cunningham concluded that the white category was comprised of 205 Canadians, 101 Scandinavians, 78 British, 35 Austrians, 28 Greeks, 23 Finlanders, 19 Italians, 17 Spaniards, 8 Germans, 10 French and 7 Russians; there were 9 who "defied the efforts of the fisheries office to classify them and were described by Inspector Cunningham as indescribables."

For the first time, the canners were preparing for a season with no "attached licences" handed directly to cannery owners. Time and experience had converted the canners to the virtues of an unlimited licensing scheme in which all comers would be granted permits. The canners were counting on their rental fleet, the disorganization of fishermen and their ability to control Japanese fishermen to retain their control over the price of fish.

Not only was the number of boats increasing, the cost of each vessel was rising as well. Gas engines were becoming widespread, adding between $200 and $600 to the cost of a $200 boat. The first twenty Easthope "Fisherman's Automatic" gas engines were installed by B.C. Packers' in its Imperial cannery fleet in 1912. Ranging from 7 to 12 horsepower, they dramatically increased the boats' efficiency. Since the canners could not take measures to increase the amount of production overall, they could compete only by intensifying the harvest of what was available. The cost of this more intensive harvest was high, but of no consequence to the canners provided it was borne by the "independent" fishermen.

A boat rental would cost a fisherman either $100 for the season or one-third of the gross catch, probably a better deal in view of the low prices. "Those fishermen owning boats have the power to sell their catches to anyone they wish," wrote one reporter in the Vancouver *Sun* on 24 April, "but this right is hardly of great value, for a uniform price is always maintained by different concerns on the rivers."

Nonetheless, the promise of a big year was stimulating plenty of interest. Early in June, native fishermen on the river reported catches of large sockeye, a sure sign of a massive run.

The first harvests that June, however, were small. After the usual consultations in cannery offices, an opening price of 25 cents a fish was posted on the river. That price was accepted by the Steveston Japanese Fishermen's Association, which represented the majority of the fishermen on the river, but to the canners' surprise, the settlement was countered by a leaflet issued by the Industrial Workers of the World (IWW, nicknamed the Wobblies), advising strike action if the price was cut. By early July, when native cannery crews were taking up residence along the Fraser, posters appeared on the boardwalks of Steveston, appealing to both fishermen and cannery workers. "Let no nationality or anything else get between you and the price of your fish," said the broadside from the IWW. "It makes no difference whether you are a Japanese, Chinese, Italian, Indian or Britisher, the bosses rob you all alike. You all belong to one nationality, the working class. The boss is the foreigner. Let him get out of the country if he does not like it, let him go to work for once in his life, then he will know what working for wages is." The offended canners demanded a roundup of Wobbly organizers, and Bowser readily complied.

The Wobblies, riding a wave of labour discontent then sweeping the province, were offering a new kind of industrial unionism that embraced every part of the workforce, regardless of race or place in the production process. For the first time since 1901, the canners faced a strategy that stood a chance of success.

Throughout July the sockeye played hide and seek with the fleet, with boat averages as low as ten fish per day. On 31 July, however, the word flashed through Steveston of increasing catches. "Salmon now running, million in the Gulf," reported the *Province*. The canners promptly cut the price to 15 cents, but the proof that the Wobblies had struck a nerve came on 3 August. "Four thousand to 5,000 strike when price cut," shouted the New Westminster *Daily News*. "Women workers join Indians, Whites and Japanese. All Walk Out Together."

It was the Japanese fishermen, however, not the IWW, leading the strike on the Fraser. Multiracial crews were dispatched on the picket boats to round up scabs and bring them to shore. B.C. Packers' tried to break the strike with trap fish, but the canners were flummoxed by the walkout of shoreworkers. "By their action in calling out the women, the Japanese and the Indians have evidently served up even the trap-owning canners," reported the 4 August *Daily News*. For the first time, the women made their own demands, insisting on 25 cents an hour and time and a half for overtime.

Some fishermen, however, could not be brought into the fight. In New Westminster, white fishermen continued to fish. Within twenty-four hours, independent canners approached the Japanese union in Steveston and offered 20 cents a fish. Although below the 25-cent target, it was 5 cents above what the major canners were paying scab fishermen. A number of Japanese fishermen returned to work, while the native and white fleet continued picketing. On shore, there was even greater confusion. Native women returned to work, in some cases accepting their old pay scale of 20 cents an hour. Japanese women remained on strike, "their places taken by Hindoos." IWW organizers were rounded up.

The strike disintegrated under an avalanche of fish. Steveston canneries were glutted with catches from American traps and from New Westminster gillnetters.

As soon as the full fleet resumed fishing, it was overwhelmed. Sockeye swarmed in every reach of the river, overflowed the cannery scows and clogged the cannery floors. The price fell to 15 cents across the board, and by 7 August, sockeye taken in excess of the boat quotas set by the canneries were being given away at Steveston docks and rumours of price cuts to 5 cents a fish swept the floats. Surplus fish putrefied at dockside, and scow after scow was dumped at Sand Heads lightship at the mouth of the Fraser. Desperate fishermen were selling sockeye in New Westminster at a price of three for 25 cents. Rotting fish discarded by fishermen and canners lined both banks of the Fraser, mixing with spilled crude oil and polluting the beaches at every tide.

As the strike ended, Cunningham wrote to Ottawa in great excitement to report the size of the run. "This year has proved that the sockeye are not depleted by any means and if they had no trap nets to content with in Puget Sound, this river would retain its reputation for the fourth year run."

Federal authorities suspended the annual 25 August to 15 September closure. It was not until 27 August that catches began to decline, but still the fleet kept working. Canneries that had thrown away fish two weeks before raised prices back up to 25 cents in an effort to keep the wheels turning.

As September turned into October, the run began to decline, but still the fishermen set their nets and the canners eagerly bought up the catches. In October, however, there came disquieting news of a demand from Victoria for a complete closure. Rumours of a slide in the Fraser Canyon swept the docks but were ridiculed by the canners.

Finally, four days later, the truth exploded into the press. Attorney General William Bowser, who doubled as the province's fisheries minister, released details of a catastrophe at Hell's Gate and of his unanswered appeals to the federal authorities for action.

On 5 August, as gillnet fishermen were ending their strike in Steveston, B.C.'s deputy fisheries commissioner J. P. Babcock was clambering down the rocks of the Fraser Canyon to Hell's Gate. Below the thundering waters of the Gate, a stunning sight awaited him: a massive school of sockeye swirling in the foam downstream for a distance of 16 kilometres. As he worked his way upstream, Babcock heard disturbing stories from native fishers. Above Scuzzy Rapids, their catches had been small, and the only sockeye on their racks had been landed some weeks before. From Seton Lake hatchery, Babcock's pride and joy, came reports that only 1,000 fish had arrived. Deeply troubled, Babcock telegraphed C. H. Gilbert, the province's leading salmon scientist, to come to the canyon immediately. As he wrote later, the source of the problem was obvious: "The road-bed was blasted through the solid rock immediately above White's Creek, Hell's Gate, China Bar and the Scuzzy Rapids in the fall and winter of 1912–13. The rock displaced by these operations and the great slides incidental thereto was tumbled into the river, further narrowing the passage-way for salmon and so increasing the difficulties that at times the channel was rendered impassable."

Babcock and Gilbert met at Hell's Gate on 19 August and observed an appalling disaster. "The entire surface of the large bay at the foot of and to the right of the Scuzzy Rapids was darkened with a milling mass of sockeye," Babcock wrote later. "Clinging closely to the shelter of the rocks on both banks of the rapids there was a thin line of advancing sockeye and a few spring salmon, which extended from the bay below to within a short distance of the head of the rapids.

"Immediately above the rapids the channel of the river widens to thrice its width just below, where the currents are mild and the eddies placid. At the head of the rapid a natural wall of rock projects from the right bank into the channel. Almost directly opposite on the left bank, immense masses of rock from the railroad-cut above had slid into the channel, constituting a great wing-dam. The rapid currents striking these two rock projections were deflected violently towards the centre of the stream. Upon attempting to pass around these two points, the sockeye were obliged to jump at right angles to the current and were swept away from the shore out into the channel, where the major portion disappeared from view beneath the chocolate coloured water."

Walking farther downstream, Babcock and Gilbert saw that for many kilometres the "sockeye were massed in incredible numbers. . . . They filled every inch of space where they could make headway against the stream and even in the most rapid parts of the channel, fish were seen struggling to advance. It was a wonderful sight." Yet most of the advancing run was unable to breach the waters of the Gate to reach the river above.

Still hoping for a miracle, Babcock contacted residents and native bands in the Quesnel, Thompson and Chilcotin districts to ask if any sockeye had arrived. Although all the areas had received some early run fish, no late run sockeye had appeared at all. There could be no doubt that the Fraser Canyon had been blocked. Finally, more than four weeks after first detecting the blockade, Babcock returned to Hell's Gate, finding the massed sockeye now joined by pink salmon. Convinced at last, he rang the alarm, dispatching his assistant to Victoria with the dreadful news.

Bowser at once telegraphed federal fisheries minister J. D. Hazen: "Through rock and gravel slides consequent on railway construction, Fraser Canyon above Yale practically impassable to salmon with the result that ninety percent of sockeye cut off from four-fifths of river during entire season. In view of extreme serious nature of situation, which threatens to wipe out big year on the Fraser, would urge you to send engineer to co-operate engineer this department."

But Ottawa was prepared to move only at a very deliberate speed. Cunningham, although ordered to inspect the scene immediately, did not reach Hell's Gate until 27 September, where he found the river almost filled "with huge rocks. The water rushes through with terrific velocity and where rocks jut out at a certain point, it forms a regular chute and comes down in such a way that even if the fish get above it, they are caught in a whirlpool, thrown out into the centre of the river and thus go down again." He assigned the department's engineer, D. W. R. Wilby, to blast a passageway for the salmon.

Channels blasted open during the next few days at Scuzzy and Hell's Gate began to carry some fish. Satisfied his job was done, Wilby returned to Victoria. A sad trickle of sockeye began to ascend the river, until falling water levels left Wilby's channels high and dry.

As Wilby packed his bags for home, Babcock was exploring the Fraser between Agassiz and Hell's Gate. From Hell's Gate to Spuzzum, the river was black with fish for 13 kilometres, with hundreds of thousands trapped below the falls that now cascaded over the site of Scuzzy Rapids. Every snag and bar was covered with dead and dying fish. From Hope to Ruby Creek and for some kilometres west, Babcock wrote, "the air was foul with the stench arising from the dead fish that covered the exposed parts of the river. The shelving bars and banks were covered with great numbers of seagulls and crows feeding on the eyes of the dead sockeye, which rose lazily upon our approach. . . . The dead sockeye were so numerous that the appetite of the birds, numerous as they were, was satisfied without turning over the bodies to obtain the other eye." On this trip and a second visit two weeks later, Babcock was unable to find a single sockeye that had spawned. "The living were not spawning and the dead were unspawned," he wrote.

News of the blockade at Hell's Gate quickly travelled to the far reaches of the Fraser and the Thompson. At scores of fishing sites, native fishers counted their catches and knew something was terribly wrong. Hundreds of people had gathered in the canyon, as their ancestors had for millennia, to gather their winter food supply, travelling by pack train from the Merritt region, down the

Nicola. Below Hell's Gate, where the water teemed with fish in tragic abundance, there was no shortage, but in the Interior, famine loomed.

A CPR inspector travelling his right of way in September "did not see a single sockeye or humpback in any of the streams or in the Thompson proper at this time. There had been so few salmon in the Thompson this year up to that time that [the tribes] could not catch more than enough to supply their daily demands." Those that could travelled to the Gate, but for the rest there was no relief. At Adams Lake, where hundreds of thousands of spawners were anticipated, only 2,000 appeared. A frantic harvest of fresh-water fish began. As autumn turned to winter, Fraser River bands normally well stocked with fish tried to migrate to lakes in the Nicola region for supplies; women and children died in the attempt as their pack trains struggled over treacherous trails in freezing rain and snow. From Lytton to Stuart Lake came calls for relief.

Meanwhile, the canners were profiting handsomely. Henry Doyle noted in his diary on 24 September that "the market has been quite excited. Price for half-pound flats of sockeye now up to $8 a case. Talls are now in demand for export with few available outside the B.C. Packers. The Wallace Fisheries are completely sold out, Todd and Bell-Irving practically so and all the small Fraser River canners."

On 4 October, provincial fisheries official D. M. McIntyre demanded a closure on the Fraser. The sockeye then being caught were "unfit for canning," he wrote to his federal counterpart, and all possible spawners were needed to perpetuate the run.

The quiet Cunningham found his voice when the interests of his canner friends were threatened. "Sockeyes now in the river in good condition for canning," he wired Ottawa. The salmon were again ascending the Fraser, he claimed, and a "closure would prove disastrous to cold storages and fishermen. I recommend fishery be allowed to continue." Ottawa overruled Cunningham and ordered the closure, but in one of the most disgraceful betrayals in the history of the fisheries service, Cunningham ignored his instructions. Not only did fishing continue, but local federal fisheries officers ridiculed the idea that the sockeye faced any problem whatsoever in their passage up the canyon.

On 6 October, Bowser again pressured Ottawa for action, but Hazen was receiving counterpressure from New Westminster MP J. D. Taylor, who warned that "industry and provincial representatives as well as federal members for Fraser District opposed to irresponsible suggestions for closing." On 10 October, Hazen formally rejected the closure and ordered fishing to continue just as Babcock was arriving at the Gate for the third time to find the passageways dry.

While federal fisheries officials wrote memos to Ottawa from the warmth of their New Westminster offices, Babcock's crews, assisted by native people from the Hell's Gate area, blasted new channels and ensured the passage of at least 1.3 million fish.

The cynicism of the federal authorities outraged even Bowser, who was no stranger to the task of prostituting the public interest. He delivered a final salvo to Ottawa by telegram and leaked it to the press. Bowser directly accused Hazen of negligence and corruption: "I regret that your officers as yet know nothing personally of conditions there and that their advice to you in the matter was coloured by solicitude that some thousands of dollars would be lost to interests, local to the places where their offices are situated, without any thought of the danger of the complete obliteration of the run in the future." He was ignored. On 11 December, Cunningham assured reporters that "all salmon, except a few stragglers, have succeeded in making the rapids."

Babcock later concluded that the 1913 Fraser sockeye run was the largest in history, with the escapement to the river the greatest since the beginning of industrial fishing, but the Hell's Gate blockade devastated the runs. Returns to the Quesnel were one-eightieth of the 1909 brood year: the Seton River received 30,000 spawners from a 1909 return of one million, and the Shuswap and Adams systems were nearly extinguished. (The abundant Upper Adams run had been devasted by a dam in 1908. The Hell's Gate blockade devastated the Lower Adams races.) In 1945, a generation after the catastrophe, federal scientists calculated the losses to the canning industry alone at between $250 million and $300 million in the first thirty years after the blockade. The human costs to those living above and below Hell's Gate were beyond computation.

Throughout 1914 and 1915, crews of workers laboured to clear the Hell's Gate blockade. They were headed by John McHugh, an experienced engineer from the federal Department of Marine and Fisheries. In the torrential rains of late October and early November, he directed operations at the Gate while CNOR crews relentlessly blasted away at their roadbed over his head. McHugh's own workers faced daunting risks as they struggled in the icy water to lay charges under massive and shifting boulders. Among them were native workers drawn from local communities and rail gangs, several of whom were injured by rock falling from above.

Continued rain brought down slides on both sides of the river throughout December, but still the CNOR carried on blasting. The CPR was twin-tracking near Yale, dumping its rock into the river with equal abandon. On 1 December, McHugh reported that both railways regularly dumped their loose rock in the river in violation of the law. He sought authority to order the removal of the spoil even if rail traffic delays resulted.

On 15 January, the fisheries department in Ottawa addressed its first warning to the CNOR and the CPR since the entire catastrophe had begun. A year later, the CNOR had not replied except to deny financial responsibility for any slides. The CPR wrote back suggesting the letter had been misaddressed and was intended for others. In fact, the CPR's own double-tracking had not been approved, and fisheries officials privately believed that a report on the impact of the double track on the Fraser "might disclose that the proper protection of the river would involve the expenditure of such a vast sum of money that the double-tracking at such points could not be undertaken."

On 23 February 1914, CNOR crews blasting a tunnel above Hell's Gate touched off a massive landslide that carried half of the mountainside into the canyon, blocking the Fraser a second time.

By mid-August, McHugh had succeeded in constructing a long wooden flume across the obstruction. Workers secured with ropes suspended themselves in the icy cataracts to drill and hammer bolts to hold the fragile flume in place. Early in September, the river carried the entire 107-metre contraption away, but McHugh's diary recorded the slow and painful contribution which native workers, dipnetting and transferring salmon one by one, made to the run's survival: 25 August, 200 sockeye; 27 August, 1,350 sockeye and 200 springs; 28 August, 1,864 sockeye and 258 springs; 29 August, 2,600 sockeye and 180 springs; 30 August, 880 sockeye. McHugh estimated his flume carried 16,500 sockeye and 850 springs over the slide that autumn, in addition to an unknown number which made it on their own.

It took McHugh a year, the life of one of his workers and more than $108,000, an enormous sum for the period, to restore Hell's Gate to a semblance of its former flows.

The last spike was driven on the CNOR on 23 January 1915, and traffic began moving in March 1917. Among the first shipments was a trainload of canned salmon destined for Europe. Salmon unable to pass Hell's Gate in the river now had a choice of routes to do so by rail.

For the Fraser, the golden age of salmon canning was over. Sockeye were scarce. Someone would have to be sacrificed to make ends meet. The Hell's Gate blockade initiated an era of expulsions from the salmon fishery, the forced exile first of native people and then of Japanese. The native people were driven out of the fishery because white society wanted their fish; the Japanese because whites wanted their jobs. In both cases, the expulsions were carried out largely by decree, by fisheries officials who knew their actions were either of dubious legality or completely illegal. Yet the actions directed against both groups were largely successful. If there are native people or Japanese Canadians in the industry today, it is due entirely to their own efforts, because almost no one could be found in the dominant white society to speak up for their rights.

PART TWO

COMPETITION AND CONFRONTATION

THE FISH OF THE PROVINCE BELONG TO THE PEOPLE OF CANADA. THEY CONSTITUTE ONE OF OUR GREATEST NATURAL ASSETS. . . . DEPLETED RUNS CAN BE RESTORED. THE RUNS OF FORMER YEARS MAY EVEN BE ENLARGED. IF THE BEDS ARE SEEDED THERE WILL BE A CERTAIN RETURN. THE FISH WILL DO THE WORK NECESSARY, PROVIDED THE GOVERNMENT GIVES THEM A CHANCE TO DO SO. THEY WILL PERPETUATE THEMSELVES WITHOUT COST. THEY WILL ENTIRELY DISAPPEAR IF LEFT TO CORPORATE AND INDIVIDUAL CONTROL.

—WILLIAM SLOAN,

B.C. Fisheries Commissioner,
Memorandum Respecting Salmon
Fishery Regulations,
December 1919

THE EXPANSION OF THE FISHERY

THE FIRST WORLD WAR ASSURED THE CANNERS THE ABUN-
dant profits of guaranteed markets, so they spent the time in intensive expansion, undertaking a new rush for the largely unharvested stocks of chum and
pink salmon in the waters north of Johnstone Strait, shipping these former
nuisance fish into new markets in Europe and the southern United States. The
insatiable demand for salmon was led by the British army, which added
canned salmon to its basic rations.

The times called for a new policy to satisfy the public clamour for an end to
"special privileges" yet allow an intensification of the harvest to ensure profits.
The architect of the policies that dominated this period was William Ambrose
Found, a meticulous, clean-shaven and unassuming man who gave the impression of indecision and mediocrity. In reality, Found had a lively intelligence
and a sure grasp of his files. He emerged from relative obscurity in the fisheries
department to assume the post of superintendent of fisheries when E. E.
Prince retired. From then on, Found's rise was meteoric. He was appointed assistant deputy minister in 1920 and deputy minister in 1927. Until his retirement in 1938, he was director of fisheries, standing at the peak of the national
fisheries bureaucracy with a decisive role in every significant policy decision.
Very soon after his appointment, Found took a firm hold of the levers of power
and began to move the salmon fishery to an entirely open system, whereby in
theory the opportunity to fish would be available to all without discrimination.

Found and his subordinates, Cunningham and Williams, were playing a
complex game. Sensitive to the public demand for an end to the canners'
power, they were moving to a licensing system in which the remaining special

fishing rights of the canning fraternity would be eliminated. The attached cannery licences that remained everywhere except the Fraser, for example, would be wiped out, as would the exclusive seine leases that blanketed much of the coast.

But in order to open the fishery to some, others had to be excluded. The policy of the fisheries department between the Hell's Gate slides and the beginning of the Great Depression was to support the canning industry by encouraging the most intensive possible harvest of remaining stocks. Since these runs included coho, chums and pinks, which now were in demand but not easy to gillnet in river-mouth fisheries, the industry required the development of a highly mobile purse-seine fishery. This economic imperative had to be balanced with the pressure to curb and then to eliminate Japanese fishermen.

The move to an unlimited seine fishery had the additional effect of negating the aboriginal fishing rights of coastal people, whose most lucrative fishing spots had often been converted to exclusive beach seine leases. Such leases were, in effect, joint ventures between local chiefs, who provided labour, and canners, who provided capital. These comfortable arrangements could not survive the economic storms which had been developing for a decade, storms unleashed by Found's policy and by the destruction of the Fraser sockeye runs.

The outbreak of the First World War hard on the heels of the Hell's Gate blockade made a further assault on aboriginal fishing rights both economically necessary and politically feasible.

F. H. Cunningham, the superintendent of fisheries, moved against the native fishery in the Fraser canyon in July 1914. As the magnitude of the Hell's Gate disaster had become apparent, he directed an immediate and comprehensive enforcement of the ban on the sale of food fish and attempted to restrict the food fishery which did occur. The use of dipnets and sidenets was banned. "This curtailment of the liberties of the Indians was very strongly resented by them," Cunningham later acknowledged, "it being probably the first time this ancestral privilege had been in any degree interfered with." Although cloaked in the virtuous rhetoric of conservation, the policy amounted to a straight reallocation of fish from the native people to the canners.

Cunningham also forced an end to the prevailing legal attitude that had tolerated the native sale of fish provided the money was used for personal subsistence. Fisheries officials attempted to enforce Cunningham's determination to prohibit all fishing between Hope and Lytton.

The enforcement of the closures above tidewater caused widespread hunger, provoked intense resistance and provided one of the sparks which led to the resurgence of the movement for aboriginal land claims. Initially, however, many bands were too preoccupied with the simple matter of survival to take up their grievances with Ottawa. At the northern extreme of the sockeye harvest, at Stuart Lake, Carrier people who had based a tenuous existence on the runs found their food supply had vanished. A few years before, they had lost their weirs to the same crusade which hit the Babine. After making extensive preparations in 1913 for a large catch, the Stuart bands were forced to trek over to the Babine watershed to take their winter supply. In 1914, the Stuart Lake fishery yielded only 800 fish for thirty families.

The famine on the Fraser was prolonged. Babcock's tour of the spawning grounds in 1916 revealed a litany of devastation. The bands on the Shuswap had only enough fish for immediate consumption—their drying racks stood empty. The Quesnel had only 3,000 spawners, the Chilko was barren, and only 20 sockeye had arrived at Stuart Lake. These disastrous returns produced a sharp increase in the need for relief throughout the Fraser watershed, and the correspondence to fisheries officials from their Indian Affairs counterparts developed an acid tone. In one of his many futile protests to the fisheries department, the deputy superintendent for Indian Affairs, D. C. Scott, complained: "The present impoverished conditions of the Indians is principally due to the restrictions that have been placed upon the salmon fishery, which has been, as you are aware, their principal source of livelihood from time immemorial."

Poor results in the subsequent two years provoked an all-out campaign by fisheries officials in 1919 to shut the river completely above Mission. Significantly, however, the bands were promised compensation, a commitment that was not kept but which reflected the government's awareness of aboriginal rights.

The native groups of the canyon defied the renewed closure, and ten people were charged in what the fisheries department feared would become a test case. Led by Chief Benedict of the Thompson, and Chief Joseph Brown and Chief John Charley of Boston Bar, they hired a lawyer who put the case succinctly: "The commercial fishermen of the coast are allowed to fish as freely as ever for profit [while] natives who fish for their very means of livelihood alone are stopped. The right of Indians to take fish and game for their own sustenance has never been questioned since the very first days of white settlement in this country." The ten ultimately paid fines and were released.

The species of salmon now sought by the canners—particularly pinks and chums—ran to every river and creek on the coast. Although larger stocks ran up the major river systems, most chum runs relied on smaller rivers, too small to justify the construction of a cannery or the deployment of a gillnet fleet. The best gear for chum fishing was a purse seine worked from a larger vessel, which could move from stream to stream and run longer distances to deliver.

By releasing their nets to encircle the schools of fish, seine fishermen could harvest effectively in waters unsuitable for gillnetting. Once the catch was made, the net was "pursed up" and the encircled fish were brought aboard.

The technique of purse seining and the development of more powerful gas engines enabled canners to reduce labour costs and to harvest wherever the fish could be found. Initially, purse seines were used primarily in the limited herring and chum fisheries established by the Japanese for the salt fish markets of Asia. Elsewhere, however, chums were harvested almost exclusively by native people for domestic consumption.

Most of the British Columbia coast was taken up in seine leases, held by speculators who seldom exercised their rights. Where they did, their nets were almost exclusively beach or drag seines. One end of the net was secured on shore while the other was towed in a large circle by a skiff or scow. Once set around the fish, the net was towed into shore by manual labour, a team of horses or a donkey engine. At places like Nimpkish, Quashela Creek in Smith Inlet and several other locations, small sockeye runs justified both a cannery and a seine operation. In many locations, the exclusive rights claimed by fishing companies and native bands were effectively interlocked. As long as canners hired native labour—and they seldom had any alternative—the chiefs were content to allow the fishery to proceed.

Some canners and white fishermen opposed the continuance of existing seine leases, but for different reasons. Most fishermen saw them as a symbol of economic privilege which stood in the way of a modern, small-boat fishery. Some canners wished to break the legal strait jacket imposed by the outmoded lease terms. Cunningham and Found were determined to meet both objections and were prepared to override the protests of existing lease-holders in the process.

Coastal bands soon learned of an equally serious threat to their livelihoods. Found's new policy of issuing independent licences to qualified fishermen in northern waters contained a clause denying the licences to native people, a clause based on the government's unstated objective of creating a "white fishing population." The canners, no longer so reliant on native labour, were keen to keep their cannery licences for Japanese fishermen, who could be retained in conditions of near serfdom. With the independent licences offered exclusively to white fishermen and cannery licences held for Japanese, scores of native gillnetters found themselves unemployed. A petition sent to Ottawa in 1915 by the native fishermen of Hartley Bay, Port Essington, Kitsegukla, Kispiox, Glen Vowell and Kitselas reported that fewer than 50 per cent of them seeking jobs in 1914 had found work. They demanded independent licences and a commission of inquiry.

Native leaders quickly took the gillnet licence issue before the McKenna-McBride Commission, a federal-provincial royal commission then touring the province to determine reserve boundaries. In Bella Coola, Chief Peter Elliott testified that of seventy native gillnetters who had worked in 1912, none received independent licences in 1915, despite the issuance of thirty licences to whites in the area. "All we ask is to have equal rights with the whites," he said. The McKenna-McBride commissioners concluded that the native complaint was fully justified. In an appendix, they quoted the testimony of Cunningham, who said the licences were restricted to white men as an inducement to settle. Commissioner McKenna was thunderstruck when Cunningham vowed to double the number of white fishermen in Smith Inlet without allowing a single licence to native people. "You discriminate against the Indians," McKenna asked, "who were the first settlers on the coast, who built the first boats and knew the harbours and knew the places where the fish ran, and these Indians cannot have the same privileges as these white men because they are bronze skinned?" The commissioners unanimously recommended an end to the practice, but Found would agree only that canners should be encouraged to hire native people before giving licences to Japanese. The ban on independent licences for native people would remain.

The continued hiring of Japanese on attached licences while native people remained on the beach added salt to the wounds of the chiefs and their band members in every community. They readily joined in the clamour for Japanese exclusion and were supported in this and their call for independent licences by white fishermen's organizations in the north. At the same time, however, coastal bands increased their sale of "food fish" to the canners.

The Great War intervened to reduce some of the pressure. As white workers were fed into the trenches, more openings appeared in the gillnet fleet for native fishermen. By late 1916, the newly formed Native Fishermen's Association of B.C., an organization claiming 114 members, was applauding the department for the increase in native employment. A year later, cleric and NFA leader the Rev. William H. Pierce advised the department his organization could speak for 500 members and 21 bands. By urging its members to be sober and industrious, he wrote, the NFA hoped to prove they were "deserving of unattached licences."

The issue of the aboriginal right to sell fish also absorbed the time of the commissioners, a question which was linked to the creation of exclusive fishing reserves and fishing stations by earlier reserve commissions. There was no doubt, the commission said, that previous reserve commissions had granted "exceptional or even exclusive rights to fish in certain particularized waters" to dozens of bands. Not only should Ottawa and Victoria determine whether or not to confirm those rights, the commission said, the two governments should also consider the fact that many of the rights had "been wholly or in large measure destroyed by the subsequent allowance of cannery seining licences." The commission recommended that these rights be clarified and that native people be granted the right to sell fish in specific limited quantities, provided the proceeds were for personal use and reduced the demand for government aid.

In the conclusion to their report on fisheries issues, the commissioners drew to the attention of Ottawa and Victoria certain remarks which appeared "to disclose the mind of the officials of the Fisheries Department in their administration of the Regulations as affecting the Indians of this Province." The remarks are contained in extracts of minutes from two special conferences with fisheries officials in Victoria:

April 9, 1914:

CHIEF INSPECTOR CUNNINGHAM: . . . The time will probably come when it will pay the Government to provide for the Indians by other methods than the extension of fishing privileges . . .

December 23, 1915:

MR. CUNNINGHAM: . . . If he [the Indian] is not taken care of, why do they have Indian Agents to look after them? Why do they give them farming implements and cattle and in fact everything that they want . . . I think it would be in the public interest to feed the Indian on white men's food and don't let them eat any more fish at all . . .

MR. BABCOCK: . . . I think the fishing regulations should be changed; I would like to see above all things the Dominion Government buy up all the privileges in regard to fishing that the Indians have, because the fish are worth more to the Dominion Government than they are to the Indians . . .

Babcock's view became provincial policy. In 1919, provincial fisheries commissioner William Sloan urged that Ottawa purchase and eliminate aboriginal fishing rights. Ottawa agreed that the fishing rights should be eliminated but saw no need to pay. That bill could be borne by future generations. For Found, Cunningham and their associates, the immediate task at hand was to ensure the profits of the canners. That required the creation of a mobile purse-seine fleet. Once such a fleet was in place, talk of aboriginal fishing rights would be so much hot air.

Throughout the First World War, Cunningham was besieged by attacks on the seine lease system. Typical was the petition produced in 1916 by citizens in the Duncan area who opposed the seine lease in Crofton Bay. Signed by 113 people, including labourers, longshoremen, sawmill workers, truck drivers, clerks, an oyster farmer, loggers, carpenters and one hotel keeper, the petition also demanded an open fishery and an end to privileges. Similar controversies erupted at Cowichan Bay, around Prince Rupert and in Port Alberni.

Cunningham introduced regulations to create a series of seine districts up and down the coast. The number of purse seines licensed for each area would not be limited. As for the drag seines or beach seines on which so many native communities relied, "it is my desire to eliminate this class of fishing as much as possible," Cunningham told Found. Found warmly approved. When he obtained ministerial approval late in 1919 to end the limitation on licences, he directed Cunningham to issue seine licences to members of the white race only.

Within thirty days, Cunningham had issued regulations to open purse seining in ten northern areas. Seines would be restricted to a single area, but an operator could own vessels in several areas. The goal was to compel independent owners of seine vessels to deliver to the cannery in their area, thus reducing the possibility of upward pressure on prices. In January 1920 Cunningham explicitly rejected any thought of protecting native beach seine fisheries. "Purse seines can be fished where the Indians now operate their drag seines," he ruled. "It is no use considering except under the most extraordinary conditions the protection of any person operating in the fishing industry."

This sudden revolution in fishing regulations caught both native communities and the Department of Indian Affairs entirely by surprise. By March, Indian agents were predicting serious trouble "if the cannerymen carry out their threat to have white men fish in waters fronting all Indian reserves where there are fish," but that was precisely what Found and Cunningham planned. Desbarats deflected protests from D. C. Scott of Indian Affairs with the suggestion that the native people could find work on purse seines. To ensure that such work was done on the canners' terms, he directed his officials to reject applications for seines from native people. The same day that Found spelled out this policy to his officials, he also ordered that troll licences should be denied to Japanese fishermen.

This edict from Ottawa precipitated chaos on the coast, as Indian agents and even some canners had predicted. To their anger and dismay, many native bands set out their gear that summer only to find two, three and four purse seines setting just offshore, devastating the run and effectively denying fish to them. At Minktrap Bay near Kitkatla, Chief Amos Collinson ran off white fishermen at gunpoint when they attempted to set at his hereditary fishing spot near Deer Point. On 26 July, Found was cornered in Port Essington by the Rev. William Pierce, founder of the Native Fishing Association, who headed a delegation of northern chiefs demanding exclusive rights on their creeks and access to the newly minted purse seine licences. They were denied both requests. Chief Campbell of the Kitkatla band feared the salmon would be "killed out." He wanted a ban on seining around creek mouths and sought licences for his own people. The Skidegate people sought protection for eight streams on the Queen Charlotte Islands. Joseph Bradly of Port Simpson told Found that "wise men always prevent trouble and preserve life. We come now to ask the Government to prevent fishing the creeks and rivers with purse-seines. . . . We feel it is not right for us to have to buy a licence to fish at all, because the rivers belong to us." The native people would take licences, he said, but wanted their creeks reserved. More than 2,000 members were represented by the delegation, Pierce concluded, and threats of gunplay could become reality if Found did not act. Found refused, but promised to consider issuing some seine licences to native people.

The countless creeks and rivers traditionally owned by native people thus remained open to all comers, and the salmon stocks paid a heavy price for the new policy. Found was more eager, however, to protect the interests of canners whose exclusive sockeye leases now were rendered worthless. Two prominent cases were the B.C. Packers' leases on the Nimpkish and at Lowe Inlet, both consistent sockeye producers. At Nimpkish, the company had effectively acknowledged the Kwakiutl title to the fish by paying a rent for the use of the foreshore, by paying the going commercial rate for all fish landed and by hiring labour exclusively through the chiefs living at Alert Bay. When seiners owned by Preston Packing fished within view of the B.C. Packers' lease, the band passed a number of resolutions demanding protection for the old arrangement. Not all the native people favoured B.C. Packers'; some liked the fact that Preston Packing had offered a substantial price premium for fish delivered to its boats.

The situation was equally difficult at Lowe Inlet, where cannery manager William Curtis became a staunch defender of aboriginal rights. Clearly, the days of his operation were numbered if purse seines were allowed to intercept the Lowe Inlet run. The fisheries department had always acknowledged at least a native "moral" right to the creek, Curtis wrote, but now "this is all to be changed, the Indian 'moral' right is to be no longer recognized and all these Indian creeks are to be thrown open to white men only. It is quite likely that thirty or forty purse seine licences will be given out in Lowe Inlet district alone, and as each and every of all these purse seines may fish at every creek you will readily see that the early extermination of the salmon must follow, so that there will be none for either Cannery or Indian."

The purse-seine policy, although it was directed at coastal bands, united both Interior and coastal groups. Andrew Paull, who was organizing protests on Howe Sound and the Fraser to oppose restrictions on the native fishery on the Fraser, again raised the call to legalize the sale of all native-caught fish. Found turned him down. Early in 1920, Nisga'a elder Peter Calder joined Paull to confront Found in Ottawa, where both "very strongly objected" to the denial of purse-seine licences to native people because it compelled them to work for the canneries. It was after this meeting that Found pasted into his files an undated newspaper clipping of a poem on the issue, aptly entitled "God and the Millionaires."

After consulting with his friends in the canning industry, Found adjusted the regulations to allow drag seines to remain at Lowe Inlet and Alert Bay. Fisheries files do not record how many drag seines were eliminated in this regulatory coup, nor do they record what happened in native communities which lost first their fishing traps, then their gillnet licences and finally their opportunity to seine. It is safe to assume that hardship and some hunger resulted from Found's policies, although coastal bands often had more food available from the sea than Interior tribes could gather from hunting or trapping. In 1923, Found tightened the noose by banning any form of seining within 365 metres of a creek or river mouth. This effectively did away with most of the remaining drag seines which had sheltered under the protection granted to existing canneries.

Native resistance to the attack on their fisheries was prolonged, determined and soon merged with the growing demand for a comprehensive settlement of the land claims question. In 1914, Ottawa was moving to counter the increasing pressure, particularly from the Nisga'a, for recognition of their land claims. Then, as now, the Nisga'a were demanding a comprehensive treaty between their nation and the crown, as promised in the Royal Proclamation of 1763. They were not alone. Chiefs from many areas had met on several occasions with Sir Wilfrid Laurier during his 1910 tour of the province, and almost a hundred chiefs had travelled to Victoria the next year to pressure Premier Richard McBride. By 1916, Andrew Paull and Peter Kelly, a Methodist minister with ties to the fishing industry, were able to convene a conference of native people from every part of the province to form the Allied Indian Tribes of B.C. to press for resolution of the land question.

For the next four years, the Allied Tribes lobbied, petitioned and pressured Ottawa for action. The question of fishing rights assumed greater and greater importance as the Fraser closures continued, although the Allied Tribes tended to restrict the issue to one of fishing for food rather than for sale. Their efforts reached a peak in 1927 when a special parliamentary committee was struck to investigate their claims. In lengthy hearings, Paull and Kelly defended aboriginal claims and insisted on "the right to catch fish in all rivers, lakes and tidal waters of the province without permit and without any limit with the explicit understanding that the fish will be used by the Indians for food only." They further demanded the right to fish or troll without licence in tidal waters and to be granted seine licences at half the prevailing fees. Finally, the Allied Tribes demanded that "in all fishing districts certain waters be reserved for the exclusive use of Indian bands or tribes."

The Allied Tribes' position of 1927 was remarkably close to the solution offered forty years before by A. C. Anderson. Although the Allied Tribes had made a significant concession on their right to sell their catch, their proposal essentially consisted of a demand for exclusive fishing rights in certain locations combined with access to the commercial fishery on the coast. But the special committee not only urged rejection of the Allied Tribes' petition, it laid the groundwork for the repression of native organizations. In 1920, Ottawa had begun coastwide enforcement of its ban on the potlatch ceremony with a wave of arrests and jailings. By 1927, the government felt strong enough to deny the existence of any aboriginal rights whatsoever. The special committee rejected any land claims, and amendments to the Indian Act passed in 1927 made it a crime to raise money for the pursuit of aboriginal claims.

Those amendments destroyed the Allied Indian Tribes and forced the struggle for native rights underground. The battle for fishing rights went with it. As the years passed, the fisheries department slowly relented on its closure in the Interior, allowing food fishing to resume with a permit. By 1927, most local fisheries officers even gave up attempting to curb the sale of fish because of the difficulty of proving it was illegally caught. A fishery that a century before had supported tens of thousands of native people, as well as the Hudson's Bay Company's export trade, was reduced to a closely watched food fishery which eked out a meagre harvest from the Fraser's shattered runs.

The situation on the coast was little better. Found's regulations had led to a dramatic expansion of the seine fleet and a consequent heavy harvest of small stocks. Between 1922 and 1925, the number of purse seines doubled from 142 to 302. By 1925, the industry was virtually unanimous on the need to regulate the size of seines to eliminate the shallow nets used in river and creek mouths. The decision to make seines a minimum 10 fathoms (18 metres) deep eliminated the many 8-fathom and 6-fathom nets then popular. The minimum length later was fixed at 150 fathoms (275 metres). Although a necessary measure, it hit hard at native fishermen, who often now were relegated to smaller and less efficient cannery gear which they fished from flat-bottomed scows, sometimes equipped with power winches.

At the other end of the scale were company-financed seiners with powerful gas motors, large enough to inaugurate the sockeye fishery in the Strait of Juan de Fuca by 1925. The number of seiners continued to grow, rising to 406 in 1926. Increasing numbers were owned by independent operators, who typically operated smaller vessels as little as 9 or 12 metres long with double-ended hulls and a small wheelhouse. Quarters were cramped, the hours long, and the work all by hand, but there was money to be made. The rules restricting the work to British subjects were twisted to allow Yugoslavs to participate because of the growing demand for experienced fishermen. Native people were less welcome. As late as 1927, Found still was seeking ways to eliminate small seines 60 to 80 fathoms [110 to 146 metres] long "used chiefly by Indians . . . with deliberate intention of fishing illegally."

In fact, these small purse seines were sometimes also deployed by canneries working in shallow inlets. J. J. Petrich, the manager of Nootka Packing, told the Port Alberni Indian agent that his fleet of fifteen boats, crewed entirely by native workers, used nets of between 75 and 90 fathoms (137 and 165 metres). The fleet employed forty-five fishermen in the fall fishery, and their combined earnings of $16,000 between 10 September and 29 October could be added to the native women's combined cannery earnings of $8,000 to suggest the economic importance of these jobs. Found's ruling may have saved some fish, somewhere, but it also spelled the end of the Nootka Packing operation.

Although the department had permitted drag seines to remain in certain areas, it had not restricted the operation of purse seines in the same districts. By 1926, the Nimpkish boasted twenty-seven drag seines and thirty purse seines where a handful of drag seines had worked for decades. All of the new nets were fishing four days a week and all were losing money. Found again laid plans to eliminate the remaining drag seines on "conservation grounds," although conservation regulations governing the purse-seine fishery were virtually unenforceable.

By 1927, however, Found's concern with drag seines had dwindled. The economic forces unleashed by the policy of open fishing had created a far deeper crisis. With the assistance of local officers, he began tightening the regulatory screws to force the canners to confront the consequences of their latest assault on the stocks. In ten years, he had not only dramatically curbed the Interior native fishery, he had reduced the coastal people to supplicants for jobs on the decks of seine boats.

THE RISE OF THE CANNERS'

NORTHERN EMPIRE

THE COLLAPSE OF THE FRASER SOCKEYE RUNS ACCELERATED
the move to pillage the province's northern stocks. Canneries had long been
established on the Skeena, at Rivers Inlet and near other sockeye runs, but
now new plants rose in a dozen other locations to can the coho, pinks and
chums previously discarded as pests. Just as sockeye had been developed as the
food of working people, so these new products were sold in mass markets of
the working poor. The chums sold well to sharecroppers of America's Deep
South, and large shipments of the coho and pinks were sold to Mediterranean
countries.

The new salmon rush in northern British Columbia was dominated by investors whose fortunes were not reliant on the strength of the Fraser runs.
Among the newcomers were Richard E. Gosse, Francis Millerd and the backers of the New England Fishing Co. Gosse was a Newfoundland fisherman
who rose to the command of his own vessel at the age of twenty-one. He immigrated to British Columbia in 1887, and in 1894 was engaged to build a
cannery for Dinsmore Island Canning. He was so successful that he soon
moved into cannery construction full-time, building either for others or for
companies he established himself. In 1908, he hired another recent immigrant
to operate one of his Fraser River canneries, Francis Millerd, an Irish veteran of
the Boer War. Together they built Gosse-Millerd, a canning empire in the
northern coast that was to last until the great collapse of 1928, although the
two parted ways in 1921. Hard on the heels of Millerd came Alvah Hager, the
agent of New England Fishing of Boston, which was seeking new supplies of
halibut. Hager took over a small Vancouver company called Canadian Fishing
on New England's behalf and began to build it into a diversified firm, starting

first with cold storage work and then moving into salmon canning. These men and many others became the new generation of canners.

These firms gained added financial strength from new canning technology which cut labour requirements by up to 35 per cent. The solderless sanitary can, which used a lock and lap seam to eliminate the painstaking hand-soldering performed by skilled Chinese workers, drastically reduced the number of defective cans as well as lowering labour costs. The sanitary can and further automation of other aspects of the canning line eased the transition to the cheaper grades of salmon by reducing the cost of production.

The canners set up a regulatory system in northern waters which exactly duplicated the palmy days on the Fraser before the rise of trade unionism. To avoid wasteful competition for fish, they had conspired in 1908 to establish a "boat rating" to limit the number of boats fishing in each area. Each canner was assigned a quota of boats. These licences were attached to the cannery as they had been on the Fraser. On the Skeena the fleet totalled 850, and 750 gillnetters were allocated to the waters of Rivers Inlet. To eliminate the prospect of more competition, in 1914 the canners secured federal and provincial legislation putting a freeze on the construction of any new canneries.

Between 1913 and 1915, the pack of Fraser River pink salmon soared from 9,973 to 128,550 cases. Sockeye prices reached a new high of 50 cents a fish, and even the lowly pink salmon were worth 15 cents each. Despite the poor performance of the Fraser sockeye, the industry began exceeding the packs of the big years by harvesting fish it previously had spurned.

Cunningham and John Williams, supervisor of District 2, fought a bitter rearguard action against independent fishermen who sought the right to fish in northern waters. These fishermen, including many Finns and Norwegians then settling in Johnstone Strait and in the little community of Sointula on Malcolm Island, won commitments from the government that any white fisherman seeking a licence would get one. As they had been on the Fraser, these "independent licences" were drawn from the total pool of licences established by the boat rating. All the rest of the licences were "attached" to specific canneries.

During the early war years, Cunningham and Williams carefully limited the independent licences to 300 for the entire area from Johnstone Strait to Rivers Inlet, but public opinion saw the creation of an open fishery as an important tool in developing the coast. Early in 1917, W. D. Burdis, secretary of the B.C. Canners Association, was horrified to learn that B.C. members of Parliament, meeting as a Fisheries Advisory Board in Prince Rupert, had urged the government to eliminate the boat rating and open up fishing coastwide. Even more incredible. they proposed to legalize gas-powered gillnetters in District 2, where the sail gillnetter reigned supreme. Burdis pound-ed out a letter to J. D. Hazen, minister of fisheries, in which he launched the canners' offensive in defence of their profits. Elimination of the limits on the numbers of canneries, seine leases and fishermen would result not only in depletion of profits but also of salmon, Burdis wrote.

Aemilius Jarvis, now vice-president of B.C. Packers, considered the very concept of living in northern B.C. ridiculous. "Have you ever had the pleasure of visiting these northern districts and seeing where the inhabitants are clinging on by their eyebrows to the pine-covered rocks on the margin of these outlandish parts?" he asked Hazen. But under Found's influence, the department stood firm. With the Grand Trunk Pacific Railway about to begin service to Prince Rupert, new business interests were determined to have their share of northern B.C.'s wealth. In words that struck like cold steel into the canners' hearts, deputy minister G. J. Desbarats declared that the boat rating would be discontinued and "such licences as are issued will be independent of any cannery."

Insistent pressure by fishermen's associations had compelled Cunningham to issue independent licences for northern waters in every year of the war, but the independents could do little without gas engines, which still were banned to save the canners from the high cost of conversion. An open fishery meant all the nightmares the canners had fled on the Fraser: unions, high costs, real competition. Now thoroughly on the defensive, the canners campaigned feverishly for a postponement of open fishing until it could be considered by "a commission of practical businessmen, non-political in character."

As always when the canners pulled out all the stops, Ottawa complied, but limited the terms of reference of the new commission to issues affecting District 2, thus shelving some burning issues such as oriental exclusion and a Canada-United States salmon treaty, which were left to fester. Named to head the commission was economist Sanford Evans. Between the commission's appointment and the release of its report, Prime Minister Robert Borden won re-election at the head of the Unionist government. The new fisheries minister, C. C. Ballantyne, received a report from Evans which met most of the canners' demands. Evans recommended that the freeze on the number of canneries continue for at least five years, along with the prohibition of gas boats in District 2 for the same period. In a concession to the fishermen, however, Evans recommended the end of attached licences, urging the government to issue gillnet licences to any British subject who was a bona fide fisherman, or could prove some competence in gillnet fishing.

Evans's recommendations simply fuelled the controversy. Northern fishermen, particularly in the rowdy railway town of Prince Rupert, deluged Ottawa with demands for action. They not only demanded an end to attached gillnet licences but also an end to seine leases, whose ownership was so concentrated that five firms controlled seining on 4,800 kilometres of B.C.'s twisting coast. The Rupert fishermen also provided Ottawa with convincing proof of depressed prices in District 2, where fishermen had no alternative but to deliver to the main canners. Sockeye worth 35 cents each on the Fraser were only 25 cents in the north. Coho were 5 cents on the Fraser, 4 cents in the north. Pinks were 15 cents in the south, only a nickel on the Skeena; and chum salmon worth 35 cents on the Fraser had to be sold for 7 cents on the Skeena.

Ballantyne deferred action on the Evans report until after the 1918 season, then implemented most of its demands. His guide in these actions was Found, who contrived a policy which would allow Ballantyne to continue the moratorium on cannery licences while still protecting the public interest. In exchange for the continued limit on canneries, the government announced it would levy a tax on production to raise revenues from canneries to $300,000 a year from the existing level of $50,000. (The fee for a cannery licence was raised from $50 a year to $500 plus 4 cents for a case of sockeye and 3 cents for each case of other salmon production.)

The canners resented the royalty but could not complain. Although the boat rating was abolished, the implementation of the rest of Evans's recommendations represented a major victory for the canners. It seemed their northern kingdom was safe, but it could not last. The fall of 1918 brought the end of the war and the return of Canada's soldiers. After years in the trenches, they were angered by privilege and profiteering and eager to make their own fortunes. For the veterans, the stink of corruption from the canners' cartel was too much to bear.

In December 1918, the Port Alberni *News* broke the sensational news that eighteen fishermen, native and white, had sworn affidavits condemning the destruction of fish by company seines operating in Barkley Sound. Conservation was their first concern, they told reporters, and private ownership of the seine leases was the root of the problem. Because they believed F. H. Cunningham, chief superintendent of fisheries, was "a party to the abuse of seining privileges," they declined to lay their charges before him. Their testimony implicated Wallace Fisheries, Gosse Packing and Canadian Fishing in the destruction of stocks in both the herring and sockeye fisheries. One affidavit said Wallace was using both purse and drag seines to take sockeye in the mouth of the Anderson River in contravention of the law.

Other affidavits described the destruction of salmon fishing in Uchucklesit Inlet, where in 1913 three purse seines had taken 10,000 to 20,000 fish a day. The result of this massacre was that the catch in 1918 was only one-tenth of its former level. Similar overharvests afflicted herring stocks. Witnesses described the destruction of tonnes of herring, which were left to sink to the bottom because the salteries could not handle the catch. (The herring was salted for export to Japan.)

Found directed Cunningham to go immediately to Port Alberni, "investigate fully and fearlessly deal with the situation." Cunningham went, but the people of Port Alberni would have nothing to do with him. Better to send someone to investigate Cunningham, said the Great War Veterans Association, than to send Cunningham to investigate the fisheries. Local fishermen formed the Barkley Sound Fishermen's Protective Association to press their charges, most of which centred on the activities of Wallace Fisheries.

Ballantyne needed little urging to investigate the crimes of the previous administration. In January 1919, he appointed Mr. Justice D. M. Eberts to conduct a public inquiry. Eberts's hearings provided reporters with sensational copy. Leading the attack was MLA Major Richard Burde, who denounced the fisheries department as a "standing disgrace." "There never was a bigger graft in Canada than there is where one must wait for a fishing licence," he said. "You can sell a fishing licence any day in a real estate office for $3,000 or $4,000." The racist mood of the time was inflamed by the fact that Wallace subleased most of its privileges to Japanese operators.

The specific charges against Cunningham included allegations that he had denied licences to those not linked to Wallace, that he had offered a licence to a man on condition that he fish for Wallace and that he had charged a gillnetter for fishing in Uchucklesit Inlet where Wallace seiners were at work. The arrest of the gillnetter had proved a major embarrassment. Police were forced to release the fisherman because his arrest had been illegal—Cunningham had neglected to prohibit fishing by others after the leases were granted.

Most astonishing of all was the claim that fisheries inspector Edward Taylor "in the presence of Chief Shewish, moved forward the legal stakes indicating the boundaries for fishing so as to enable Wallace and other large cannery interests to operate their seine within illegal distance of the Nahmint River, Mr. Taylor stating at the time that it was not right that these people with large investments should not be taken care of."

Hearings in the Port Alberni opera house were packed. Wallace was running scared, threatening to shut down if denied the right to seine. Provincial fisheries commissioner William Sloan turned up to testify and added more bombshells, revealing that an American firm had been given exclusive rights to seine at the mouth of the Nitinat and that a Toronto friend of the government, a fish broker who had served on the Sanford Evans commission, had won similar rights for the Cowichan River. Over Cunningham's protests, Found and Ballantyne ordered Eberts to expand his inquiry to cover all of Vancouver Island.

Eberts's report, when it finally came down in October 1921, exonerated

Cunningham, but the vote of confidence came too late. Cunningham was forced from his job by the Barkley Sound scandal and took up full-time work with the canners, promoting their interests openly rather than covertly.

The Barkley Sound investigation came as thousands of veterans returned to the coast, impatient for peace and prosperity. There was also a pent-up anger among B.C. workers at the sacrifices they had made during the conflict while corporations grew fat. Labour organization was at all-time high, and when the Winnipeg General Strike began in May 1919, sympathy strikes hit Victoria, Vancouver, Prince Rupert and several smaller centres. The public was in no mood to grant legal protection to monopolies, and wise politicians took note. The Eberts inquiry confirmed that it was the time to end special privileges for the business class.

The outcry provoked by the Barkley Sound affair produced irresistible pressure on Ballantyne and Found to withdraw the remaining concessions they had granted the canners after the Evans report. The chief target of the fishermen was the continued limitation on seine privileges, but they were determined as well to demolish the vestiges of the boat rating system. The department was attempting to hold the number of licences at the levels dictated by the boat rating, but to issue them to all qualified gillnetters. At the same time, returned soldiers demanded priority. The result was chaos. To issue licences to all returned soldiers would displace many white fishermen from coastal settlements, not to mention Japanese and native fishers who used the attached licences. A quota was established for returned soldiers but that quickly proved unenforceable. In desperation, Found directed that all returned soldiers be granted licences for gillnets or seines, even if this rendered the boat rating meaningless. Veterans soon took up the offer, reselling or leasing their seine privileges to canners and fish dealers.

By the end of 1919, Found had prepared a list of proposals and carefully polled the B.C. members of Parliament. Despite the howl of anger he knew would come, he then took a deep breath and recommended that "there would not only not be any restriction on the number of cannery licences but on the number of fishery licences as well, and that we must safeguard the situation by decreasing the fishing season where necessary and putting on sufficient Fishery Officers to prevent illegal fishing." Found was recommending a revolution in fisheries management. Instead of guaranteeing the canners a profit, the department would in theory occupy itself with conservation of the stocks. The economic direction of the industry would be the responsibility of the canners.

Found's philosophy seemed radical to the canners, but was moderate compared to that proposed by William Sloan, fisheries commissioner for the provincial government. "The time has come when the Government should step in and take over our salmon fisheries and administer them for the benefit of the people as a whole and for all time," he said. "Instead of licensing existing and new companies and individuals to take and handle our salmon fisheries, the Government should take them over and handle them. By so doing the fish will be given full protection. There will be a radical reduction in equipment and a consequent reduction in overhead expenses that will materially reduce the retail price of both fresh and canned salmon." Neither the canners nor the federal and provincial governments, however, were ready, for all-out nationalization.

Public support for an end to the cannery monopoly was intense. The canners, unable to fight the political winds, elected to exploit racism in a desperate bid to retain an element of their privileges.

The fishery would be open, but only to whites.

DROPS OF SWEAT AND BLOOD

THE HUNDREDS OF VETERANS RETURNING TO THE FISHING IN- dustry not only demanded an unlimited supply of independent licences coastwide, they called for the elimination of the attached licences that had provided an assured supply of jobs for Japanese and native fishermen. In particular, they directed their fire at the Japanese in a renewed outbreak of virulent racism.

Japanese Canadians had used the period of the war to put down deeper roots. Some volunteered to fight in the Canadian forces, where their great heroism was noted in many battles, including Vimy Ridge. Those who stayed home pushed out to the frontiers of the fishing industry, pioneering in regions and with fishing gear that others did not care to try. Their first efforts at trolling off the west coast of Vancouver Island were so successful that scores of fishermen moved to isolated communities at Ucluelet, Tofino and Clayoquot to harvest spring salmon, coho and halibut that could be sold to American packers delivering to the fresh fish markets of Seattle. Other fishermen began prospecting the same area for chum salmon, refining their seining techniques on schools of herring.

The canners, unable to appeal openly for the protection of their own privileges, decided to ride the rising tide of racism then flooding the province. Leading the offensive on the canners' behalf was Conservative MP H. H. Stevens, who warned Ballantyne that open fishing "would give full control of fisheries to Japanese and American interests." A meeting of canners took a similar tack, claiming that open entry would lead to waste, Japanese control, intensive fishing and "would shortly be followed by the extermination of salmon in the north as has been the case on the Fraser."

Leading the white fishermen was William Maiden, a returned soldier who had developed a special ability to handle a machine gun in the trenches of France. Maiden built a career on persecution of the Japanese Canadians. Through his membership in both the Great War Veterans' Association and the B.C. Fishermen's Protective Association, he exercised considerable political clout. He had close ties to the Liberal party through friends like W. G. McQuarrie, Liberal MP for New Westminster, who often passed his views on to Found. In the wake of the 1919 crisis, Maiden claimed to have "bullied the canners" into providing gear for 500 returned veterans to enter the fishing industry. It was this group of gillnetters on which Maiden based his strength for twenty years, urging them to fanatic policies against Japanese Canadians and exploiting their charter from the Trades and Labour Congress to undercut efforts at gear unity and collective bargaining. Minutes of the canners' association often noted Maiden's actions with an approving tone, as when he offered to send reliable fishermen into Rivers Inlet in 1923 in the wake of a bitter strike with the goal of "eliminating as far as possible industrial warfare." Maiden was a classic case of an industry demagogue, inveighing against the canners' monopoly one day, appealing to the fishermen to support the canners the next. For a number of years, he was a fixture on fisheries patrol boats undertaking the annual sea lion slaughter, where his wartime skills as a machine gunner came in very handy.

The Fishermen's Protective Association declared itself, as reported in the Vancouver *Daily World* on 1 December 1919, "in favour of the policy of throwing open all salmon fishing areas to all British subjects whose names appear on the voters list, whether British-born or naturalized." The key qualification was the reference to the voters list, which was closed both to native Indians and to Japanese.

Found quickly secured Ballantyne's agreement to end limited entry to canning and fishing. The only problem remaining was the ticklish question of how to deal with the licence applications of Japanese fishermen who were naturalized or Canadian-born. Ballantyne accepted Found's proposal to admit them to the fishery on an equal basis, though members of Parliament wished to allow only Japanese veterans. It was Found's only political slip, one from which he quickly recovered. On 22 November, Ballantyne sent his fateful telegram, advising the canners that he proposed "withdrawing the restriction on the number of canning and fishery licences and grant such licences to all resident British subjects, whether by naturalization or birth."

Pressure on Ballantyne continued to mount. Cy Peck, a member of Parliament, a returned war hero and army commander at Vimy, produced a thick wad of telegrams from Prince Rupert constituents demanding open entry, gas boats, a stream clearance program and, above all, no Asians. Clearly, Ballantyne needed to exclude the Japanese Canadians if his overall policy was to be saved. But could such a policy be adopted without falling afoul of the Anglo-Japanese treaty and the laws of Canada? It fell to Found to propose a solution. "From the nature of the industry, it is undesirable that Asiatics should engage therein, whether they are naturalized British subjects or not," Found wrote on 18 December. "Therefore, there should be no increase in the fishing privileges available to such naturalized subjects, and a process for their gradual elimination from the industry should be started by annually decreasing the number of gillnet licences that may be available to them. No salmon cannery licences should be granted to such Asiatics." In his own hand, Found added in the margin: "No cannery or seining licences should be granted to Indians."

Cabinet was dubious. It sought a legal opinion from the justice department on whether the anti-Asian rule was consistent with the treaties with Japan, which stated that the subjects of both countries would "have the right, equally with native subjects, to carry on their commerce and manufacture." E. L. Newcombe, deputy minister of justice, replied that it would be best to give the minister absolute discretion in the granting of licences without spelling out an anti-Japanese clause.

Found elected to follow only part of Newcombe's advice, a decision he would deeply regret. He directed his officials to prepare the necessary amendments to the Fisheries Act to legalize an open fishery. The Asiatic exclusion policy, however, was not included in the changes. The control on the Japanese, Found decided, should be considered "a departmental policy only." He also directed his officials to move some boundaries seaward and to extend closures as necessary to ensure some conservation, but the new fisheries policy was fundamentally a form of apartheid, not fish conservation.

The Japanese exclusion policy thus was implemented despite the government's conviction that it violated a treaty with Japan. From that day forward, Found had the power to eliminate the fishing rights of both Japanese Canadians and native people without recourse to Parliament or any other public process. As a concession to public sentiment, Found decided to give licences to Japanese-Canadian war veterans, provided an equal number of other Japanese Canadians were retired. When the Canadian Japanese Association appealed to the department to allow Japanese-Canadian veterans to take licences without displacing others, the department stiffly turned them down. Canners who sought to protect Japanese-Canadian workers on existing seine leases, however, were given every consideration.

The freeze on Japanese-Canadian licences went into effect immediately, but the postwar downturn in salmon markets sent the industry into a depression. To ensure that the canners obtained every available fish at the lowest possible price, Found delayed implementation of his gradual reductions. The licence freeze alone, however, worked severe hardship on Japanese-Canadian communities. Because the attached licences had created a system of debt, the canners rehired those engaged in previous years so they could retire their debts. Inevitably, however. some fishermen who had left their jobs or whose licences had been given to someone else were left on the beach. Those who lacked their own naturalization papers soon found themselves victims of an iniquitous racket. Japanese labour contractors holding naturalization papers were demanding large advances and a bonus of $25 a boat for providing fishermen. Other fishermen found themselves exploited by the canners, who held their own naturalization papers and offered jobs to Japanese "who will fish the cheapest." The Steveston Fishermen's Benevolent Association protested this system as "verging upon slavery." Much worse was yet to come.

According to Found's figures, the licence freeze left 2,332 Japanese-Canadian gillnetters in a total fleet of 5,105 and 584 Japanese-Canadian trollers in a coastwide fleet of 2,259, most of them concentrated in the Strait of Georgia and a few locations on the west coast of Vancouver Island. Of the Japanese-Canadian gillnetters, more than half, or 1,187, were fishing in the north, where canners had built up their Japanese-Canadian fleets during the wartime labour shortage. These northern gillnetters were the most vital to the canners and would be the most difficult to eliminate. Another 876 remained on the Fraser, and the rest were scattered around Vancouver Island.

The continued depression in world salmon markets prompted several canners to close their Rivers Inlet and Smith Inlet operations in 1921. To protect their attached licences, the canners retained their Japanese-Canadian fishermen and laid off whites. The vigilant William Maiden, who found an ally in Comox-Atlin MP A. W. Neill, made haste to renew his crusade.

Neill was a populist MP from a sprawling riding that included the northern half of Vancouver Island and much of the north of the province. His interest in excluding the Japanese Canadians reflected his strong support in the labour movement as well as his own virulent racism. He was supported by local veterans, organized in groups like the White Fishermen's Union of West Vancouver Island, who believed that the presence of Japanese-Canadian trollers was somehow stopping them from earning more money. Local canners supported the action because the Japanese Canadians sold to their own buyers, often Americans interested in coho and springs for the fresh market. Together, Maiden and Neill would do more to expel the Japanese Canadians from the fishing industry than anyone, other than Found himself.

The call for action from Maiden and Neill offered the chance to begin the expulsions in earnest, but Found hesitated. "It is very questionable if our policy in this connection is fundamentally sound from a legal standpoint," he said, "but it has stood the test for a good many years." Ultimately, however, Found overcame his fears and approved Neill's call for a one-third reduction in the Japanese-Canadian troll fleet to 334 boats. He thus signed an economic death warrant for 166 fishermen and their families.

In many respects, the trollers were an ideal target for Found's first attempt at fleet reduction. Isolated on the west coast, they were far from any potential support from the Steveston Fishermen's Benevolent Association. Because they delivered their catch to American buyers for the fresh fish markets, not to the canners, there was no danger of protest from that quarter. The Japanese-Canadian trollers attempted to circumvent the loss of licences by fishing outside Canada's three-mile (5.5-kilometre) limit, but Found quickly passed a regulation making it illegal to leave a Canadian port to fish salmon outside Canadian waters.

Significantly, the main protest came from the white communities of the west coast which Neill claimed were indignant at the successes of the Japanese-Canadian fleet. A petition from the white community at Ucluelet urged that the policy be amended at least enough to ensure licences for local Japanese-Canadian residents and a further petition contained the appeal of the Japanese Canadians themselves. On arrival in Ottawa, the petitions were clipped unanswered into the file where they remain to this day. There was no protest from any other quarter. Despite the losses they suffered, the Japanese Canadians never forgot the whites in their community who stood by them in 1922. Ten years later, when the son of one of those white supporters from Ucluelet was lost at sea, the entire remaining Japanese-Canadian troll fleet of fifty-two vessels left the fishing grounds to search until the boy's body was found.

Found stood firm. Emboldened by this success, he recommended a 10 to 50 per cent reduction in the number of Japanese-Canadian gillnetters fishing Rivers Inlet and Smith Inlet, a change he calculated would affect seventy-eight men. Once more, however, political opportunity knocked. The collapse of negotiations with the United States for a sockeye treaty had prompted B.C. members of Parliament, many of whom sat on the House of Commons Standing Committee on Fisheries, to begin hearings into the plight of the industry. Always alive to the prospect of good publicity, committee chairman William Duff and his colleagues convinced fisheries minister Ernest Lapointe to anoint them as a royal commission of inquiry into the B.C. industry. Lapointe and Found gratefully assigned them a number of hot potatoes, including the difficult question of Asian exclusion.

The Duff Commission was a catastrophe for Japanese-Canadian fishermen, who had looked to it for a fair hearing of their case. Instead, the commissioners made their hearings into a political grandstand. Already committed to Asian expulsion before they left Ottawa, they declined even to invite Japanese-

Canadian representatives to speak. The only question before them was how quickly they should be eliminated. The canners, smelling the political winds, secretly opposed elimination of the Japanese Canadians and the attached licences which kept them bound to their bosses, but publicly they dared to urge only a gradual elimination of their most productive employees.

Many working fishermen, however, were anxious to deal with other issues, including the canners' renewed demands for a five-year closure of the Fraser and legalization of traps to deal with the depletion of the sockeye runs. It was this mood that Japanese-Canadian spokesman P. E. Kuwabara tried to capture when he went before the commission in September in New Westminster. "We are not responsible for that decreasing [of the sockeye]," he told the commissioners. "We wish you to undertake increase of salmon and development of industry without curtailment of licences."

Kuwabara was pilloried for his poor English and driven from the stand by the commissioners, but Duff and his colleagues were stung to real anger by the intervention of eighteen-year-old Yoshio Oda, already a five-year veteran of the Fraser sockeye fishery, who electrified the hearing with an all-out assault on the expulsion policy. "Everyone knows there are fewer sockeye each year, but I do not know why, for that reason, the licences should be cut down," he said in unaccented English. Japanese-Canadian fishermen outfished others because "the white men loaf in town until it is time to go fishing," he charged, "while the Japanese will sacrifice two or three weeks and get there at the start and get the best gear." Duff, hoping to silence this upstart, demanded to know why Japanese-Canadian women worked in canneries with babies on their backs, a fact which scandalized the commissioners and always was blamed on the Japanese, never the canners. How could white men compete with people prepared to adopt such a low standard of living?

Oda's eloquent reply, spirited but brief in the transcript, was elaborated with the retelling in the Japanese-Canadian community. "The standard of living means more than material things," Oda replied. "To me, the standard of living equates [to] the quality of life. One should not be judged by how much money one has, what one eats, what one wears or where one lives, but rather should be judged by the way one lives. A man should be loyal to his country, obey the law of the country and serve his society. And more important, his main concern should be to be honest with himself, so that he can examine the self-serving motives which are at the root of racial prejudice and other forms of injustice. In light of my definition, the standard of living of the Japanese fishermen is far higher than that of the wealthy class." The audience broke into applause and Oda stood down.

A few hours later, Oda insisted on returning to the stand. "There is a reduction of 15 per cent in the licences of the Japanese next year on the Fraser," he said. "That will mean a reduction of 38 Japanese. One man has gear valued at $2,500 to $3,000. They will be tying up boats valued at $400,000. My father wants to know if that is British justice." "Your father wants to know?" asked Duff. "And so do I," said Oda. Duff made no reply.

Hozumi Yonemura made a final effort to intervene with the commission on behalf of his 1,500 members in the District 2 Japanese Fishermen's Association. Once again, Duff and his fellow commissioners derailed the discussion onto the topic of women packing children into canneries. Yonemura also was condemned for his organization's failure to control trafficking in naturalization papers and ultimately was accused of holding illegal papers himself.

The commission's final report, issued in February 1923, recommended an across the board 40 per cent reduction in the number of Japanese-Canadian gillnet licences to be issued that year. Those that remained in District 2 were to be allocated to the canners on a pro rata basis based on the number of Japanese Canadians they had employed in 1922.

Found had news of the commission's recommendations well before the report was formally submitted. He urged a further one-third cut in the Japanese-Canadian troll fleet in a memorandum to Lapointe. This reduction, later moderated to 25 per cent to make room for a handful of Japanese-Canadian veterans, was approved soon after Duff's 40 per cent figure became known. Disheartened and demoralized, the Amalgamated Fishermen's Association of B.C. offered to assist in determining who should have the remaining licences. Major J. A. Motherwell, who had replaced Cunningham in 1919, hastened to accept.

In 1921, Motherwell's officials had licensed 6,229 gillnet and troll fishermen coastwide. Of that number, about 1,200 were native people, of whom 969 gillnetted for northern canneries. Another 2,200 were white, including 1,600 gillnetters: again, the majority—some 868—gillnetted north of the Fraser. The Japanese Canadians made up more than one-third of the fleet, operating 2,600 boats; of these, 1,100 were working in northern waters, another 873 on the Fraser and almost all the rest were Vancouver Island west coast trollers. According to Found's information, the total Japanese-Canadian population of the province was only 15,000 men, women and children, of whom 9,800 were male. Found proposed to eliminate more than 600 jobs in the first year of the reduction, throwing 15 to 20 per cent of all Japanese-Canadian wage earners out of work.

In the communities of the west coast of Vancouver Island, where no alternative work was available, the policy spelled catastrophe. "Practically all of your petitioners have a wife and family to support," read an appeal to Lapointe signed by 138 fishermen. "We have with few exceptions been fishermen all our lives and if compelled to abandon fishing we will be thrown out of work altogether, for owing to the present serious state of the labour market in B.C. and the widespread condition of unemployment, it will be impossible for us to find other work."

The pleas of fishermen could easily be ignored. The concerns of the canners were another matter. Driven by contractors and economic necessity, the Japanese-Canadian gillnetters consistently outproduced their white and native counterparts and were cheaper to employ. Three northern canneries reported that in 1922 the average Japanese-Canadian fisherman landed 5,451 fish on the Skeena. Native fishermen landed 3,220 and whites 3,192. The reasons lay not in any genetic superiority but in the fact that Japanese fishermen started the season earlier, often were given better gear and worked together to mend nets and equipment.

Throughout the spring of 1923, the canners and Found engaged in a bitter war over the distribution of the remaining Japanese Canadians. While the fishermen themselves waited in ignorance to learn their fate, politicians, bureaucrats and bankers squabbled over them. B.C. Packers enlisted its bankers and shareholders to lobby William Lyon Mackenzie King, who had been elected prime minister in the 1921 election which returned the Liberal government to power.

Found had barely subdued the canners' ire over the allocation of gillnet licences when they erupted once more over his intention to eliminate Japanese-Canadian workers from seine crews. Found was implacable, claiming his hands were tied by the Anglo-Japanese Treaty! "If unnaturalized whites [are] licensed on seines, we must also grant licences to unnaturalized Japanese," he explained. "Therefore, none other than white British subjects or native Indians may be licensed." Even the Chinese cooks had to go, he ruled, and so it was done.

While memoranda and petitions flew back and forth from Ottawa to British Columbia, the Japanese-Canadian community began the difficult task of selecting the fishermen who would face expulsion. In the three years between 1922 and 1925, more than 1,000 men would be driven from the industry. In community meetings, it was agreed that married men would have priority to retain licences. Those newest in the region or with the best alternative prospects were expected to withdraw from the industry voluntarily, and hundreds did. Fishermen's organizations tracked down those fishing on illegal papers and asked them to leave as well, to improve the position of those remaining. For those losing a licence, the community itself paid compensation of $150 to $300 for each head of a family, an obligation the government had rejected.

It was a dark time. Racist sentiment was in full flood. In 1922, Mackenzie King negotiated a voluntary limit on emigration from Japan of 150 men a year in return for the government's promise not to enact legislation against the Japanese in Canada. Under the circumstances, it is hard to imagine how legislation could have been worse than the conditions already faced by Japanese Canadians. In 1923, however, King's government passed a Chinese Exclusion Act, and throughout the decade, provincial authorities agitated for the forced "repatriation" of Japanese Canadians.

By the fall of 1923, however, Found's policy was faltering. Even members of the Asiatic Exclusion League, enthusiastic supporters of the cuts, had observed that the numbers of white fishermen were not increasing no matter how hard Found laboured to expel the Japanese Canadians. And Neill, whose constituents were seeking a 40 per cent cut in the troll fleet, said he would settle for a 10 per cent cut in the gillnet fleet "in view of the opposition of the cannery men." A troubling contradiction existed on the west coast of Vancouver Island, where Found had drummed eighty-four Japanese Canadians out of the industry. There, the number of white and native fishermen had declined even more sharply, by ninety-two. It seemed that white and native fishermen were leaving to take the place of Japanese gillnetters and trollers displaced from more desirable fisheries.

Those Japanese Canadians lucky enough to retain access to an attached cannery licence worked in conditions of unparallelled subservience. As prisoners of the licensing system, their bargaining power was nonexistent. The Canadian Fishing Co. calculated in 1923 that its Japanese-Canadian fishermen delivered fish to the dock for half the cost of white fishermen because of their higher boat averages. This fact was not lost on businessmen who hoped to find a niche in the canning industry. Francis Millerd, who was unable to obtain a share of the attached licences, told fisheries minister P. J. A. Cardin in April 1926 that "the canners who have an allotment of Japanese can compel them to fish at the price they name and this power enables them to insist that their white fishermen fish at the same price. Plainly it means giving the other canners a number of slaves and asking us to compete." Millerd had reason to be bitter. Departmental files confirm his suspicion that some canneries were kept in operation strictly to retain the attached licences, even though Found had assured canners they could concentrate their entitlement in central locations.

But once the expulsions began, they moved relentlessly through every fishery: 40 per cent of gillnet licences in 1923, 40 per cent of cod licences in 1924, 40 per cent from seine licences the same year, a further 15 per cent across the board in 1925 and so it went. It was clear that only token numbers of Japanese Canadians would be left in any fishery by the end of the decade. On 21 January 1927, Found took stock of his achievements in a memorandum to the minister. According to his calculations, he had eliminated 1,374 people from their jobs on grounds he and his government knew to be of dubious legality.

Their contemptible treatment at the hands of the Duff Commission had convinced the Japanese-Canadian community of the need for strong action. Since they lacked the right to vote, a court action was their only recourse, but the community was divided both by geography and by the conflicting political agendas of the fishermen and the consul. When the Steveston Fishermen's Association took the initiative to launch a court action designed to halt the 1924 reductions, they turned for financial support to the consulate, which had paid the Japanese Community Association a steady commission for handling various immigration matters in B.C. The fishermen asked for access to this fund.

The consul, however, was reluctant. From the comfort of his desk job, he urged the fishermen to co-operate with white and native fishermen to mobilize public opinion against the reductions, proof that he was completely out of touch with the virulent racism of the Canadian community. The community association quickly endorsed this recommendation and refused to release the funds. For two long years the court action was stalemated.

Despite the paralysis in the Japanese-Canadian community, some pressure did come to bear on Ottawa from other sources. Motherwell pestered Found with clippings from as far afield as the Washington *Times,* criticizing Found's policy. The *Vancouver Sun* appealed to Ottawa to consider the country's trading relations: "Good will between Japan and Canada is just as important to this country as the jobs of a few white fishermen." More ominous were the warnings of the new Japanese consul, who told the external affairs department that his government viewed the expulsions as a violation of international treaties. Japan raised the issue during negotiations over immigration, and alarmed officials at the Canadian ministry of justice warned Found that "there can be no possible room for doubt that it would not be competent to refuse a licence" if qualified Japanese-Canadian fishermen decided to press for their rights.

Early in 1926, the Japanese-Canadian fishermen finally decided to tackle the case on their own. A co-operative committee chaired by Shinya Yoshida, chairman of the Steveston Fishermen's Association, was elected. It included representatives of fishermen from the Skeena, the Nass, Rivers Inlet, the upper Fraser, Celtic Camp, Ucluelet, Tofino, Clayoquot, Chemainus and Nanaimo, as well as salt herring and salt salmon producers. The new consul, whose name is not recorded in the surviving accounts, directed the Japanese Community Association to release the funds. The association now shamefacedly revealed that most of the money had been spent. Hundreds of jobs had been lost while the two factions squabbled.

The cost of the case was expected to be enormous, a staggering $20,000 to $30,000. Despite the assistance of the consul, the fishermen had to raise much of the money themselves. Early in 1927, the action finally began, precisely as the justice ministry feared that it might. Throughout the spring, twenty-two

Japanese-Canadian fishermen applied for northern gillnet licences, each carefully swearing out an affidavit asserting his status as a British subject. In eighteen of those twenty-two cases, the fathers had been naturalized citizens as well. Typical was the case of Kunataro Fukuda of Dollarton, whose son was born in Canada in 1903. Young Fukuda had a $500 boat and a $300 net, but Found's policy denied him a licence.

The Japanese Canadians hired Toronto lawyer W. N. Tilley to represent them, and in April 1927, he demanded a reference to the Supreme Court to determine the legality of the anti-Japanese policy. Without such a reference, Tilley warned, the Japanese Canadians would demand their licences. Found had little doubt that Tilley would make the refusal of the twenty-two applicants the basis for a court appeal if a reference was denied. Tilley was promised his reference. Suddenly Found had his hands full. In a separate action, Francis Millerd, unwilling to accept Ottawa's decision to deny him the right to can salmon in northern waters, had challenged the law and won. Found quickly appealed to the B.C. Supreme Court, but Millerd won his case hands down.

The department's policy was threatened with disaster. Without the right to licence canneries, the department could neither control Millerd nor limit Japanese-Canadian entry to salting and canning. Working feverishly, Found convinced fisheries minister Lapointe to request an immediate Supreme Court reference to determine the department's powers on both questions—the control of canneries and the limitation of the Japanese. The request was soon granted, but Found's heart must have skipped a beat when he looked over the panel of Supreme Court judges. Among them was E. J. Newcombe, who had warned of the dubious legality of the anti-Japanese policy when it was initiated in 1919. Newcombe had not changed his mind. In the decision he wrote, the Supreme Court of Canada rejected the fisheries department arguments on every point. In desperation, Found arranged for yet one more appeal, this time to the Privy Council in Great Britain.

The Supreme Court victory elated the Japanese-Canadian community. Not only had the licence reductions been halted since the court action began in 1927, there was a prospect they could be ended altogether. The entire fate of the community would rest on the decision of a distant group of jurists in London whose thinking could be influenced by only a few hours of argument. The heavy extra costs were borne by the Japanese-Canadian herring fishermen, who paid for a fisherman from Vancouver to travel to London to advise their legal counsel. He was John Simon, later finance minister in the Baldwin government. The case was hard-fought. The Canadian government tried to have the case thrown out by on the grounds that it was purely a domestic matter. Simon fought back, telling the judges that such discrimination against human rights and natural justice was not only a blot on the prestige of the British Empire but also contrary to treaties with Japan. The Privy Council decision, delivered on 15 October 1929, upheld the Japanese-Canadian fishermen.

The Privy Council decision was an unmitigated disaster for Found, whose policies on cannery limitation, cannery taxation and elimination of Japanese-Canadian fishermen were swept away. The Privy Council also settled once and for all the division of powers between the provinces and the federal government with regard to fisheries. Ottawa now was charged solely with the management of the harvest. Henceforth, Ottawa would have no authority over fish after they were caught unless they were destined for export markets. The power to limit entry into salmon canning now lay exclusively with the province.

With the onset of the Great Depression, however, there was no further need to limit canneries, and no taxes to be had in any case. After careful study of the Privy Council ruling, which found "there is no express provision for withholding a licence where a qualified applicant submits a proper application," Found hurried through new amendments to the Fisheries Act, giving the minister absolute discretion in the issuance of fishing licences, the course suggested by Newcombe in 1919. The powerless Japanese Canadians were sent brusquely back to square one, but Found never regained the political momentum necessary to resume the expulsions.

The Japanese Canadians, in fact, took advantage of Found's disarray to press for the abolition of attached licences and an end to the ban on their operating gas boats in District 2. Leading this battle was Jun Kizawa, a charismatic fisherman and self-taught lawyer, who travelled the coast from one end to the other to organize the fishermen. In June 1929, he deliberately fished from a gas boat to test the law, but wary fisheries officers released him because of the uncertainty surrounding the Privy Council decision. Emboldened by this action, which destroyed the prohibition on Japanese Canadians fishing from gas boats, he next tackled the attached licence system. After a long battle, in which the labour contractors found support from both Motherwell and the canners, Kizawa was able to end the attached system. "Fishermen to Become Free," the *Province* headlines read on 22 December 1931. Japanese-Canadian fishermen appeared to be on the brink of a new era.

That new era never arrived. As the industry sank deeper into the Depression, Japanese-Canadian fishermen faced a tough struggle to survive. Still denied the vote, they were unable to win restoration of the licences stripped away between 1922 and 1927. Both Motherwell and Found continuously sought opportunities to roll them back even further, moving in 1938 to abolish the old boat pullers' licences that allowed several hundred fishermen to maintain a toehold in the industry. In the end, the victory of 1929 proved to be merely a stay of execution. In reality, most of the fishing industry had barely noticed the long struggle of the Japanese-Canadian fishermen.

THE MESS ON THE COAST

ON 18 JUNE 1926, FISHERIES PATROLMAN JAMES BOYD COMmitted a blunder by hiring a more-or-less honest and qualified man to fill the post of fisheries guardian for Smith Inlet. Maurice MacKay Williams knew the area well, he was not a drunk, he was not interested in graft, and he was happily married. By the time Williams ended his fisheries career a few weeks later, he would know what the canners really meant by conservation—and he would tell the world.

Boyd gave Williams a government gas boat and sent him to Rivers Inlet to meet the department's top man in the Central Area, fisheries overseer R. Saugstad, hailed by the canners as "a most efficient and painstaking official."

Five days later, Williams found himself in action for the first time. While on patrol in Smith Inlet, he surprised two fishermen gillnetting with their nets tied to the shore, contrary to the provisions of the Fisheries Act. He issued summonses to the two men to appear before Saugstad, but when Williams arrived on the appointed day to testify, neither Saugstad nor the accused were present. The cases were put over for one week. The next time, Saugstad was on the scene and grudgingly agreed it would "look very bad if nothing was done." He told the accused: "Your cases are not serious ones. I will overlook it this time, but it will not be overlooked should this occur again. Case dismissed." The thunderstruck Williams was forced to run a gauntlet of raucous laughter from fishermen as he returned to his boat. The next morning, Williams cast off for Smith Inlet on a bizarre voyage that would reveal more about the operations of the fishing industry than a score of royal commissions.

Sockeye returning to their natal streams on Long Lake above Smith Inlet must pursue a complex path. The waters of the lake drain through the Docee

River into a 9.7-kilometre lake called Wycleese Lagoon. The lagoon is neither salt nor fresh. At one end, it is fed by the Docee, at the other by salt water pushed over a series of tidal rapids in a channel called Quashela Creek. To reach Quashela Creek, the sockeye must first leave the inlet and pass through a narrow channel into a small, circular cove bounded on the east by a shelving beach, which stands at the entrance to the creek. Here the sockeye school by the thousands to await a favourable tide to run up into the lagoon. The shore was a natural location for a beach seine, and since a fishing lease here would control the entire sockeye run to Long Lake, the rights to the Quashela seine lease was a glittering prize. To this day, this spot is known as the Seine Hole.

In 1884, the exclusive right to fish the creek had been given to Andrew Welch and R. P. Rithet, who made Quashela Packing a cash cow for their Victoria Canning Co. When Henry Doyle purchased Victoria Canning during the assembly of B.C. Packers', he assumed that the lucrative seine lease would come with it. It was a costly mistake. Early in 1902, the lease came up for renewal, but before Doyle could act, the lease was handed to William Hickey, along with exclusive fishing privileges for all of Smith Inlet, for nine years. B.C. Packers' owned the land on which the seine was operated but could do no more than charge a token rent for its use. In just one of those years, 1906, Hickey took out 28,000 cases and sold them for more than $6 each. Thanks to the lease, the cost of the fish was about 40 cents a case and gross profits were $3.28.

In 1911, Hickey renewed the lease and sold out to Wallace Fisheries for a hefty $325,000. Richard Kelly, one of Wallace's owners, used his influence to buttress the lease by innovative means. Since gillnetters could outfish the seine if they fished above the Seine Hole, Kelly got fisheries officials to declare that the lagoon was entirely fresh water. As a result, gillnetting was banned upstream of the seine.

For more than thirty years, Quashela Creek had been synonymous with power and privilege. When returned soldiers found Asian labour working the Wallace seine in 1919, they burned it on the beach, and officials in Ottawa, wary of the political winds then blowing, cancelled the lease once and for all. From now on, fishermen were promised, the harvest would be conducted in the waters of Smith Inlet only, and sockeye would find sanctuary upstream of Quashela Creek. A fisheries guardian was posted on a float house in the Seine Hole to enforce departmental policy.

It was this vigilant guardian, Fred Christensen, whom Williams expected to meet as he travelled to Quashela Creek. As Williams and Christensen chatted, fisherman A. L. Hall came alongside and asked for the privilege of fishing in the lagoon. Christensen said the fee would be $50.

During the following week, Williams prowled the waters of the Seine Hole, observing a steady stream of gillnetters pouring in and out of the lagoon, laden with illegally caught sockeye. Williams watched one day as George Gory, a collector boat operator for Gosse Packing, stopped only long enough to drop off his wife on Christensen's raft. Word of the scene that greeted Williams on his arrival at the float house reverberated the length of the coast. "On entering the shack on the raft I saw Mrs. Gory on the bed with Christensen," he told police. "They were conducting themselves in an improper manner," he said, or as he later delicately phrased it in Latin, they were "in flagrante delicto." He turned and headed back to Margaret Bay where he complained to Saugstad, who fired him on the spot.

Saugstad's dismissal of Williams was too late to save the racket in which he was just a small cog. The traffic in poached fish was becoming so massive that word was spreading throughout the coast. The embittered Williams returned to Quashela Creek to collect evidence for another entire week, watching as gillnetters illegally set their nets all around the fisheries raft. The arrival of fisheries inspector Adam Mackie did nothing to slow the traffic. Unable to beat the thieves, Williams joined them, spending much of August gillnetting in the lagoon himself, free of charge. All might have ended there had Saugstad not made the final and amazing mistake of cheating Williams of his pay.

Within days of this final insult, word reached Found in Ottawa of extensive and organized poaching at Smith Inlet. Under pressure from the B.C. Fishermen's Protective Association, he ordered a secret RCMP investigation. The Mounties collected affidavits pointing to a conspiracy between canners and top department officials to pillage Smith Inlet. Motherwell rushed a summary of the RCMP report to Ottawa. Fisherman Pete Larsen had sworn an affidavit charging that Mrs. Gory was an integral part of the poaching operation, which rewarded Christensen both financially and sexually for his compliance. "Tell the boys to go out and fish 'til daylight," a cannery manager had said. "I have the fishery officer in bed." The right to fish in the lagoon could be secured by payment of $10 to the guardian and 10 cents a fish, which the canners deducted from settlements and remitted to Mackie and Saugstad.

Those participating in the ring, which affected at least 60 of the 380 boats in the inlet, were richly rewarded with tremendous catches. Fishing in the lagoon throughout the closed period, the poachers could be assured of several hundred fish per day, a catch that normally could take a week.

Found was confronted with a difficult political bombshell. The RCMP had been unaccountably reluctant to interview the canners because they "would be on their guard," but Motherwell was facing demands from the Fishermen's Protective Association to launch a public inquiry. Found finally complied in the spring of 1927. The sensational testimony dominated the Vancouver and New Westminster papers for more than a week. Under the protection of the

Canada Evidence Act, more than fifty fishermen testified as to their poaching. On 1 May 1927, Christensen and the luckless Williams were jointly charged with accepting bribes. Inquiry commissioner David Mackenzie declined to recommend charges against any canners for "lack of evidence."

The fishermen's testimony, however, left no doubt that the canners were sponsoring the entire affair. Not only were the gillnetters towed to the lagoon by cannery boats, in some instances, but they also delivered to cannery collectors working inside the fishing boundaries. Catches of up to 1,900 sockeye per boat per day were handled during the closed period by every company on the inlet. Had the independent fishermen not come forward to press for the inquiry, the ring might have continued for years. Reports of similar scandals elsewhere, some implicating Motherwell, soon bubbled to the surface, but Motherwell convinced Found that any further inquiry "would result possibly in leaving the impression in the minds of the public that things were not right."

As far as fishermen were convinced, things were not right at all. The police received a telling letter from one fisherman who carefully guarded his anonymity. "All the fishing laws, boundary lines and the patrolling here in B.C. are hardly any more than a joke. It is not only at Smith Inlet but more or less all over. The most of the fishermen are for the government law and regulations, but a small per cent of them are running wild. The most of the cannery managers are patting them on the back and always buy their fish. If anyone gets caught, it is not the cannery who suffers, but the fishermen.

"Patrolmen are the lowest paid in government. The canneries don't need to bribe the commissioners or the patrolmen, but maybe they feel sorry for them and help them with a little $50 a month or so. . . .

"I have often wondered if it is not the influence of the cannery companies that the government pays such small wages. . . . If anyone of the cannery bosses finds out about this letter, I would be out of luck for a job, but I thought maybe some of what I have written would be to your help. I do hope that you would be able to clean up all the mess on this coast."

The mess was far worse than anyone guessed. Despite unlimited numbers of gillnetters, hundreds of seines, virtual elimination of the native fishery and a crippling of the Japanese-Canadian fleet, still the canners poached from the meagre runs left over—and still they went broke.

After the initial postwar depression, the 1920s had been boom years. The canners were able to reinforce their profits with still more technological changes like the updated "Iron Chink." Henry Doyle estimated the new machinery could produce an average profit increase in northern canneries of $2 a case, with "a further saving if your Chinamen can be induced to work for two cents a case less." In 1924, gas boats began their invasion of the north, with eighty-six in operation in the first year alone. The purse seine fleet tripled in size to 406 vessels by 1926 as the canners scoured the coast's creeks for chums and pinks to fill their canning lines.

The old firms that had dominated the industry found themselves challenged by aggressive upstarts who forced their way into the market with consignment sales systems, particularly in the domestic market. Canadian Fishing, a relative newcomer to salmon canning, took over four northern canneries in 1923, three more in 1925, and another six in 1926, giving it a coastwide presence.

Canadian Fishing and Gosse Packing achieved gains at the expense of the B.C. Packers' Association, reorganized in 1921 as the B.C. Fishing and Packing Association. That year the shareholders had been able to pay themselves the equivalent of a 100 per cent stock dividend. Profits in the company's first two decades had been close to $2 million. But by 1927 the company's 42 per cent share of the coast's salmon catch had been eroded to 30 per cent, as northern catches assumed greater importance. Canadian Fishing, which had no salmon landings in 1918, controlled 15 per cent of the catch in 1927; and Gosse Packing, which accounted for about 9 per cent of the landings in 1916, took in 21 per cent the same year.

Aemilius Jarvis, revitalized after serving a jail term in Ontario for stock fraud, engineered the 1926 takeover of Wallace Fisheries' seven canneries by B.C. Fishing and Packing. The new firm had twenty-six canneries, three cold storages and two fishmeal plants, as well as shipyards and a substantial fleet. The pack in 1926 was a record 1.47 million cases, which spurred even more cannery construction the following year.

Among the optimistic investors was Francis Millerd, who had left Gosse-Millerd in 1922 to form Somerville Cannery; by 1927, his reorganized firm was called Millerd Packing, and boasted five canneries and two salteries. His erstwhile partners had done even better. By 1928, Gosse Packing, now operated by R. C. Gosse and R. J. Gosse, sons of the founder, controlled thirteen canneries and three fishmeal plants.

To feed their new acquisitions, the canners spent hundreds of thousands of dollars to secure the deliveries of independent seine and gillnet fishermen. But softening retail prices and a downturn in catches in 1927 brought them face to face with reality. Since the volume of fish could not increase, the time was right to increase profits by the time-honoured tactic of amalgamation.

One who was alert to the possibilities of such a project was Henry Doyle, still bitter at being ousted from B.C. Packers' head office a decade before. In the intervening years, he had collaborated with R. V. Winch to vindicate himself by building up Northern B.C. Fisheries, but that venture collapsed in 1923 after his Namu cannery's pack spoiled in processing. The Royal Bank withdrew its financing, and Doyle's life work was wiped out. Effectively forced from the industry, he obsessively compiled statistics and information about every aspect of salmon, using his remaining shares in Cassiar Packing and in B.C. Fishing and Packing to monitor developments. As the 1927 crisis unfolded, he deluged Jarvis with plaintive appeals to allow him to repeat the triumph of 1902, but Jarvis's replies were cold and noncommittal. Doyle was yesterday's man; bigger and even more audacious plans were afoot now.

In September 1927, the canners reviewed their results and discovered the bubble had burst, despite a pack of 1.3 million cases. Runs coastwide had been late and weak, with the sockeye pack totalling only 308,032 cases. Even more disturbing was the pink run; the pack of 247,617 cases was slightly more than half of the cycle year catch and only one-third of the huge landings of 1926. An emergency meeting of canners and fishermen considered means of reducing the amount of gear in the water "in the interests of conservation as well as with a view of re-establishing a more economic basis of operating."

Major Motherwell confidentially advised Found that the economic crisis had partly been induced by the department. Late runs, dry streams and the insatiable pressure of the fleet had necessitated tough closures, the major said, but the escapement had never been in doubt. "It was hoped that the more stringent regulations would have the effect of compelling the fishermen to get together and materially reduce the amount of gear in the water." The tactic was successful. A conference of canners and fishermen agreed to ask Ottawa for a 50 per cent reduction in the number of purse seines, a 30 per cent reduction in the number of gillnetters, the creation of area licensing to compel seines and gillnetters to fish and to deliver in given areas, and a pledge that no new canneries would be licensed.

Found deflected these proposals, in part because the industry delegation represented only the interests of certain gillnetters, including Maiden's B.C. Fishermen's Protective Association, and certain canners. The delegation's views were hotly opposed by Bell-Irving's ABC Packing, groups of seine fishermen, and native communities that stood to lose scores of jobs.

But Found had even more compelling reasons to do nothing. He had just lost a key test case that challenged Ottawa's power to intervene in the canning industry in any fashion. The source of this setback was Francis Millerd, who had decided to start a new canning venture in northern waters whether or not Ottawa granted him a licence or a share of the attached cannery gillnet licences. In 1924, he took advantage of a little-known clause in the Fisheries Act which permitted the use of floating canneries, provided they remained in one place. Millerd acquired the decrepit lumber schooner *Laurel Whelan*, equipped her with a canning line and towed her to Masset to can clams. At the end of the season, he was given permission to shift operations to Quatsino.

The transfer sent a shockwave through the industry. If Millerd was allowed to move from place to place, feasting on runs long used by stationary canneries, the existing operators would soon be out of business. Pressure on Ottawa produced an ultimatum to Millerd: he was to pick a single location and remain there. If he did so, his licence would be renewed for five more years. If he refused, it could be cancelled.

But Millerd, a strong free enterpriser, was not interested in Ottawa's concerns. When he finished in the Charlottes in 1925, he towed the *Whelan* to Prince Rupert. The department decided to turn a blind eye. But Millerd would not desist. In 1926, he advised Motherwell he would return to harvest the Masset pink run. Found and Motherwell could not tolerate Millerd's defiance. On 11 August 1927, fisheries officers seized the *Whelan* and shut it down for operating without a proper licence.

Once again, however, Millerd was saved, this time by customs minister H. H. Stevens, who intervened to have the charges dropped on condition the *Whelan* remain at Masset until its licence expired in 1929. Millerd, with astonishing gall, then sued Found and Motherwell for $70,000 in damages allegedly suffered as a result of the seizure.

While Found and Motherwell considered this development, Millerd applied for permission to can clams in Prince Rupert. Not surprisingly, he was refused. Undeterred, Millerd towed the *Laurel Whelan* back to Seal Cove and went to work. Once again he was charged, but this time a magistrate acquitted Millerd on the grounds that the federal government had no constitutional right to regulate canneries. On 23 September 1927, a judge of the B.C. Supreme Court confirmed Millerd's acquittal, wiping out federal authority to control cannery licensing.

At one blow, two pillars of Found's policy had been destroyed. Without the power to licence canneries, Ottawa could not limit entry to the processing sector or limit Asian ownership of canneries, salteries or fishmeal plants. With Millerd pressing for his licence, Found took the only way out and arranged for the emergency reference of Millerd's case and that of the Japanese-Canadian fishermen to the Supreme Court of Canada.

Throughout the autumn of 1927, the coast was in ferment and fishermen's associations vied with each other and the canners to press their views upon Ottawa. There was talk of another royal commission and demands for firm action, but when a new delegation visited Ottawa in November, it discovered fisheries minister P. J. A. Cardin and Found determined to do nothing. In the government's view, "those engaged in the salmon canning industry had within their own hands the regulation of the amount of gear to be used in fishing areas and . . . should enter into mutual agreements for the better regulating the amount of gear to be used in fishing."

Behind the scenes, the industry's senior canners took the minister's advice. At a series of secret meetings, they developed a plan to reshape the industry from the Fraser to the Skeena. The precise levers that key companies used to secure their objectives either have been lost or remain hidden in the archives of B.C. Packers Ltd., for it was this company that achieved a complete reversal of its failing fortunes in the dying days of 1927 to emerge as the undisputed giant of the coast.

The architects of this plan left no aspect unresolved: every major company was included, gillnet and seine salmon prices were established coastwide, and the fisheries management system of the salmon industry was overhauled. First news of the plan came on 10 February 1928 when the *Financial Post* revealed that Merrill DesBrisay would become the "new czar of B.C. fisheries," authorized to arbitrate disputes which arose from a far-reaching strategy to reshape the industry.

Under the terms of a contract agreement, which included canners handling more than 80 per cent of the province's salmon production, the coast was divided into seventeen areas. Within each zone, the canners established strict limits on the numbers of seines, gillnets and drag seines allowed to operate. The canners voluntarily agreed to a dramatic reduction in licences in 1928. The number of purse seines would be cut from 659 to 236, drag seines from 46 to 21, and gillnetters from 3,905 to 2,910. The *Financial Post* concluded that "limiting the amount of gear to be used and elimination of financial assistance to fishermen will result in great savings." More ominously, the canners pledged not to buy fish from independent fishermen and to impose penalties on fishermen who tried to deliver outside their assigned areas.

Key to the agreement's success was a side deal to eliminate the troublesome Francis Millerd from the industry. A copy of the final agreement indicated that most of the companies signed on only after Gosse Packing and B.C. Fishing and Packing agreed to acquire Millerd's interests. A new B.C. Packers Ltd. was created on 18 May 1928, with authorized capital of $8 million. Shares of the new firm were swapped for those of Gosse Packing and B.C. Fishing and Packing on a one-for-one basis. Three days later, B.C. Packers added Millerd Packing's assets.

The result was a new corporation controlling forty-four canneries. The tenacious Aemilius Jarvis, who had insisted on the merger with Wallace Fisheries a few years before, became president. The Gosse brothers took on the posts of chairman and general superintendent. Before the ink on the agreement was dry, the new directors agreed to close eight canneries, some of which had been operating for almost half a century. Canadian Fishing instituted equally sharp reductions, closing ten of its fifteen plants between 1927 and 1932.

The formation of the new B.C. Packers triggered other elements of the agreement which have affected the coast down to modern times. The operators of seventy-four out of seventy-nine B.C. canneries were committed to this section of the deal, which spelled out precisely how much gear each company was entitled to use. All canners were prohibited from offering "free provision of boats, gasoline or supplies or the giving of prizes or bonuses" to any fishermen without receiving rental or payment, nor were canners allowed to retain contractors. Side agreements with the B.C. Fishermen's Protective Association established binding prices and gear charges for every area of the coast. Each of the seventeen fishing areas was carefully defined. Boats fishing in an area could deliver only within that area, a policy that effectively eliminated the mobility of the independent fishermen, whose catch was not to be purchased in any case. A separate clause permitted canners to pool or transfer their boat ratings, so they could deploy extra gear where runs warranted.

Found and Motherwell did everything they could to sustain the agreement but could not withstand the anger of fishermen, who saw it as a pact to wipe out any vestiges of their independence. The canners, now organized as the Canned Salmon Section of the Canadian Manufacturers' Association, did nothing to calm these fears, demanding that Japanese-Canadian licences be attached to canneries so as not to place them in a position to "dictate terms."

Meanwhile, the fisheries department was under heavy fire from fishermen, both gillnet and seine, outraged by the area rules. Maiden, now blowing with more radical winds and ignoring his complicity in the deal, said the scheme would turn the market over to "a highly organized group of capitalists [and] give said capitalists a vicious power in the matter of setting prices to fishermen."

Seine fishermen J. Fiddler, J. Fiamengo and J. Steffich condemned the compulsory delivery requirements. The policy had "nothing to do with the conservation of fish," they said, "but only with compelling the fishermen to deliver them fish at the lowest possible price." In desperation, Motherwell adjusted the canners' seventeen areas to twenty-seven, adding additional divisions on the south coast, and declared a seine rating for each one. Seines would be allowed to move about freely, but if the number of seines operating in any area exceeded his rating, he would increase the closed time by twenty-four hours to seventy-two. After further pressure, the department relented to allow the transfer of raw fish among the areas.

Although the canners' efforts to control the harvesting sector ultimately were defeated, the industrial structure established by the agreement of 1928 persisted largely intact until 1969. B.C. Packers and Canadian Fishing took their places at the head of the industry, waiting patiently until the remnants of venerable giants like J. H. Todd and ABC Packing were weak enough to dismantle and absorb. They were strong enough now to guarantee by their own efforts what they had so often demanded of government—a limitation on entry to the canning industry.

The crisis of 1928 marked the end of an era for fishermen, as well. Despite the reduction of the Japanese-Canadian fleet to a ragged rear guard, white and native fishermen remained poverty stricken. A decade had been wasted while white fishermen sought to climb to economic security on the backs of their fellows. Clearly, that route was a dead end. The struggles of the 1920s, however, had ended the canners' control over independent white fishermen, who now were free to roam the coast, fishing and selling wherever they chose. The stage was set for a coastwide struggle over how much of the value of the catch would be kept by the canners and how much would be shared by the fishermen, a re-creation of the battles of 1900 and 1901 on a much greater scale. In the course of that contest, fundamental questions about the conservation of the salmon would be posed once more. The canners had rationalized production on a provincial basis in 1928, just as they had done on the Fraser in 1902. The challenge for fishermen was to succeed where they had failed a generation before. Without such a counterbalance to the canners, their future and that of the resource would be little better than the pillage of Quashela Creek on a coastwide scale.

THE MAD STRUGGLE FOR FISH

In all cases where the salmon supply is on either a constant or a declining basis, maximum levels of profit depend upon more intensive operation. It is obvious that with company-owned gear this process cannot be pushed beyond the point at which the return per boat is sufficient to cover the necessary capital outlay. But if the fishermen can be induced to assume ownership of the equipment, the number of boats operating in an area can be increased indefinitely. A large item of expense is thus completely eliminated and the unit efficiency of the gear ceases to be a matter for company concern.

—LAUREN CASADAY, *"Labour Unrest and the Labour Movement in the Salmon Industry of the Pacific Coast,"* 1933

EARLY ON THE MORNING OF 5 JULY 1936, HAROLD "BUTCH" Malyea fired up his gas-powered gillnetter *Lemae,* cast off from the floats at Anglo–B.C. Packing's McTavish Cannery and headed down Rivers Inlet toward Schooner Pass. The fishing season was only a week old, and on most Saturdays the fishermen stayed close to the cannery, working on their gear, reading the mail and catching up on their sleep.

But not today. As Malyea travelled seaward, he was joined by skiffs and gas boats streaming out from every one of the inlet's ten camps and canneries. They were all headed for Provincial Cannery and Dawson's Landing to a meeting called weeks before by the executive of the Fishermen and Cannery Workers Industrial Union (FCWIU) in Vancouver. Only one issue could mobilize fishermen this way—a strike for better prices.

Malyea had been fishing since 1923 and working in Rivers Inlet since 1929. Like many fishermen, he believed the canners were getting rich while he starved. "A can of sockeye salmon even then cost over two bits for a pound can," he recalled more than half a century later. "Why strike? Well, the prices—40 cents for a sockeye. The first year I went 40 bucks in the hole and I had to pay that back the next year. Price was the big issue."

Although the canners claimed that only a tiny minority of the fishermen supported the FCWIU, several hundred of the 1,300 Rivers Inlet permit holders crowded the floats at Provincial Cannery as Malyea pulled in. A union banner was mounted on the floats and fishermen perched on deckhouses, racks, bluestone tanks and nets as the meeting got under way.

Union officers George Miller and Alex Ramsay reported on the failure of negotiations in Vancouver. Far from conceding to the fishermen's demands for 50 cents a fish for Central Area sockeye, the canners were offering 45 cents in Smith Inlet and only 40 cents in Rivers Inlet, a cut of 5 cents from the 1935 level. Only Skeena sockeye was worth 50 cents, the canners claimed, because of its superior quality and larger size.

For several hours, the fishermen debated. Chairing the meeting was gillnetter Jim Law, a strong union man who enjoyed the respect of every fisherman on the inlet. He had delivered just 197 salmon to J. H. Todd's Beaver Cannery the previous week, and like most of the fishermen there, he was ready to call it a season. He was going broke.

One fisherman after another took the floor. Finally, union activist Gus Bokma spoke up. His landings had totalled only twenty-seven fish, but he was even more determined than Law.

"When they raised the question of how much money we were going to strike for, he says 'Fifty cents or nothing,' " Malyea remembered. "He was supported, by God. The vote was pretty well unanimous to go ahead and strike."

By the next day, the strike committee had the results of a secret ballot taken at each cannery. The result: 849 for the strike, 143 opposed. There were eight spoiled ballots. The same day the tie-up spread to the seine fleet in Alert Bay and to gillnetters on Burke and Dean channels. The strike had begun.

The Rivers Inlet strike was the culmination of years of struggle by Central Area fishermen to fight their way out of a tightening economic noose.

B.C. canners had entered the Depression in fighting form after the massive corporate shake-up of 1928. The merger that created B.C. Packers Ltd. resulted in the new firm landing 47 per cent of the 1929 canned pack. But the complex gear reduction agreements that accompanied the merger proved largely unenforceable. The canners rationalized their shore operations, then set about to divest themselves of the cost of maintaining the fleet. They also concentrated on a united front to drive down raw fish prices as low as possible and increased the charges for the cannery rental boats that many nominally independent fishermen relied on. Fishermen were given bonus payments for providing their own nets and boats. Canneries were closed to reduce operating costs, but their fleets were maintained.

As they had on the Fraser, the canners turned open entry to their advantage, transferring much of the cost of the harvest to the newly "independent" fishermen. Although they retained enough contract Japanese-Canadian fishermen to meet their basic needs and to deter strike activity, the canners benefited as well from a steady increase in the number of independent fishermen. Between 1928 and 1934, the number of gillnetters fishing Rivers Inlet had risen from 1,117 to 1,899. Average season sockeye catches for each boat had fallen in the same period from 699 to 527. As a result, fishermen's earnings were down sharply.

There were no more fish to catch, but by increasing the effort and intensifying the harvest, each canner hoped to reap a larger share for himself. The result was a downward spiral of economic misery for the fishermen, who found that debt and poverty were the fruits of their new-found independence.

Those without their own boats rented company sailing skiffs, riding out to the grounds on Sunday night on the towline behind the packer, fishing for five days and then struggling back to the cannery for the weekend closure. The skiffs typically were between 8.5 and 9 metres long, their open hulls a clutter of oars, centreboard, net lights, net, centreboard case and assorted gear. Everything was done by hand, although the lucky few with gas boats could forget about their oars.

"The living conditions in those sailing skiffs were awful," recalled Malyea. "Damn near every one of them leaked like a basket. You'd be sleeping in wet blankets. We had a single burner kerosene stove and it stunk like heck. We pulled the nets whenever we had to. If you found you weren't getting any fish you'd run the net, just run along the corkline, and if there was a fish there you'd feel him and pull it up.

"When you went to put your net out, you'd sail it out if you had a breeze, but you had to be damn careful when you did that. I went to sail mine out once and the hooks in my shoes got caught in the web and pulled me right over the roller, and I was hanging on for God's sake. The snaps in the hooks of my shoes were pulling out. Finally I was able to pull myself back aboard."

In a storm, the fishermen just held on, sheltering under the canvas or plywood doghouse in the bow. If they were injured, they had to live with it. On Kaarlo Huovinen's first season on the Skeena in 1928, his skipper dislocated his shoulder when his hand caught in the net while setting. Huovinen was just a green boat puller, but he knew the packer would not be back to collect their fish for twenty-four hours. He made his partner lie down in the boat and, racking his brain to remember the technique, popped the joint back into place.

More days were sunny than stormy and remarkably few fishermen were lost. They spent their weeks drifting, rowing, pulling nets and counting the catch, hoping the returns would be enough to keep them off relief that winter. A pot of meat mulligan bubbling on the primus stove served as breakfast, lunch and dinner, unless some pinks or steelhead turned up in the net. Sockeye were too valuable to eat. When catches were poor, the men might pull into shore, light a fire, have a barbecue and relax.

Few fishermen would have argued with the assessment of one who wrote to the *Unemployed Worker* in July 1933, to forecast even worse conditions to come. "The tremendous speed-up and cut-throat competition amongst the fishermen is absolutely unavoidable while fishing under the present system. Long sleepless hours and hard ceaseless toil are necessary in order to compete with other fishermen and one has only to watch the fishermen working through the gap on a flood tide to realize that every fish caught there should be worth its weight in gold in order to compensate the fisherman who must sweat blood in his mad struggle for fish."

Still the prices fell. From peak prices of 60 and 65 cents a fish in 1933, the price of Smith and Rivers Inlet sockeye was cut to 50 cents in 1934. Yet the number of boats steadily increased, from 1,149 in 1929 to 1,899 in 1934. The canners piled on new charges, including fees for net mending and an unprecedented $5 rental fee levied at RIC cannery for the tent on the skiff.

At 50 cents a fish, an average Rivers Inlet fisherman could expect gross earnings of $250 in 1934, according to calculations in *The Voice of the Fishermen*. Assuming costs of $150 for a new net rental, $20 boat fare to reach the inlet, $10 to rent a skiff, $25 for clothes and $75 for groceries, the return for five weeks' hard labour would be a loss of $30. Considered from the canner's perspective, the situation was rosy. One hundred fishermen landing 500 fish each would provide 50,000 sockeye for a pack of about 5,000 cases with a value of $14 to $20 each. After expenses, the fishermen said, the canners could count on gross profits of at least $8.50 a case. The canners argued they could hardly find takers for the pack at $10 a case.

Contemporary accounts of conditions in the canneries have not survived, but the militance of shoreworkers is evidence that the situation often became intolerable. Despite the seasonal nature of the work and the inherent difficulty of organizing contract labourers of several races, shoreworkers frequently exercised their power. No doubt canners were prepared to listen to grievances more seriously when the fish were running.

Lauren Casaday, an American researcher who toured the entire salmon industry of the Pacific seaboard from Washington State to Alaska in the early 1930s, concluded that canners were pursuing a deliberate policy of racial hiring to maintain tension, division and low prices. J. N. Cobb, the dean of American fisheries research during the period, claimed that "in many canneries special quarters have to be provided for certain races—more particularly the Chinese and the Japanese—in order to prevent racial hatred from engendering brawls and disturbances."

By the mid-1930s, B.C.'s coastal cannery workforce numbered about 5,000, of whom 15 per cent were Chinese men, 15 per cent Japanese-Canadian men and women, and the rest overwhelmingly native women. There was a strict hierarchy of living quarters, with separate bunkhouses for Chinese, Japanese and native people, and small cottages for white workers. All were employed on some form of contract labour arrangement, paid a piece rate, and provided with food, lodging and transportation to the cannery. Although this iniquitous contract system was banned by law in the United States in 1936 due to pressure from organized labour, it continued unabated in Canada until wiped out by union organization in the late 1940s. A surviving example of an American contract in force during the 1930s stipulated penalties of 25 cent to 50 cents an hour or per meal "for any period during which they were unwilling or unable to work for any reason whatever." Medical care was entirely the workers' responsibility, and the contract concluded: "I agree to forfeit my entire salary if I should be found guilty of fomenting strikes or spreading discontent among other workers."

There was no limit on the length of the working day, although in practice it lasted eleven to twelve hours. Government investigators in Puget Sound in the mid-1930s heard of twenty-hour shifts, after which the Chinese workers had to cut their boots from their swollen feet and "cried like babies" when forced back to work.

Once transported to the cannery, shoreworkers could while away the few quiet hours gambling, watching the waves roll in or spending some money at the company store. To break the monotony of rice, boiled fish and stew which was standard fare, workers could buy canned food, eggs, fruit and cheese at premium prices. "The cannery stores at all the canneries have at least three different prices," reported *The Voice of the Fishermen*. "Cheapest prices are for the net crews and white cannery workers, some of the favoured fishermen getting the same price advantages, then the next line of prices is for the white and Japanese fishermen. The last and highest price of all is for Indians. This price is never written down. The store-keeper keeps these prices in his own head and just sticks it on as he dishes out the goods."

Certainly there was prostitution at B.C. canneries and many abuses, but little evidence of the racketeering which became a feature of the U.S. system. B.C. canners were content to work the crews for the minimum possible salary.

As a consequence, most shoreworkers were happy to take home $80 to $100 for two months' work, and the majority of workers in the industry, ashore and afloat, needed relief every year of the Depression.

One shoreworkers' strike that produced some gains hit Nelson Bros. St. Mungo cannery on the Fraser in August 1934. Women on the filling line rebelled against piece rates and a shape-up hiring system in which the boss called out seventy-five women each day to fill sixty-five positions. Not knowing from day to day if they would have work, and receiving only 2.5 cents for filling a tray of forty-eight half-pound or one-pound (227- or 454-gram) cans, they threatened a strike. They won a half-cent raise, but Motherwell reported that a man named James Munro "who had been advising the females and agitating for a strike of all staff, was discharged."

Although shoreworkers remained virtually unorganized, fishermen had formed several associations and unions in the early 1930s to protect their interests. In 1931, seine fishermen formed the United Fishermen of B.C. and secured a charter from the Trades and Labour Congress. Although organized to represent all fishermen, the union—later named the United Fishermen's Federal Union—took in skippers and crews on company-owned salmon and herring seiners. Trollers organized a number of co-operatives and associations. Gillnetters, the largest group of fishermen, still relied on the old BCFPA.

But the BCFPA had become moribund, more preoccupied with persecuting Japanese-Canadian fishermen than with advancing the lot of all who worked for the canners. When BCFPA leaders undercut a strike for improved sockeye prices at Barkley Sound in 1931, fishermen answered the call of the militant Workers Unity League to organize a new union called the Fishermen's Industrial Union (FIU). Its founding meeting was held in Vancouver in early 1932.

The Workers Unity League had been founded only a year before by the Communist party of Canada as a response to the Depression and a challenge to existing trade unions to confront the economic crisis by renewed organization. Committed to industrial unionism, which would bring all workers in a given industry into a single organization, the league was founded on rank-and-file control and urged all-out struggle, including militant strikes, to make gains. Although industry observers then and since have been baffled by the persistence of strong radical politics among fishermen, the early success of the FIU was completely natural. In the 1930s fishermen learned radicalism on the job, their hardships, according to a gillnetter quoted by Lauren Casaday, "a living denunciation of a parasitic industry, an industry that depends for its profits on exploiting to the limit both men and resources." " Is it any wonder," one fisherman asked, "that many fishermen are radicals?"

Many were radicalized in the industry, but others learned their politics elsewhere. One virtue of open entry for white fishermen was that it created a refuge for labour militants blacklisted in other industries. Early supporters of the FIU included Nick Stevens, the son of the same John Stevens who had assailed the canners in 1893, and Marko Vidulich, a veteran of the 1900 strike. Many others among the white fishermen had been members of other unions and supported the numerous strikes that had broken out in B.C. in 1919 in support of the Winnipeg General Strike. For these men, the class struggle was not rhetoric, it was a fact of life. "This fishing is more or less a struggle between hope and despair," wrote a Sointula fisherman in 1932 in the *Unemployed Worker,* a description that well fitted the task of building the union.

The fishermen faced formidable obstacles. They were divided by gear and they belonged to different ethnic organizations and regional associations. The FIU not only argued that all fishermen and shoreworkers should be in a single organization, it actively sought unity with Japanese-Canadian fishermen and shoreworkers.

The union changed its name in 1934 to the Fishermen's and Cannery Workers Industrial Union (FCWIU) and began to grow. Raids on union offices by the RCMP—"they didn't leave enough paper to light a pipe"—failed to stem the tide.

Angered by their sellout leadership, a section of the United Fishermen of B.C. rallied to the FCWIU in 1934. In June of that year the FCWIU made a breakthrough. After a hard-fought strike, the union signed an agreement for troll blueback production in the Strait of Georgia with Deep Bay Packing. Organizers then moved to Rivers Inlet, where support was running high. The canners enlisted Motherwell's assistance to thwart a strike. The size of the fleet normally would have dictated at least a seventy-two-hour weekly closure, but Motherwell arranged to rescind the closure for fear it would "be the necessary ammunition required by the Reds to gain their point and wreck the season's fishing." When the threat of job action eased, Motherwell added extra closed time in the following week, prompting an angry protest from fishermen.

Struggles on other fronts were paying dividends as well. Aware that the drive for unlimited salmon licences was eroding the earnings of real fishermen, the FCWIU campaigned to limit the fishery to bona fide fishermen. Six new locals were formed in 1934, and fishermen began to raise the call for Workers Compensation Board coverage and universal unemployment insurance.

The union also exposed the hypocrisy of government and corporate cries about depletion of the runs. "In their greed for larger profits, the word conservation is being used to camouflage further exploitation of the fishermen," warned *The Voice of the Fishermen* in 1934. In another issue of the magazine, a Rivers Inlet fishermen protested, "As there were no fish elsewhere and the canners wanted the fish, they robbed the spawning grounds to swell their profits. This instant clearly illustrates the fishery patrol is controlled by the boss canners."

The time had come to challenge the rule of the canners. Rivers Inlet was a natural battleground. During the spring of 1936, FCWIU organizers attempted to draw all the fishermen's organizations into a single front under the umbrella of a Fishermen's Joint Committee. Some early skirmishes with the canners won a price increase in early-run Fraser fish, but the Canned Salmon Section of the Canadian Manufacturers' Association (CMA), which represented the canners, stood firm against any increase in Rivers Inlet. The union's allies on the Joint Committee quietly faded into the background. By June, it was clear that if the FCWIU wanted to take on the central coast canners, it would have to do so alone.

The union's organizers, George Miller and Alex Ramsay, headed for the grounds. They travelled by gas boat, raising money for fuel as they went. Costly though a gas boat was, it made union organization a possibility, enabling organizers to link canneries and communities in united action for the first time. A meeting of 125 white and native seiners at Alert Bay on 21 June voted full support. The strike deadline was 5 July, one week after fishing was to begin in Rivers Inlet. As the deadline neared, most fisherman were in a buoyant mood. Many felt that a strike would last less than a week.

For the first week, their optimism seemed justified. From Alert Bay, where seiners joined in the strike, to the gillnet fleets at Namu, the central coast was shut down. On 12 July, the canners turned up the pressure. They posted notices promising police protection to anyone who would scab, and in Alert Bay they attempted to intimidate the grocer and butcher into denying supplies to the strikers. The businessmen refused. The strike committee's offer to resume negotiations was ignored. The canners clearly wanted a fight to the finish.

The struggle that ensued shaped the fishing industry for the next half-century. From busy kitchens in Sointula, strikers ferried bread and other groceries all the way to the head of Rivers Inlet, where company stores were locked to union members. In tense nighttime confrontations on the fishing grounds, pickets stared down the barrels of police guns, cut scab fishermen's nets and seized the catches of strikebreakers to feed strike-bound shoreworkers. But after weeks of determined picketing, both fishermen and canners were forced to concede that the season had been lost. Native fishermen, who broke ranks at Alert Bay because they believed their interests had been betrayed by their white counterparts, formed a new organization to counter the union's strength. White fishermen, who doubted the militance of Japanese-Canadian fishermen, acknowledged that the solidarity of the Japanese-

Canadian fleet in Rivers Inlet had been unmatched anywhere on the coast. And fishermen realized that it was possible to shut down the canneries and survive. When eighty scabs were moved in under police guard late in July, union fishermen recognized the canners' action as a desperate move to salvage a lost cause. The strike ended short of victory, but far from defeat. Instead of the 100,000 cases of sockeye the processors had hoped to take from Rivers Inlet that year, there were just over 46,000.

The lessons of the strike were studied by fishermen coastwide. When the seine fleet struck in Alert Bay in 1938, fishermen like Elgin "Scotty" Neish who had learned from the errors of 1936 drove the canners to the wall with disciplined picketing. The momentum of 1938 carried the industry through to the formation of the United Fishermen and Allied Workers Union in 1945.

The Rivers Inlet strike had shown both the power of united action and the obstacles that stood in its way. Just months after the strike ended, the FCWIU voted to dissolve and merge its various gear sections with the American Federation of Labor affiliates then being established in the seine and gillnet fleets south of the line. Across North America, affiliates of the Workers Unity League and its American counterpart were taking the same course in an effort to consolidate the labour movement. In Canada, FCWIU gillnetters became members of the Pacific Coast Fishermen's Union. Seine members joined the Salmon Purse Seiners Union. In 1937, the threat of united job action won an arbitrated price settlement from the canners, the first fruit of the struggles of 1936. But the goal of a signed net salmon contract eluded fishermen until 1938.

In September of that year, the canners unilaterally cut the price for seine-caught chums from 10 cents to 8 cents a fish. Their action ignited a strike among Yugoslav, Italian and Canadian-born seine fishermen in Johnstone Strait that soon won the support of key figures in the native seine fleet, which fished exclusively on company boats. Strike leaders Murphy Fiore, "Scotty" Neish and Marijan Ruljanovich, backed by a large strike committee, agreed that to maintain solidarity the crews would remain on board their vessels and anchored offshore. On 18 September, the negotiating committee marched up to the Canadian Fishing offices in Alert Bay to present their demands to spokesmen for Canadian Fishing, B.C. Packers and ABC Fishing and Packing.

The exchange that followed showed how much had changed in the industry. Years later, the events in that crowded office remained engraved in Neish's memory. In a December 1987 article in *The Fisherman,* he recalled: "When we said we demanded the increase in price, Doorman, of the New England Fishing Co., objected and said 'You mean you are asking for an increase.' John Hanson—he had only one eye—got up and whipped open the drapes. He

pointed to the fleet tied up and said, 'We're not requesting any more, Doorman, we're making our demands. There's our solidarity. You get on the phone
and tell Vancouver that.' "

The canners responded by cutting off food and credit at the company stores
and pressuring fishermen to turn in their gear. The fleet voted 225 to 5 to
keep their nets. When the canners persisted, the fishermen called their bluff.
They would turn in the nets, but strip them first into their component parts,
rendering them useless for fishing. "The companies said, 'You can't do that,
it's private property,' " Neish recalled. "We said, 'Like hell it is, we built
them and we're taking them apart.' "

With the nets turned in, the majority of the seine fleet voted to take the
boats back to Vancouver to tie up for the season. The subsequent trip, with a
stop at Blubber Bay to assist striking members of the International Woodworkers of America, became a legend in the history of the industry. As the
fleet approached Vancouver, it formed up two columns, each thirty vessels
long, and sailed into port in formation. Still the canners stood firm. It seemed
that this strike, like the battle in 1936, would be a stalemate. But the seine
fishermen were heartened by the news that gillnetters, confronted by the same
cuts, were joining the strike as well. When gillnetters at Port Renfrew voted
to join the tie-up, the canners finally conceded and signed a coastwide agreement at 10 cents a fish.

The 1938 strike was a breakthrough, not only for what it achieved but for
how it was done. For the first time since 1900, fishermen had overcome not
only racial differences but differences in gear and region to confront a common
enemy. It seemed at last that the end of the canners' empire was within reach.
To some veterans of the struggle for unionization, however, the fight for good
prices was only the first challenge. Until fishermen had the security of licence
limitation, any other gains would be built on sand.

THE DRIVE TO ORGANIZE

THE B.C. CANNERS ALWAYS FLOURISHED DURING WORLD wars. As the battle was joined in Europe, B.C. Packers and Canadian Fishing were undertaking their first major expansions since the shakedown of 1928. Despite the pressure of organized fishermen, times were good, and both companies added new product lines, expanded existing plants and ventured into new areas, consolidating operations on Vancouver Island and the Queen Charlottes. New seine boats began to slide down the ways, and canneries were equipped with the latest vacuum-canning technology. Radio telephones and echo sounders made their first appearance, diesel engines were installed on new vessels, and ice-packing of fish extended the range of the packer fleet. In 1939, Ottawa signalled the end of the era of sail by eliminating boat-pullers' licences for B.C. gillnetters. Early that year, ABC Packing, B.C. Packers, Canadian Fishing, Nelson Bros. and Nootka Packing demonstrated their patriotic spirit by loaning a total of forty vessels to the federal government for the Royal Canadian Navy Fishermen's Reserve.

Despite the battle over 1938 seine prices, which the companies had predicted would destroy their profits, the year-end results were excellent. The value of the pack rose 15 per cent, although the volume was the same as 1937. During the decade from 1931 to 1940, the volume of landings rose 30 per cent, while value rose 100 per cent. The number of canneries was reduced from sixty-three in 1929 to thirty-eight in 1940, and the value of individual canneries rose sharply as a result of plant consolidation.

Economist J. Wigdor concluded in 1940 that "the industry is operating with less overhead, is achieving greater labour and operating economy and is achieving a greater return in value per pack per unit of operation" than it had a decade before. During the First World War, the value and volume of the pack had actually doubled. Now the main companies were well placed to repeat the feat. ABC Packing, B.C. Packers, Canadian Fishing and J. H. Todd, the four largest operations, accounted for more than $10 million in capital assets. Their six smaller competitors together amounted to only $275,000. B.C. Packers had emerged from the turmoil of the 1928 consolidation to take over fully one-third of the industry's total output and controlled 60 per cent of the province's fish exports. Like the rest of the Big Four, B.C. Packers was planning for expansion and was virtually debt-free as the Second World War began. The long-awaited signing of a Canada–United States salmon treaty in 1937, which created the International Pacific Salmon Fisheries Commission, had opened the door to rehabilitation of the Fraser. The processors could count on better returns in the 1940s even without the bonus of wartime profits.

The exigencies of war required a single-minded dedication of all government resources to what the canners did best: harvest and preserve every available fish. Concerns about conservation and the underlying structural problems of the industry were pushed aside. Persistent demands from fishermen's organizations to eliminate the Sooke salmon traps and to place controls on the expansion of seine fishing were explored by a royal commission in 1940. Commissioner Judge Gordon Sloan rejected elimination of the traps, although he conceded they played no role in redressing the imbalance in Canadian and American salmon catches. (American traps had been banned for five years.) He also recommended continued seine harvests in the Strait of Georgia, despite the opposition of Fraser gillnetters, who had suffered from the lifting in 1933 of a ban on seining off the river's mouth.

With markets assured and runs strong, the industry put up its largest pack to date in 1941. Export controls on fresh troll salmon were tightened, and salmon salteries, still managed largely by Japanese Canadians, were denied licences entirely. (Their owners were expelled from B.C. soon after.) Despite paying record high prices to fishermen, the canners racked up handsome profits. Buoyed by the injection of confiscated boats from the Japanese-Canadian fleet, guaranteed access to virtually every salmon, and assured of unlimited markets and a minimum rate of return under wartime pricing regulations, the canners enjoyed yet another golden age.

At war's end, the industry's economic structure was significantly changed. In 1944, B.C. Packers reported net profits of $544,379, a hefty increase over the $132,801 reported in 1938. This figure included an unknown amount of "excess profits" taxed away under wartime legislation. Although the cost of sockeye had risen 35 per cent and labour costs had almost doubled, retail prices had increased by the same amount and other costs were down sufficiently to give canners an increase in their net returns. How was this miracle accomplished? By a combination of factors. Wartime legislation fixed prices, guaranteed profits and controlled price increases for necessary supplies. The supply of raw fish was assured and the harvest intensified. Because most of the pack was consumed in the United Kingdom, Canada or the British Commonwealth, the war left most markets intact but eliminated competition from Japan's domestic and Siberian production. It was a situation tailored to the canners in every way. The only cloud on the horizon was the relentless expansion of union organization. After forty years of struggle, fishermen and shoreworkers were about to realize Frank Rogers's dream.

The drive to organization, which had begun in the wake of the 1928 crisis and was spurred by the Depression, affected every sector of the industry. Although native Indian, Japanese-Canadian and white fishermen had responded at first by building separate organizations, the benefits of united action were so compelling that ethnic divisions were beginning to crumble by the end of the 1930s. The outbreak of war, particularly the expulsion of the Japanese-Canadians, shattered the balance of power within the fishing fleet. The immediate beneficiaries of the expulsion were the canners, who acquired the Japanese-Canadian fleet and made it available, in large part, to native fishers. It is a tragic fact that the catastrophe of Pearl Harbor achieved for native people a partial redress of the losses they had suffered as a result of the industry's institutionalized racism. They did so as a consequence of a paroxysm of racism that realized the long-standing dream of hundreds of fishermen to eliminate the Japanese Canadians. The transfer of vessels to native fishermen consolidated the creation of the first coastwide native organization.

The economic impact of the Depression had been devastating to native communities, many of which were effectively driven out of the wage economy. Only in the fishing industry did they retain an economic base, however weak.

Native leaders in coastal communities knew a new organization was a necessity. The man who provided the spark was Alfred Adams, a commercial fisherman, Anglican lay minister and Haida, who had been inspired by Alaska Indians and their movement called the Native Brotherhood. In late 1931, he met in Port Simpson with leaders of a number of Tsimshian communities to form the Native Brotherhood of British Columbia. Although based on fishing industry communities, the Native Brotherhood was not initially a fishermen's organization. From its earliest days, it spoke out on all questions confronting native people, from education to aboriginal rights. Because it was illegal to organize for land claims, that issue remained the unspoken motive behind the rest of the Brotherhood's program. A key demand at the first conference was a call for recognition of the right of native people "to fish for domestic consumption without permits."

Fraser River gillnetters, using the earliest version of planked skiffs built for the fishery, deliver to a cannery in the late 1880s. EDWARDS BROS. PHOTO/CITY OF VANCOUVER ARCHIVES/256-23

Pioneer canners meeting in 1889. Left to right: (seated) D. J. Munn, E. A. Wadhams, *Alexander Ewen, M. M. English, Ben Young;* (standing) *Mike Leary, H. Harlock, T. E. Ladner, J. A. Laidlaw, Robert Matherson.* DELTA MUSEUM AND ARCHIVES

Britannia Cannery's 1895 pack of 1.6 million gleaming cans was shipped to markets as distant as the United Kingdom and Australia, where canned salmon was cheaper than fresh beef. CITY OF RICHMOND ARCHIVES

The Columbia River-style boats that dominated the Fraser River by 1900 carried a crew of two who rowed and sailed to and from the fishing grounds. B.C. ARCHIVES AND RECORDS SERVICE/43095

The Duke of Connaught's Own Regiment, dubbed "the Sockeye Fusiliers" by fisherman, was dispatched to Steveston in 1900 to suppress a pivotal strike. VANCOUVER PUBLIC LIBRARY

An early gas-powered gillnetter (foreground) *ties up alongside a pot scow, which collected salmon, while sail gillnetters and a sail gillnetter converted to power wait their turn.* B.C. ARCHIVES AND RECORDS SERVICE/52933

Japanese-Canadian boatbuilders became a force in the industry very early. Above, flags snap in the breeze at a double launching at Scotch Pond in Steveston in the early 1900s. CITY OF RICHMOND ARCHIVES

Fish trap workers, probably at the J. H. Todd traps near Sooke, stand over part of the massive sockeye run of 1913, which overwhelmed the industry but died in the Fraser Canyon at the Hell's Gate blockade. B.C. ARCHIVES AND RECORDS SERVICE /84170

Canadian Fishing workers at the Home Plant load frozen spring salmon for rail transport to Montreal and New York in the early 1920s. Railway expansion made the frozen trade possible.
CANADIAN FISHING CO.

Hell's Gate after the CNOR blasted most of the east bank (right) into the canyon in 1914. James McHugh's engineers cleared a bench and put up the overhead tramline to remove tonnes of debris.
SPECIAL COLLECTIONS, UNIVERSITY OF BRITISH COLUMBIA LIBRARY/BC5 1 8-6P

A cannery tug tows sail gillnetters to the fishing grounds on the Skeena River during the 1930s. B.C. ARCHIVES AND RECORDS SERVICE/82342

Native Indian fishers clear salmon from a beach seine at Nimpkish in the 1920s. Changes in regulations wiped out the beach seines. NATIONAL ARCHIVES OF CANADA/PA 40978

Cannery work remained arduous and dangerous despite technological changes like this gang knife, which by the 1930s had eliminated much labour previously performed by Chinese workers.
VANCOUVER MARITIME MUSEUM

Rivers Inlet gillnetters gather for a strike meeting at Dawson's Landing in 1938. The strike proved a turning point in the battle over fish prices. THE FISHERMAN

Women at work building nets during the 1940s. Throughout the industry's history, women formed a large part of the shore workforce. VANCOUVER MARITIME MUSEUM

Granite Bay in 1938—the seine fleet is tied up for its breakthrough strike. THE FISHERMAN

Chinese cannery workers in the 1940s operate an iron butcher, called the "Iron Chink" by the industry, in sarcastic acknowledgement of the workers it eliminated. VANCOUVER MARITIME MUSEUM

Unloading a seine catch in the 1940s, when the seine fleet underwent a new period of expansion and upgrading. STEFFENS-COLMER STUDIO/CITY OF VANCOUVER ARCHIVES/5577

Advances in technology eliminated hand-filling of quarter-pound (114-gram) tins by the late 1960s. Above, in the 1950s, twins L. and D. Wilson join A. Hamilton at Canadian Fishing's filling tables at the Home Plant. CANADIAN FISHING CO.

The native fishery on the Fraser River during the 1950s; despite years of efforts to suppress it, the native harvest has continued and grown.

Gillnetters mend their nets at Nelson Bros. cannery on the Skeena in 1949; open entry to the fleet meant poor earnings. J. LONG PHOTO/NATIONAL FILM BOARD COLLECTION/NATIONAL ARCHIVES OF CANADA/PA 141283

Buck Suzuki building a gillnetter in the 1960s. He helped lead Japanese Canadians back into the industry in the 1950s. THE FISHERMAN, SPECIAL COLLECTIONS, UNIVERSITY OF BRITISH COLUMBIA LIBRARY/BC1532-2776-5

Three generations of UFAWU leadership. Left to right: *Homer Stevens, variously president and secretary-treasurer from the late 1940s to 1975; Jack Nichol, elected president in 1975, and Steve Stavenes, president from 1952 to 1968.* THE FISHERMAN, SPECIAL COLLECTIONS, UNIVERSITY OF BRITISH COLUMBIA LIBRARY/BC1532-371

Herring processing in Vancouver during the 1980s. The money flowing from the new roe fishery made the 1970s a boom period which disguised many underlying problems in the industry. THE FISHERMAN

In 1984 fishermen from almost every industry organization flew to Parliament Hill and donned survival suits to dramatize their opposition to Liberal government plans to implement drastic changes in licensing. THE FISHERMAN

Dr. Peter Pearse (left) meets with reporters in 1984 as fisheries minister Pierre DeBane (centre) listens in after a news conference announcing a sweeping restructuring of the industry. THE FISHERMAN

Juvenile coho rise for a feeding at a Sunshine Coast salmon farm in 1987. Despite problems with disease and markets, farmed fish are replacing both wild fish and the incentive to protect salmon habitat. THE FISHERMAN

Striking seine crew members in 1989 when the union and the industry battled to a standstill over changes demanded by the processors as a result of free trade rulings. THE FISHERMAN

Herring seiners manoeuvre for a chance to set their nets during the roe fishery in Nanoose Bay in 1984. The dramatic expansion of the seine fleet was a major inheritance from the Davis plan. THE FISHERMAN

J. S. McMillan women workers set up their picket line in the 1984 salmon strike. By the 1980s shore sector issues were gaining in importance. THE FISHERMAN

Rivers Inlet sockeye confound the experts by returning according to cycles of abundance that remain poorly understood. Logging of watersheds where they spawn casts a shadow over their future. THE FISHERMAN

As early as 1932, however, the Native Brotherhood was acting as bargaining agent for fishermen engaged in strikes on the Skeena. Uniting the disparate bands of the north coast was not an easy process. Linking up with the strong fishing communities scattered along both sides of Johnstone Strait took even longer. A turning point was the 1936 Rivers Inlet strike, viewed by white union fishermen as a major advance but recalled to this day in native communities as a serious betrayal. The source of the dispute was the conflicting assessment of the strike's end in Alert Bay, where white and native seine fishermen had tied up in support of the Rivers Inlet gillnetters. The decision of native fishermen to return to work in Alert Bay was deplored by union members as a serious blow to the strike, but native leaders were disturbed by the canners' denial of groceries to strikers and by reports that whites had scabbed the strike.

James Sewid, a Kwakiutl seine fisherman who became a central figure in the Native Brotherhood, recalled in his autobiography (edited by James P. Spradley) that "we weren't allowed to go up to Knight Inlet to see our wives and children and we wanted to know how they were getting along. They finally settled it but we didn't make hardly anything at all because we had been tied up nearly all season." Harry Assu, whose father participated in the strike, remembered that he "lost out on our whole summer fishing season. What we lost out on was not just a job. Fishing is our living, our way of life! We own these waters and we have to be able to fish them."

The Kwakiutl responded to the conflicts of 1936 by forming the Pacific Coast Native Fishermen's Association. At a September meeting at Cape Mudge, Chief Billy Assu, George Luther, Chief Harry Mountain, Chief Bill Scow and many other senior leaders created the new organization not only to represent them during collective bargaining but also to push for more native participation in the commercial fishery. In 1942, their association merged with the Native Brotherhood to produce the first major native organization in the province since the demise of the Allied Tribes.

Although the Native Brotherhood participated in collective bargaining, it was not a union. Its organizational structure, its membership base and its broad objectives were fundamentally different both from the trade unions and the gear associations and co-ops. The men responsible for organizing the Native Brotherhood were chiefs, acting in their traditional role as spokesmen for their people. During the strikes in 1893 and 1900, the chiefs had determined their people's course of action, although there were instances of native people enrolling in the unions of the day on a rank-and-file basis. On the coast, this responsibility of leadership was reflected in the chiefs' negotiations with canneries seeking leases on reserves or a supply of labour. With the end of the drag-seine fishery, this relationship was threatened. As a result of Found's licensing policy, native people had been denied seine licences. In 1922, however, they had convinced the department they should at least be allowed to be skippers on company seine boats. Companies like ABC Packing and B.C. Packers soon made company boats available to key native leaders to maintain a relationship that dated back to the days of the earliest beach-seine leases.

So it was that Heber Clifton, who combined his role as a chief with religious duties as a lay minister in his community, was able to put a seine boat at the disposal of Adams and others organizing the Native Brotherhood in the north in the early 1930s. Sewid and Assu were two other prominent examples of native leaders who combined the stature of a chief with substantial economic resources which they used to help build the new organization.

"When the first cannery men came to this coast, they put up the canneries at places where our people were living, at the best salmon rivers," recalled Harry Assu, "and we knew how to take fish in our own waters. The cannery managers needed Indian men to bring in the fish and women to work in the canneries. . . . My father was recruiter for native workers at the cannery at Quathiaski Cove." When cannery owner W. E. Anderson sold out his interest in Quathiaski Cove in 1938, he asked the chiefs who they would like to work for. They told him B.C. Packers, and that was who got the cannery. "We were always able to take care of ourselves," Assu said. "Indians don't join unions. I look at it this way. There is no help from the unions. If you are fired, the union cannot give you a job. It's the company that gave you the job. In the early days, before I bought a boat of my own, I ran a company boat. In the company, if they thought you were a strong union man, they wouldn't have anything to do with you."

Sewid's story was similar. From his earliest childhood, he travelled with his mother on an annual cycle from their home on Turnour Island to the Nimpkish sockeye fishery, then to cannery work in Knight Inlet and finally to their smokehouse at the mouth of the river in Vinea Sound, where the entire community would harvest and prepare the salmon, wrapped fifty to a bundle in cedar bark baskets, for the winter. He worked in the seine fleet from the age of ten and was given command of his own boat by ABC Packing at age twenty-one. By 1942, he was able to buy his own boat, the first native fisherman to do so, and he bought a second boat in 1944. But from 1938 on he also played a vital role in the development of the Native Brotherhood.

Although the Native Brotherhood grew steadily, it really won its spurs in 1942 with its successful campaign to stop the government from levying income tax on native Indians. A major expansion followed on this success, and the organization was able to retain Andrew Paull as business agent that year. During this period, the remaining large coastal groups, including the Nisga'a, finally joined the Brotherhood, which established branches in most communities. Although increasingly involved in commercial fishing matters, the Brotherhood's roots made it a contradictory force in collective bargaining. It was not a labour organization. Owners of large boats were barred from membership in the United Fishermen's Federal Union, but dominated the leadership of the Native Brotherhood. They had close and long-standing ties to the canners as well as deep-seated suspicions about the motives of white union leaders. Strongly religious and politically conservative, the Brotherhood leaders built an organization that opened the way for the modern aboriginal rights movement. In the fishing industry, however, the Native Brotherhood acted as a brake on the actions of the burgeoning union movement.

Japanese-Canadian fishermen had been organized from the earliest days of the industry into associations which not only negotiated fish prices but also lobbied to end discriminatory regulations. Despite some tough strikes, however, these associations were dominated by labour contractors, fishing bosses and community leaders from the small merchant class in the Japanese-Canadian community. By 1919, Japanese workers, like their white counterparts, had begun looking for a more democratic and militant alternative. That year, Japanese-Canadian millworkers struck a sawmill at Sawnong Bay near Ocean Falls. When some of the strikers were fired, they travelled to Vancouver to found a new organization called Nihonjin Rodo Kumiai to defend their interests. Elected to lead this new union was Etsu Suzuki, a left-wing journalist, who hoped the organization could counter the Anti-Asiatic League. The union's first organizer was Ryuichi Yoshida, a Skeena fisherman who had immigrated to Canada in 1910. After years of tireless organizing, Yoshida and his fellow workers succeeded in building the membership to 1,600 in several industries. In 1926, the union was admitted to the Vancouver Trades and Labour Council, thanks to the efforts of unionists like Ernest Winch and Angus McInnis of the Co-operative Commonwealth Federation, but this advance did not reflect the decline in racism the Japanese Canadians were hoping for.

Although union organizers had succeeded in welding the disparate Japanese-Canadian fishermen's organization into a province-wide council, their own base remained secure only on the Skeena. In Steveston and Vancouver, conservative forces headed by Etsuji Morii took a direct role in the leadership of the fishermen's organizations. Morii was a gangster, convicted of manslaughter in 1921, who ran gambling operations in Vancouver's Japantown and had close ties to fascist elements in the Japanese-Canadian community. Later, when white fishermen and labour leaders resisted unity with Japanese-Canadian fishermen because of their alleged subservience to Imperial Japan and its agents in Canada, they had Morii in mind. It was the rising tide of racism, however, that isolated the Japanese Canadians and increased their dependency on their own conservative leadership, not a predisposition to fascism.

By the 1930s a new generation of Japanese Canadians was organizing to break out of the ghetto in which their community was imprisoned. Born and raised in Canada, they wanted the right to full participation in Canadian life. One of this new wave was Tatsuro Suzuki (no relation to Etsu Suzuki), the son of a fisherman, who was born in his family's float house at Don Island on the Fraser in 1915. From the age of nine, Suzuki—his nickname was "Buck"—was fishing the river from a rowboat. The eldest child of a family of nine, he was able to attend school for only eight years before economic necessity forced him to find work. "I got a job in a fish cannery at 25 cents an hour," he recalled. "I worked very long hours, sometimes even 22 hours a day. We had no union and conditions were very bad." Working conditions were poor, but Suzuki felt more oppressed by the racism he had encountered from his earliest school days. In 1930, at the age of fifteen, he became a founding member of the Japanese Canadian Citizens Association, which was organized to fight for the rights of Japanese Canadians. By 1938, he was an elected officer of the Upper Fraser River Japanese Fishermen's Association, recognized as a spokesman for the Japanese-Canadian fleet on the Fraser.

With the assistance of Hideo Onotera, a close friend, Suzuki spearheaded an intensive effort by second-generation Japanese-Canadian fishermen to find some basis of unity with white union fishermen. The decline of the B.C. Fishermen's Protective Association, which maintained a racist policy, and the rise of new unions that professed a commitment to organize without regard to race, colour or creed, seemed to offer some new hope. But it was an uphill struggle.

When a debate over organizing Japanese-Canadian fishermen began in the columns of *The Fisherman,* the paper published by the new unions, Suzuki was quick to contribute. "We are not angels," he wrote on 29 July 1941. "But neither are our ranks polluted with fifth columnists or soldiers who have served with the Japanese army. Most of us have been in the industry for years, or have grown up as sons of fishermen fathers. We are average human beings, with the same likes and dislikes as every other human being, despite our different physical characteristics. I have grown up myself with white Canadian fishermen on the River, have laughed with them in time of joy and wept with them in time of sorrow.

"We Canadians of oriental origin are the weak link in the long chain of Canadian workers," he concluded, "not because we want to be, but because of the way other Canadians look at us and treat us. . . . What we need is a real get-together of white Canadian and Japanese Canadian fishermen, with a neutral chairman, so that each side may give its own opinions on the situation."

The maelstrom that broke with Pearl Harbor destroyed the Japanese-

Canadian community. During 1941, all Japanese Canadians were required to register with the Canadian government. They were denied the right to serve in the Canadian armed forces. Despite these restrictions, Japanese Canadians did their best to prove their support for the war effort. Just days before Pearl Harbor, Suzuki's Upper Fraser Japanese Fishermen's Association donated 3.8 tonnes of canned chum salmon for distribution in Britain. Yet within twenty-four hours of the beginning of the war in the Pacific, Japanese-Canadian fishermen were being rounded up and their boats impounded. Joining the rising public clamour for evacuation of the Japanese Canadians was *The Fisherman.* Union fishermen "will join with the rest of organized labour in condemning any violence against the Japanese here," the lead editorial said on 9 December. "They will denounce all attempts to stir up racial prejudice. But, in the light of their own knowledge and experience, they will demand the taking of stringent precautions against dangers they have long recognized, even though such precautionary measures work hardships upon Japanese loyal to our country."

Suzuki quickly assumed an important role in the six-person Japanese-Canadian committee which advised the authorities on the evacuation. In this capacity he was able to observe the close relationship between the RCMP and Morii, who exploited the chaos and his relationship with the government to his own advantage. When this collusion with a known fascist sympathizer became the subject of a public inquiry some time later, Suzuki courageously testified against Morii.

While the Japanese Canadians were dispersed, their fishing fleet was impounded and then put up for sale. The cash-rich canners were quick to move in, buying 660 of the 887 vessels offered for sale. B.C. Packers alone acquired 27 per cent of the fleet, taking 11 seiners, 183 gillnetters, 25 packers, 9 trollers and 9 cod boats for $250,854. The entire fleet was liquidated for only $1.4 million. The canners quickly resold the boats to fishermen at cost on liberal terms that assured the canners delivery of the catch. The majority of the vessels were transferred to native fishermen.

After the 1938 strike a consensus began to build in the various unions that a single organization was required, but it took several years of negotiations to accomplish the series of mergers that produced the United Fishermen and Allied Workers Union (UFAWU). The conservative leadership of the United Fishermen's Federal Union (UFFU) was thrown out of office in 1939 by a group dedicated to more militant unionism. Among the new leaders was Steve Stavenes, a Norwegian immigrant who had arrived in British Columbia in 1925 and soon found his way to the gillnet fishery on the Skeena. Bill Burgess, president of the UFFU, Stavenes and their allies, with Miller as their paid organizer, quickly led the union to a dominant position. George Miller, secretary of the Salmon Purse Seiners Union, negotiated its merger with the United Fishermen's Federal Union in 1940. In 1941, the UFFU organized salmon tendermen and negotiated a substantial pay increase for them. That same year the Pacific Coast Fishermen's Union merged with the UFFU as well, leaving only the B.C. Fishermen's Protective Association outside the fold. It formally joined in 1944.

In mid-1941, the UFFU sought approval from the Trades and Labour Congress to begin organizing shoreworkers. When the congress refused, the fishermen sponsored the creation of a new union, which was accepted by the congress. The Fish, Cannery, Reduction Plant and Allied Workers Union Local 89, headed by Bill Gateman, quickly organized several hundred machinemen and tradesmen employed in southern canneries. In March 1945, it merged with the UFFU to form the United Fishermen and Allied Workers Union, creating at last the single industrial union so long sought by industry workers.

Rank and file organization was the key to the UFAWU's success, but the young union also boasted some extraordinary leadership. Miller was acclaimed founding president of the union, and Stavenes stepped down to a position on the General Executive Board. Two other full-time officers and a young gillnet fisherman elected to the new General Executive Board would shape the union's policies and direction. They were Bill Rigby, the secretary-treasurer, Alex Gordon, the business agent, and Homer Stevens.

Gordon, who had been recruited in 1944 to replace Gateman, was a gifted organizer and negotiator. Gordon had built on Gateman's beginnings to achieve several major agreements for shoreworkers even before the merger, including sick pay, vacation pay, the industry's first overtime clauses and double time for work on holidays.

Homer Stevens was the son and grandson of fishermen (his grandfather, John Stevens, was one of the original licence-holders on the Fraser in 1889). At the UFAWU's founding convention in 1945, Homer was only twenty-two.

Bill Rigby, a quiet, pudgy, smiling, balding man, had been in the industry less than three years. If one person could be called the architect of the UFAWU, it was Rigby. Born in Montreal in 1906, Rigby was something of a mystery. From the age of fourteen, he was on his own, making his way in the garment factories of Montreal. Very soon he was drawn into left-wing politics and the Communist movement. For security reasons, he changed his name. Almost no one in the fishing industry knew that Bill Rigby's real name was Isaac Levine.

How Rigby moved from work as a union and Communist party organizer in Montreal to the leadership of a B.C. fishermen's union is a story he seldom told and is only partly known. He was living in Vancouver with his family in 1940 when the Royal Canadian Mounted Police tracked him down and packed him off to an internment camp. It was almost two years before Ottawa became convinced that it had little to fear from the release of Communist party activists. On his return to Vancouver late in 1942, Rigby was in desperate straits until George Miller hired him to be editor of *The Fisherman*. From that day forward, the union movement in the fishing industry was Rigby's life.

Although Miller, Rigby and many other activists were Communists, the leadership of the unions they sought to bring together represented many tendencies. The broad leadership team included important non-Communists like Stavenes and Reg Payne, elected president to replace Miller in 1951. Stevens was an active member of the CCF and did not join the Labour Progressive party, as the Communist party was then called, until 1949. It was Rigby who recruited Gordon, encouraged Stevens to move into leadership and then stepped aside in 1948 so that Stevens, a working fisherman, could take his place as an officer. Significantly, the staff job Rigby returned to was neither an organizational post nor editor of *The Fisherman*. The union's General Executive Board named Rigby the new union's research director and asked him to tackle the industry's most fundamental problem—the threat that uncontrolled fishing could destroy the salmon resource.

FREEDOM AND LICENCE LIMITATION

AS EARLY AS 1943, WHEN THE WAR'S OUTCOME STILL RE-
mained in doubt, union fishermen had begun to consider how returning soldiers could be integrated into the fleet. Fearful of "overcrowding in the industry," with its attendant impact on bargaining power and earnings, the
UFAWU urged consideration of some form of limitation on the numbers of
fishermen. The union also joined the canners to develop a brief to the government, urging a comprehensive conservation program for the postwar period,
including a suggestion that returning soldiers be employed to inspect spawning grounds.

Neither the canners nor the government had any interest in limiting entry,
especially if it served to consolidate union strength. Even before the end of the
war in the Pacific, the new union had begun flexing its muscles. The entire
northern area was hit by a gillnet strike for a week in June 1945 and again in
July as fishermen and canners clashed over sockeye and chum prices.

With end of the war, hundreds of veterans were looking for work, and Ottawa loaned them money to purchase fishing gear. The new fishermen were
competing for a reduced supply. Overcrowding, which had been obvious to
fishermen even before the conflict, now became a serious concern. The new International Pacific Salmon Fisheries Commission was ordering closures to ensure that sufficient sockeye spawners passed through the new Hell's Gate fishways. New boats and new technology were transforming the seine fleet. Fisheries officials reported early in 1949 that a Butedale seine fishery, which had
averaged 25 vessels during the 1930s and early war years, was attracting 141
vessels by 1948. The Bella Bella area had been harvested by 48 vessels between
1930 and 1943; as many as 118 crowded into the area in 1948. As a result,

weekly fishing times dropped to forty-eight hours from seventy-two or more in most areas of the coast.

The gillnet fishery was changing as well. With new nets, better engines and innovations like the gillnet drum, fishermen were expanding into areas like Johnstone Strait and the Strait of Georgia. In the south coast, part-time fishermen working on weekends and summer holidays began to crowd the Fraser River. Mechanization also swept through the troll fleet, replacing the handtrollers of the 1930s with bigger boats boasting power gurdies for running the gear. The entire salmon harvest was intensifying and moving seaward.

The question of fleet size was linked to one of the most difficult postwar issues the industry confronted, the return of Japanese-Canadian fishermen. As early as mid-1944, the Mackenzie King government had begun sounding public opinion on whether or not Japanese Canadians should be allowed to return to the coast. James Sinclair, future fisheries minister and Liberal MP for North Vancouver, declared that "for security reasons alone I believe no Japanese should be allowed in B.C. for years after the war." Native Brotherhood official Ed Nahanni warned, "We flatly do not want the Japs back in our coastal region." The end of the war, however, seemed to cool these passions. On 15 June 1948, the House of Commons amended the Elections Act to give Japanese Canadians the vote.

Just a few days later, Homer Stevens received a letter from Buck Suzuki, who remained in exile in Ontario with his family. Unable to enrol in the Canadian forces during the war, Suzuki had enlisted in the British Army and had done intelligence work and translation in the Far East. Now that he had the vote, he wanted a licence, he told Stevens, and would prefer to get it with the union's backing rather than with the help of the Canadian Legion. When the government announced that Japanese Canadians would be allowed to return to the coast in March 1949, Stevens, Rigby and other UFAWU officials arranged meetings with Suzuki, George Tanaka, Seijiko Homma and U. Sakamoto of the Japanese Canadian Citizens Association. The two groups agreed that those Japanese Canadians who wished to return to fishing should do so through the UFAWU. The union leadership promised to support their return, provided that the evils of the past—special licensing, area restrictions, segregated bunkhouses, a parallel bargaining organization—were avoided. A resolution supporting that policy passed the UFAWU convention later that month with almost no opposition, although a strong minority had fought hard against any return of the Japanese Canadians for several years.

The return itself was not as smooth. Stevens and other union officers went out to the floats on more than one occasion to confront fishermen attempting to discriminate against Japanese Canadians. The union also succeeded in defeating a canner's attempt to recruit Japanese Canadians on the basis of demand loans and similar types of financing that would quickly return them to prewar economic status. By 1950, more than two hundred Japanese Canadian fishermen had rejoined the industry.

The union's role in the reintegration of the Japanese Canadians was just one indication of its ability to direct industry policy. To both the canners and the fisheries department, there were disturbing signs that this new organization posed a direct threat to their power. In 1946, union seine fishermen harvesting Fraser-bound sockeye actually tied up and stopped fishing for one day to ensure that gillnetters would achieve what the UFAWU considered was a fair share of the pink salmon catch. The tie-up was unprecedented—a closure imposed by fishermen themselves to ensure a proper distribution of the catch. Each fishing season and almost every fishery brought tie-ups over minimum prices. Yet union convention delegates still were unsatisfied. They served notice they wanted still more fundamental changes to the industry.

A 1948 convention resolution declared that "there is no lack of fishermen on this coast but only lack of fish and adequate conservation programs to compensate for past reckless depletion." In a submission to the union's General Executive Board that year, Bill Rigby proposed to "start a study of issuance of licences in various fisheries with particular reference to quantity of fish taken per licence issued over last 10 to 20 years with a view to the GEB or the next convention working out concrete plans for the control of each fishery."

Year after year, the UFAWU urged government action to limit the number of licences. From the beginning, union policy linked conservation of the resource with protection of fishermen's income: "Conservation of fish resources is of no value unless it leads to conservation of fishermen." In 1950, a union convention resolution declared that "the catch of fish per boat has been declining over a period of years" and that "in many areas of the coast there is indicated a depletion of salmon resources necessitating conservation programs which would require serious restrictions upon operations to rebuild runs." The problem was compounded, the resolution continued, by the issuance of licences to people who were not "dependent on the fishery as a means of livelihood" and "not interested in conservation of our salmon resources in perpetuity." The union demanded a freeze on the issuance of new licences and a royal commission "to study and bring in recommendations on all aspects of licence limitation in the salmon fishery."

The union's policy, however, remained a series of generalities until 1954, when the issue again assumed importance in the wake of a bitter public debate between Sinclair and Stevens. At the UFAWU's 1954 convention, Sinclair made one of the most popular moves ever by a fisheries minister, challenging seine fishermen to go outside the Canadian fishing boundaries and intercept Fraser-bound pink salmon before they hit the American fleet. (The fleet did so, and the Americans quickly came to the table to negotiate a treaty covering pink salmon.) It was the first time—and last—that a Liberal minister would challenge American power over the salmon, and it came after a year in which U.S. harvests exceeded 80 per cent of the total pink catch. But Sinclair combined the challenge with a withering attack on union secretary-treasurer Stevens, who had condemned Sinclair for his failure to impose some form of catch division on the Canadian fleet to protect gillnet fishermen who had become the cannon fodder in this salmon war.

Sinclair had provoked Stevens's anger with a lengthy newspaper interview in which he laid out the fundamental objectives of fishing licensing policy that remain in place today. "The trend is to fewer fishermen but wholly professional fishermen who work all year round with the most efficient methods and earn excellent and dependable incomes," Sinclair said. These fishermen would use seine gear in the interest of efficiency, accept lower prices to make the industry more competitive and move the harvest seaward to improve quality. Conservation and job protection were not part of Sinclair's vocabulary.

Stevens had answered Sinclair with a point-by-point rejection of his policy. The union demanded a catch division program, licence limitation, a treaty covering pink salmon, an immediate moratorium on new licences and a royal commission to study the licensing issue.

Addressing the union convention with Stevens seated just a few chairs to his left, Sinclair subjected the union's position to a scathing attack. Limitation of effort was "the most important economic problem facing you fishermen," he said, but the union offered criticism, not advice. With heavy sarcasm, he lashed the union for the vague nature of its licence limitation demands.

Sinclair committed his ministry to developing a licence limitation scheme with three goals—controlling the number of fishermen, encouraging efficient equipment and restricting fishing areas to move harvests farther away from spawning grounds to improve quality. As a first step, he promised to limit licences to Canadian citizens and to eliminate pink and chum catches above Mission bridge. There would be no more action, Sinclair declared, until fishermen spelled out their wishes.

A year later, after lengthy research, analysis and painstaking rewriting, Rigby submitted a slim 25-page brief to the 1955 convention, giving Sinclair his answer. For Rigby, the issue was not the cost of fishing, but the benefits. He started from the standpoint of conservation, which Sinclair had not mentioned. He rejected out of hand any limitation linked to canneries and limitation based on race. Licence limitation, he wrote, might become necessary and desirable "a) when danger of depletion is evident if unrestricted fishing is permitted to continue; b) restrictions on production are introduced to conserve the fishery in perpetuity and c) such restrictions on production as are necessary for purposes of conservation tend to make the fishery operation uneconomic from the viewpoint of earnings obtained by the producer or in relation to the cost of production that must be paid ultimately by the consumer.

"Licence limitation is thus intimately connected with the need and the consequences of fishery conservation, but it cannot be considered solely as a problem of conservation of fish. It is a social question: how to 'conserve' the produce and protect the consumer when the fishermen can no longer increase or even maintain real earnings by increasing total production. The purpose which any system of licence limitation must serve under present circumstances is to provide maximum employment consistent with adequate earnings by Canadian standards and at reasonable costs, whilst maintaining adequate stocks of fish in perpetuity."

The union position put the resource before revenue, jobs before efficiency, and benefits before costs. It came down firmly in favour of licensing fishermen, not boats: "There is as yet no boat which can catch fish without men aboard." These fishermen would be issued licence books, Rigby proposed, in which their fisheries and their landings would be recorded annually. Above all, they would be "dependent on fishing as a means of livelihood on a regular basis from year to year" and would fish actively on every day that fishing was permitted. Initially, all existing bona fide fishermen would be licensed. As fishermen died or left the industry, their places would be filled from a waiting list. Eliminating the transferability of licences would ensure that the fishing privilege could not be bought and sold. "We consider," Rigby concluded, "that freedom and licence limitation are not incompatible."

UNLAWFUL CONSPIRACY

AND COMBINE

THE UNION'S CONCERN FOR CONSERVATION CUT NO ICE WITH the canners, who were concerned only with reducing the cost of fish. However, the UFAWU and the Native Brotherhood had succeeded in retaining and building upon the high raw fish prices obtained during the war. In the seven years after its formation, the UFAWU extended its organization to cover the overwhelming majority of fishermen, shoreworkers and tendermen in the province. Whalers, herring and halibut fishermen, and even fish-trap workers joined the union's ranks.

Even the modest ling cod fishery was affected. When union fishermen struck the Gulf of Georgia cod fishery in 1947, James Eckman, president of Canadian Fishing, was outraged at their decision to issue a hot declaration against all nonunion production. The hot declaration amounted to a union boycott of all nonunion fish, ensuring that UFAWU shoreworkers would not handle any cod production. Eckman complained to fisheries minister H. F. G. Bridges that this "in our opinion is clearly a case of a union acting in restraint of trade and definitely making a combine to force the fishing companies to pay prices which they may dictate regardless of whether they are fair or in line with market conditions." Enclosing clippings reporting antitrust suits against Massachusetts fishermen, he demanded government action. Bridges replied with an explanation of how Canada's Combines Investigation Act could be put to use, advice that was studied carefully.

Across the line in the United States, where the International Fishermen and Allied Workers of America had built an organization similar to the UFAWU, Eckman could observe the antitrust strategy in action. As early as 1947, some Los Angeles fishermen had been convicted of conspiracy to fix prices because of their participation in collective bargaining. Although the fishermen insisted they were workers, federal attorneys won a ruling that they really were "independent businessmen" engaged in price-rigging. Within five years, the American union's ability to strike and picket had been all but eliminated by antitrust actions undertaken by American trade authorities.

The Los Angeles ruling awakened new hopes among B.C. processors that they could end collective bargaining by a bizarre reversal of reality. They would convict the union of running a monopoly. "Is this unionism or restraint of trade?" they asked in a newspaper advertisement during a UFAWU trawl strike in 1947. The question was repeated in 1952, when UFAWU pickets compelled two Japanese-Canadian fishermen—who claimed to be Native Brotherhood members—to dump fish harvested during a strike. The two strikebreakers retained lawyer T. G. Norris to seek a B.C. Supreme Court injunction declaring that the UFAWU was not a lawfully constituted union and should be dissolved as an "unlawful conspiracy, association and combine" under the Combines Investigation Act. Norris initially was granted an injunction against picketing by Mr. Justice J. V. Clyne, but the action subsequently failed. Undeterred, Norris was back in court in 1955 on behalf of four gillnetters who had fished during a 1954 tie-up in support of striking tendermen. When the tendermen refused to handle the catches of the strikebreakers after the settlement, Norris again sought a declaration that the union and its officers were an "unlawful combine within the meaning of the Combines Investigation Act."

Once more, Norris succeeded in obtaining an injunction against picketing, but the case then went into legal limbo. The UFAWU had just instructed its lawyers to seek dismissal of the action for nonprosecution when investigators from the Combines Investigation Branch burst into the union's offices on 15 May 1956, with orders to view more than 1,200 documents "in the matter of an enquiry into the production, purchase and sale of fish and related products." Union officers immediately told their lawyers to seek orders restraining the investigation, basing their arguments on Section 4 of the Combines Act which stated "nothing in this Act shall be construed as applying to combinations of workmen or employees for their own reasonable protection as such workmen or employees."

Newspaper reports linked the anonymous complainants in the combines action to clients of T. G. Norris, an allegation that could never be confirmed. Elements of the labour movement, as well as the processors, hoped to benefit from the complaint. As the impact of the Cold War penetrated the Canadian labour movement, unions like the UFAWU were under heavy pressure to alter their policies and to dump left-wing leadership, particularly Communists. Leading the attack was the Seafarers' International Union (SIU), which had been given an American Federation of Labor charter in 1949, authorizing it to organize fishermen and seamen "in all waters of North America and Canada." The SIU used this charter and the backing of the Liberal government to destroy the Canadian Seamen's Union. In 1953, the SIU issued its own charter to the B.C. Gillnetters' Association, which was led by elements of the old B.C. Fishermen's Protective Association, and began a raid of the UFAWU. Many of the SIU's backers in the fleet were linked to the antitrust actions organized by Norris, but the raid was stillborn. Despite frantic Red-baiting, the SIU could find only a handful of supporters, and the incumbent union officers easily defeated a challenge at the 1954 convention.

When the Restrictive Trade Practices Commission finally initiated hearings into the combines complaint in 1957, it insisted that all proceedings be held behind closed doors. Union requests to open the hearings to the public were rejected because the other parties to the action, who were never named, opposed an open trial. The reasons became clear after Stevens emerged from four days of closed-door interrogation to reveal that virtually all questions posed to him related to strikes, strike rules and membership trials of strikebreakers.

For two full years, the Combines Branch investigators pored over documents and transcripts. Working in the netherworld of the Combines Investigation Act, they were not required to make public who had made the original complaint, what evidence they had collected or to report by a particular deadline. The growing tensions in the industry were brought to a head by a ghost from a dimly remembered past.

In 1958, the Adams River run returned in strength for the first time since the Hell's Gate blockade. Preseason predictions and dockside rumours placed the potential total run at a staggering 15 million fish, only half of the historic runs of 1913 but ten times the off-year production of the prewar years and double the best runs of the cycle. Only once before, in 1942, had the Adams shown any of its historic abundance with a pack of more than 700,000 cases. To the dismay of veteran fishermen who had conserved for decades to achieve this kind of return, a substantial part of the harvest was taken by part-time fishermen who swarmed into the industry at the eleventh hour. By late October 1958, the Adams run had served notice it was back with a vengeance, filling canners' warehouses with 988,000 cases of sockeye, the largest Fraser pack since 1905. The coastwide pack exceeded 1.8 million.

Although the International Pacific Salmon Fisheries Commission had been working to rebuild the Adams River run for more than a decade, its sudden resurgence caught them and the canners by surprise. As millions of fish built up in the Strait of Georgia, the Fisheries Association, as the canners' organization now was called, announced that it would not buy late-run sockeye. The federal government simultaneously lifted the embargo on the export of raw salmon, leaving fishermen only the nonunion canners of Washington State as a potential market.

Still holding in the Strait of Georgia in late September were 3 million sockeye, of which 1.75 million were needed for spawning. The union fishermen considered themselves the victims of a carefully orchestrated conspiracy. Canadian canners refused to buy and American buyers offered 14 cents a pound (454 grams), just half of the contract minimum price of 28 cents. To protect the agreement, the union demanded and won restoration of the embargo, but the Canadian canners maintained their refusal to buy what they considered "low quality" fish. Millions of sockeye, deemed unnecessary for spawning, escaped to the river.

Now the salmon commission had a novel worry—too many salmon on the spawning grounds! Fearful that the sudden abundance of fish would lead to overcrowding, the commission took a drastic and unprecedented measure at the very mouth of the Adams River. Of the nearly 3 million fish that made it up the Fraser river, only 1.7 million were allowed through to spawn—999,340 were killed at the mouth of the Adams River by an electric fence. The remainder were caught in the sporadic Fraser fisheries of late fall, with the exception of some 51,178 that "leaked" around the fence. The total commercial catch of the Adams run was 10.5 million fish, about 1.25 million short of what could have been taken with better management. Under questioning from fishermen, salmon commission director Loyd Royal denied that more fish could or should have been taken commercially. All those that had died at the fence were "undesirable."

The controversies of 1958 set the stage for a much greater confrontation in 1959. The influx of part-time fishermen, the collusion over late-run fisheries and the final farce of electrocuting spawners at the mouth of the Adams reminded fishermen how vital their organization was. In 1959, shoreworkers, tendermen and fishermen all were going to the bargaining table at the same time. For the first time, the prospect of bargaining a coastwide, industry-wide settlement was within the union's grasp.

The companies, bolstered by the record pack of 1958, were equally determined to break the union's strength once and for all. They refused to retreat on any front. Their militance was strengthened by the passage of provincial legislation, known as Bill 43, which made unions liable for damages resulting from picket action. Industry bargainers demanded concessions from both shoreworkers and tendermen, who were demanding important improvements in wages, overtime and job security clauses. They sought a clause requiring the union to agree that it would not "authorize, call, cause, condone or take part in any strike, picketing, sit-down stand-in, slow-down or curtailment or restriction of production." Their resolve was strengthened by the knowledge that sympathetic officials in Ottawa were ready to co-ordinate government action to support the canners' agenda.

Union fishermen, whose bargaining was linked with the Native Brotherhood, submitted their price demands late in April. They wanted an increase in sockeye prices from 28 cents to 32 cents a pound, a raise for pinks from 9.25 cents to 13 cents and substantial raises for other species. But before talks could begin, combines investigator T. D. MacDonald's report was released in the House of Commons. It alleged that UFAWU members had "knowingly assisted in arrangements having the effect of fixing prices" and that the effect of tie-ups and strikes was to "interfere with free competition." In fact, MacDonald concluded, "the position of fishermen is no different from any primary producer or company such as the members of the Fisheries Association."

The canners moved quickly to exploit MacDonald's ruling. James Sinclair, who had left politics to assume the presidency of the Fisheries Association, advised the union that the processors would not risk violating the law by continuing to bargain. From now on, Sinclair told Stevens, they would "proceed on the basis that member companies will post their fish prices." The herring fishery was already shut down by strike action. In effect, Sinclair was seeking a voluntary return to work by herring fishermen and agreement from the UFAWU that it would return its members to the conditions of the 1930s.

The UFAWU responded with a coastwide strike vote by its members. The results were overwhelmingly in favour of strike action. Fishermen voted 95 per cent for strike to win a collective agreement. The canners had a choice: either accept collective bargaining or risk losing the season. An emergency meeting of the canners reviewed the results of the combines investigation and established the basic outline of the strategy for the coming days. Fisheries Association secretary John MacDonald had already returned from a flying visit to Ottawa where he found the doors of the Department of Justice and the Department of Fisheries open. An all-out confrontation over the combines report could "embarrass the government," MacDonald warned, because if minimum prices were against the public interest then "losing the fishery through union strike [is] more so."

MacDonald's report to the canners revealed that the government's top bureaucrats had their own reasons for encouraging an attack on an organization that had defied their catch allocation, condemned their international failures and directed unremitting criticism at their regulatory shortcomings. At the fisheries department, MacDonald said, deputy minister George Clark believed it was "time to clip Homer Stevens' wings." Fisheries minister J. Angus McLean was more circumspect: "he felt [we] should curb Stevens' actions but should not lose fishery."

The canners and the government were agreed that the combines action should be used to "clear up [the] union position on intimidation," to open the field for strikebreaking and nonunion activity in the fleet. The heavy union strike vote gave them pause for thought. "Do we yield and let Homer resume collective bargaining?" one canner asked. The minutes, reflecting a reluctance to writing anything down, are silent on the decision.

Confronted with the union's strike vote results, Sinclair met with union officers and asked them their intentions. "We will strike until we win an agreement," Stevens replied. "I was hoping you'd say that," Sinclair responded. Within hours, he was on a plane bound for Ottawa. By 6 July, the Liberal former fisheries minister had secured an astonishing announcement from E. Davey Fulton, justice minister in Diefenbaker's cabinet. Fulton rose in the House to announce a two-year moratorium on the application of the Combines Act to fish-price bargaining. Thinking their problems were at an end, the processors tabled new fish price offers close to the union demands.

But fishermen shocked the processors by rejecting this offer by more than 80 per cent. The union established a 25 July strike deadline and began taking strike votes once more, this time in all three sections. The results were less convincing: 68 per cent of fishermen, 70 per cent of tendermen and only 63 per cent of shoreworkers were ready to take job action.

The strike began and continued for almost two long weeks, shutting down all salmon production coastwide for the first time in the history of the industry. The main propaganda war was fought in the north, where Sinclair sought to exploit a very weak shore strike vote and the presence of an independent union, the Deep Sea Fishermen's Union, at the Prince Rupert Co-op, to break the strike. But the pressures of bargaining told heavily on the normally dignified and urbane Sinclair, who was driven to frantic Red-baiting in his effort to break the union's front. Declaring he would rather deal with Nikita Khrushchev than Homer Stevens, he concluded it was "impossible to negotiate with a pair of such dedicated Communists as Homer Stevens and [business agent] Alex Gordon."

Ultimately, it was the company front that crumbled as the Prince Rupert Co-op and tiny Tulloch Western Fisheries sought their own back-door deals. To forestall this development, the Fisheries Association made a new offer which was accepted by coastwide balloting completed on 7 August. The two-year agreement provided further important gains for all three sections, including 32 cents for sockeye in the second year, but the processors easily passed on the raise with two successive price increases to consumers during the fall.

In the fishing industry, the ultimate test of power is a group's ability to control fishing. For almost a century, the processors and the government had that power to themselves. The 1959 strike ended that monopoly.

The UFAWU followed up that breakthrough with a legal blow to the combines action. As the dust settled on the 1959 bargaining, the Restrictive Trade Practices Commission announced that its inquiry into the fishing industry would resume with a new round of public hearings. To the shock of the canners, the commission also announced it would release transcripts of company testimony made at the earlier investigation. The date for the new inquiry was set for July 1960.

The news of a public inquiry sparked dismay among the canners. B.C. Packers' president John Buchanan objected that testimony "would be made public by the union," and Richard Nelson of Nelson Bros. warned that "union members employed by our company [might be] seriously affected by wrong impressions formed by reading excerpts from *The Fisherman*." Canadian Fishing president Donovan Miller was more frank. Public disclosure could reveal "the fact that the plaintiff [Canfisco] has confidential sources within the union membership."

There was ample reason for the canners' discomfort. Even the summary of evidence contained embarrassing revelations about the canners' understanding of free markets. The commission's review of company documents had revealed evidence of direct collusion by canners on prices as recently as 1953, after which it was continued on a secret basis. For example, Canadian Fishing and B.C. Packers had met weekly during the early troll season of 1948 to establish prices for all but a few camps on the west coast. The two companies set firm prices and "these were maintained throughout the balance of the season."

A key figure in these price-setting meetings was B.C. Packers' Ken Fraser, who frequently had chaired meetings to determine Fraser River prices for net-caught salmon. MacDonald's statement of evidence noted that the issuance of circulars establishing prices was supposed to have continued until 1956, but no copies could be found later than 1953. An April circular for that year contained a suggestive handwritten note: "K. F. will phone in future." One further price circular ended with the notation: "NOT FOR CIRCULATION. FOR YOUR INFORMATION ONLY." Perhaps coincidentally, this tightened security designed to obscure the extent of price-rigging came just as T. G. Norris was preparing his first antitrust actions against the UFAWU on behalf of strikebreakers. MacDonald was compelled to conclude that the companies had colluded to fix prices. "Bearing in mind the substantial control of the market exercised by members of the Fisheries Association in the purchase of raw salmon, the effect of such agreements would be to prevent or lessen competition unduly or to the detriment of those parts of the public made up of trollers, seiners and gillnetters respectively."

The commission delayed hearings for two months, over union protests, while company lawyers sought injunctions barring the release of the information. Finally, in September 1960, the canners were successful in obtaining a court order barring the commission from "conducting in public any hearing" or "admitting into the said hearing any person, firm or corporation, or any representative thereof, against whom any allegation or allegations may have been made by the director" and "making public any information obtained by the defendants in the course of such hearing." The B.C. Supreme Court justice who handed down the order had little difficulty understanding the case—he was none other than T. G. Norris, now raised to the bench, whose clients had launched the first such action seven years before. The injunctions were granted the afternoon before hearings were to begin and effectively stopped the investigation in its tracks.

A union news release commented that "this is a fancy way of saying that companies are deathly afraid that their methods of exploiting the public, the shoreworkers and the fishermen will be exposed to the people being exploited."

The crushing defeat of the combines action set the development of the Canadian salmon fishery on a completely different path from that pursued in the United States, where collective bargaining by fishermen was virtually destroyed. It eliminated the processors' dream that they would be able to reduce the cost of raw fish by a return to the dictatorial economics of the prewar era. It also brought the question of licence limitation to the top of the agenda, where the processors opposed its implementation until they learned of a way to turn it to their advantage.

PART THREE

COMMON RESOURCE OR PRIVATE PRESERVE

THE FREE ENTERPRISE SYSTEM DEPENDS ON SOMEONE HAV-
ING CONTROL OVER ALL OF THE FACTORS OF PRODUCTION, IN-
CLUDING NATURAL RESOURCES, AND ENSURING THAT THEY
ARE USED IN THE MOST PROFITABLE WAY. COMMON PROPERTY
RESOURCES HAVE NO PLACE IN THE MARKET SYSTEM OF ECO-
NOMIC ORGANIZATION; INDEED, COMMON PROPERTY IS
REPUGNANT TO THE PRINCIPLES OF A MARKET ECONOMY AND
THOSE THAT INVOKE THE VIRTUES OF FREE ENTERPRISE
SHOULD BE THE LEAST SATISFIED WITH THE FREE-FOR-ALL OF
OPEN FISHERIES.

—PETER PEARSE,

*Final Report of
the Royal Commission
on Fisheries Policy,* 1982

THE RISE AND FALL OF

MAXIMUM SUSTAINED YIELD

THE STALEMATE IN THE STRUGGLE FOR CONTROL OF THE postwar salmon fishery coincided with revolutionary changes in two areas that previously had little impact on the lives of industry workers: fisheries biology and resource economics. The merger of two new currents in these fields in the late 1950s provided fisheries managers for the first time with a theoretical and ideological manifesto.

Before the Second World War, fisheries department officials were primarily political appointees with little training beyond their apprenticeship in the department; their role was to deliver the maximum volume of fish to the canners at minimum cost to the government, political or otherwise. In the postwar era, a new generation of fisheries managers emerged. Some were simply dedicated civil servants very serious about their role as managers on behalf of the public good. Others were formally trained in biology. The emerging prestige of fisheries biology, symbolized by the concrete fishways at Hell's Gate, gave fisheries management new lustre. Where Cunningham and Motherwell had taken direction from the canners, the new generation of fisheries officials tried to take their cue from science and economics. Those who rose to leadership positions believed they had an obligation to fit fisheries into the national government's industrial policy. They began reordering the industry, looking beyond the concerns of the canners to meet the economic needs of a broader corporate community more interested in hydroelectric dams, mining, logging and international trade than in fishing. It was not until the mid-1960s that the canners themselves accepted their new role and adopted the new religion with the enthusiasm of recent converts.

Despite the efforts of John Babcock, fisheries management had been largely bereft of a scientific basis since the foundation of the industry. During the 1930s, the creation of the International Pacific Halibut Commission and then the International Pacific Salmon Fisheries Commission had provided, for the first time, a research base relatively free of direct intervention by the industry. Pioneer efforts by biologists like W. F. Thompson, who studied the Pacific halibut, and C. H. Gilbert, who laid the groundwork for understanding the sockeye, reflected a North American effort to manage wildlife. Regulations proliferated, and fisheries scientists groped toward some understanding of what amount of harvest could be sustained before the stock collapsed.

They were "illuminated in the glow of the Gospel of Efficiency," said Canadian biologist Peter Larkin, who became the dean of Pacific fisheries biology, and their work laid the basis for the theory of maximum sustained yield. As Larkin put it, "the dogma was this: any species each year produces a harvestable surplus and if you take that much, and no more, you can go on getting it forever and ever (Amen). You only need to have as much effort as is necessary to catch this magic amount, so to use more is wasteful of effort; to use less is wasteful of food."

In the real world, however, with stocks and substocks of fish existing in complex ecosystems and fishermen employing ever-improved technology, maximum sustained yield seldom achieved its theoretical promise. To really make it work, Larkin pointed out, "would almost certainly require research and management expenditures that were greater than the value of resources to be harvested. Moreover, it would still assume that species were ecologically separate, feeding neither on the same foods, nor on each other, which is, of course, not so."

The fisheries biologists were adrift, developing and implementing a theory that not only did not accord with reality but violated economic common sense. Time after time, fish stocks refused to respond to the dogma, returning either too weakly or too abundantly. The electrocution of the Adams sockeye, which had clearly not understood the theory, was an extreme case—and resulted in very weak returns four years later. For their own survival, fisheries managers had to find a new theory. They were saved by another group of academics called resource economists.

The resource economists, who first came to prominence in the early 1950s, were part of a new generation keen to bring logic and order to the harvesting of natural resources. Unhindered by any direct knowledge of the industry or the biological dynamics of fisheries resources, they turned their attention to what seemed like an enormous government and corporate effort to reap a relatively modest volume of fish. At the forefront was Canadian economist H. Scott Gordon, whose main contribution was "the final destruction of the pure conservation argument for fisheries management." Quoting one of his contemporaries, Scott Gordon wrote that "the management of fisheries is intended for the benefit of man not fish; therefore the effect of management upon fish stocks cannot be regarded as beneficial per se." He was aghast that fisheries managers ignored factors of fish production that should have been counted as costs: boats, labour, enforcement and other expenditures were left out of the maximum sustained yield equation.

Scott Gordon placed his finger on what he believed was the problem: open entry to the fishery. Because there was no limit on the number of people who could participate in the fishery, their number would steadily increase to the point at which no one was able to make a living. If the labour and capital used to harvest the resource were held to the minimum, a substantial economic surplus could be produced. But because of open entry, money—which might have been available for appropriation by the government in the form of taxes, or by the processors in the form of profits—was dissipated. This was bad for everyone. Fishermen could not make a living. Processors found profits scarce. Society wasted energy and capital in the fishery.

There was one reason why this was so, Scott Gordon charged: the resource was common property, owned by everyone and thus by no one. This was what became known as "the tragedy of the commons." In one famous passage, he argued that "common property natural resources are free goods for the individual and scarce goods for society. Under unregulated private exploitation, they can yield no rent; that can be accomplished only by methods which make them private property or public [government] property, in either case subject to a unifying directing power."

Scott Gordon's analysis contained a fundamental flaw. His assertion that common property implied an absence of property rights was wrong. In British Columbia, all fishers, whether native, Japanese Canadian or white, had asserted a collective right to fish. Native people had asserted an aboriginal right. The canners had long sought an exclusive right to fish based on ownership or control of the means of production or of the fish itself. There was no absence of rights in the B.C. salmon fishery, but there was sharp conflict over how those rights should be understood and respected. By asserting an absence of any rights to the fishery, Scott Gordon and his followers ignored the existence of a public right to share in the benefits of the resource. They denied as well that industry workers had the potential to act rationally and collectively in their own interest. They assumed, as political economist Wallace Clement commented, that "those working in the fishery are totally irrational—an assumption fortunately not yet proven."

From the beginning, resource economists were aware of the human cost of their efficient new world. It was a tricky problem, one they preferred to leave to others. Some conceded that unlimited entry might well be the most efficient arrangement from a social standpoint, even though it was anathema economically. If social considerations were a factor, economists F. T. Christy and Anthony Scott said, then some balance would have to be found between the economic optimum and the social one. Some fishers would have to go so that those who stayed "would be producing the maximum economic revenue [to be shared by them or appropriated by the public] and so that those who are prevented from participating will be able to produce other goods and services valued by the economy." Such reductions, the theorists estimated, might entail elimination of one-third to one-half of the fleet. These individuals would simply have to be compensated or take other jobs.

And what of the fish? James Crutchfield, a Washington State economist who was to play a crucial role in events in British Columbia, placed the matter very clearly. "It is simply impossible to make sense of conservation except in economic terms. Why conserve salmon at all? Unless the end products of the fishery are worth more in money than the cost of producing them, there would be neither a fishery nor a conservation problem." He defined fish stocks as the inventory and capital equipment of the industry. "The problem of conservation is using it up over an appropriate period of time." The existence of several competing canners, he speculated, had frustrated the ability of a single canner to achieve the goal of maximum net economic yield by cutting prices. They had financed fleet expansion "as part of a competitive scramble for a share of the declining supply."

Crutchfield was unmoved by the prospect that licence limitation would lead to greater vertical integration of canners and fishermen. Canner control was "already an accomplished fact," he said. If that integration increased, it would "improve both the accuracy and the efficiency of the regulatory program." This theory was just what the canners were looking for, but it would take time to convince them.

The marriage between the resource economists and the fisheries biologists was made in heaven. It was dictated both by the bankruptcy of the theory of maximum sustained yield and by the imperatives of the Canadian economy and the corporations that controlled it. When this marriage was consummated, both canners and government officials had an answer to proposals advanced by the fishermen, whose well-being depended so directly on the resource. From now on, the success of fisheries management would be measured not in the survival of stocks or the incomes of fishermen but in cold cash.

The merger of maximum sustained yield with maximum economic rents produced optimum sustained yield, which Peter Larkin defined as the "maximum sustained yield of social benefits." Since fishing was still organized around the requirements of processors, their profits were the surest gauge of social benefits. In 1977, when Larkin sanctified the new marriage of theory in a paper he entitled "An Epitaph for the Concept of Maximum Sustained Yield," he was struck by the fact that the new theory failed to state what should be sustained, the stock or the financial yield. The Canadian government's reflection of this debate, published in a national fisheries policy in 1976, long after the argument had been settled in B.C.'s salmon industry, set the nation's goals as "to maximize food production, preserve ecological balance, allocate access optimally, provide for economic viability and growth, optimize distribution and minimize instability in returns, ensure prior recognition of economic and social impact of technological change, minimize dependence on paternalistic industry and government and protect national security and sovereignty." Since not all of these goals could be optimized at a time, fisheries managers looked outside government for direction. The battle to maximize profits was rejoined.

The chaos of the 1958 Adams River run, the shock of the 1959 strike and the collapse of the combines attack finally forced the Liberal government to take action to bring order to the fishing industry. Elimination of the union was no longer an option. In 1959, fisheries minister J. Angus MacLean appointed a University of Manitoba economist named Sol Sinclair to study the problem of licence limitation.

Sinclair's report was a year in the making, and its release in March 1961 was a moment that union fishermen had been awaiting for almost twenty years, but he turned the dream of licence limitation into a nightmare. The only recommendation the union supported was Sinclair's call for a five-year moratorium on new licences. The rest of the report, the 1961 UFAWU convention declared, was "extremely dangerous and in direct contradiction to the interests of fishermen." The theories of the tragedy of the commons and optimum sustained yield had become government policy.

Almost from the first page of his report, which was to form the cornerstone for fisheries licensing policy for more than a generation, Sinclair declared war on the UFAWU's fundamental approach to licence limitation. The union's objective, he noted, was "to create a condition whereby the 'consistent and regular commercial producer' will earn a 'decent livelihood.' " The union proposed to solve this problem by protecting entry for bona fide fishermen and eliminating moonlighters. Sinclair took the opposite tack. The job, he said, was to make the industry less attractive to labour and to drive some fishermen out.

He then turned his guns on fisheries managers. Leaning heavily on Scott Gordon, he argued that conservation was not a sufficient reason to regulate a fishery. In words that would haunt the industry, Sinclair declared "the economic contribution of any productive enterprise to an economy can only be determined after the costs of its production have been deducted from the returns earned. This point has been largely neglected in most discussions or regulatory decisions regarding the halibut and salmon fisheries." Quoting freely from Scott Gordon and Crutchfield, Sinclair concluded that "in a fishery with unrestricted entry, fishing will always be intensified beyond the optimum economic level and most likely to the point where the net yield is wholly dissipated."

The ultimate solution advanced by Sinclair was private ownership, for then "only that amount of fishing effort would be applied that would maximize the net yield from the fishery." Direct sale of rights to the resource to private owners was ruled out for two reasons—the high cost of research and enforcement, and the necessity for international treaties. The task, said Sinclair, was to simulate monopoly control of the resource under conditions of public ownership. Maximum profit was the goal. Limited entry was simply the first step.

In fewer than a hundred pages, Sinclair set a course for the future. All regulations, Sinclair decreed, must assist the industry to "perform according to the standards generally recognized as sound public policy for private enterprise." These standards were harsh: no labour or capital should be used in fisheries which could be used more profitably elsewhere.

This concept spelled doom for habitat protection. Fishermen might desire more fish, Sinclair said, but "if this means wasting labour, capital and management or using these in fishing when they could be used more profitably in other production, such action should be avoided." Nor was Sinclair interested in protecting labour. His goal was to compel it to perform for the least cost. His tool was "a limit on the entry of fishermen to the fleet combined with a system of taxes on the catch and/or the fishermen."

Sinclair's plan was simple. For five years, the government was to freeze the issuance of licences. In the meantime, fishermen and boats with landings in the previous two years would retain their fishing privileges, but pay a $10 annual fee, which he believed would deter moonlighters. Then, when research had determined an ideal number of boats, that number of licences would be issued permanently by competitive auction. They would be transferable among fishermen.

Sinclair made no assessment whatsoever of existing corporate profits, nor did he consider fishermen's ability to compete in his licence auction. "Transfers, sales and rents of fishing licences, as suggested by the report, would likewise give rise to extensive, under-the-table company control," warned the UFAWU, "rampant discrimination, destruction of co-operatives, removal of native fishermen and other forms of corruption leading to peonage among fishermen and further monopoly control in an industry already suffering from monopoly dictation."

The reactions of other groups were equally harsh. The union's opposition was echoed by the Native Brotherhood and the Fishing Vessel Owners Association of B.C. The Prince Rupert Fishermen's Co-op saw Sinclair's proposals as a scheme to "enslave fishermen" which would spell the end of the co-op altogether.

MacLean, a minister in a crisis-ridden government, hesitated on the brink of this new era. The strength of the union's criticism had not been countered by strong support from the processors, who still feared that licence limitation would create a UFAWU closed shop. Nor could many industry businessmen find much enthusiasm for Sinclair's five-year moratorium, which would temporarily strengthen the position of veteran fishermen who overwhelmingly supported the union. Unable to find strong backers from any sector of the industry for Sinclair's prescription, MacLean refused to act. With the reduction of the Tories to a minority in 1962 and the election of a Liberal minority government in 1963, the window of political opportunity passed.

THE ECONOMIC RENT

OF THE RESOURCE

THE CANNERS' EQUIVOCAL AND UNHAPPY RESPONSE TO THE
Sinclair report produced a remarkable reversal in the development of fisheries
policy. For more than eighty years, it had been the processors who wanted
changes and dictated them to government. This time, it was government that
forced its views on the processors. There was no question of implementing the
union's proposal, Ottawa's officials agreed, but some form of licence limitation was essential.

Statistics collected during the preparation of the Sinclair report gave a sense
of the magnitude of the problem. In 1958, the year of the big Adams River
run, the number of licensed fishermen increased to 14,266 from 12,016 the
previous year. Although many of these were undoubtedly seine crewmen and
many others were not salmon fishermen, it was an astounding figure. Of the
26,739 licences issued between 1953 and 1958, only 4,723 fished in each of
the six years, and another 1,798 fished in five of the six years. The rest were
transient, or moonlighters. In 1961, an unremarkable fishing season, the
number of fishermen climbed to 15,660, but only 3,668 had nine years' experience. This was the core group that understood the problem, but they were
already too powerful as far as the canners were concerned.

The Fisheries Association, like the rest of the industry, had given Sinclair's
report a thorough review. By 1 May the association's economics subcommittee
had concluded that the report should be opposed as "not socially desirable"
and "against the interests of association members." Not only had Sinclair
failed to guarantee their future through some control on entry to processing,
he threatened to make fishermen more powerful. The canners also believed
Sinclair's report would either elevate native fishers to "extra special privilege"

or ignore their rights altogether. They questioned the ability of his scheme to raise fishermen's incomes, calculating that to raise incomes 6 per cent, 42 per cent of the fleet would have to be eliminated.

Most importantly, they condemned Sinclair for his failure to distinguish the salmon fishery from the deep-sea stocks on which the "tragedy of the commons" theory had been built. In theory, a majority of the salmon runs could be taken with a handful of traps at the mouths of a dozen rivers. Any increased effort over this minimum could be called "dissipated rents."

"The economic rent of the B.C. resource is proportionately enormous," the economics subcommittee reported, but Sinclair failed to conserve this golden egg for the limited number of processors already in the field. The report failed to recognize that "the entire history of the industry has been bound up by this enormous and perplexing question of distributing the great economic rent of the resource," the canners' analysis concluded. If Sinclair's scheme succeeded in increasing fishermen's incomes, their bargaining strength would grow and their financial ability to strike would increase. Fearful of this risk, the canners preferred the existing system of collective bargaining, stacked as it was in their favour, to any legislative system that could undermine their power.

The canners' formal response, however, was more circumspect and less self-centred. In a letter to fisheries deputy minister George Clark late in May 1961, the association's J. M. Buchanan raised arguments that would be forgotten in the subsequent controversy. The plan would lead to arbitrary elimination of some fishermen, Buchanan said. It was likely that after enormous dislocation, the income gains for the remaining fishermen would again be dissipated and native people probably "would be deprived of the main source of their livelihood." Buchanan underlined the issue of native rights, the first time they had been a factor in industry politics since the 1920s. "Any licence limitation proposal must spell out in detail the fact that the natives have a historic right to the fishery of B.C. and that right must be preserved," he concluded.

Internally, the canners had concluded that the current system of open entry was fine. A special committee established to review the Sinclair report recommended that the government legalize collective bargaining for fish prices by making a permanent amendment to the Combines Act. At the same time, however, the canners were opposed to any extension of formal bargaining rights to fishermen: the right to organize, to bargain and to strike. The canners wanted to ensure that their opponents remained without the basic protection afforded to other workers by labour law. The only purpose of a limitation, the committee concluded, should be to strengthen the hand of existing processors by ensuring the "passage of the buyers' licences to the most stable and continuously operating processors." This was a nostalgic echo of the canners' dreams at the turn of the century.

To achieve this restoration of their power over fishermen, the canners ultimately endorsed a full limitation program for the fleet, adding the concept of a government-funded buyback to reduce the fleet to some magic ideal figure. However, the critical problem of reducing the cost of fish remained. If the Sinclair report was unacceptable, the government asked, then what would work? Canadian Fishing Co. executive R. L. Payne, who spearheaded the Fisheries Association's committee on licence limitation, invited James Crutchfield to Vancouver for a fateful meeting on 26 July 1961 which marked a turning point in the canners' attitudes. Minutes of that meeting, stamped CONFIDENTIAL in heavy black letters, confirm that the price of fish, not conservation of stocks, was the canners' overriding concern. Crutchfield brought them good news. Far from strengthening fishermen, he argued, licence limitation could fatally weaken them. Increased financial independence would not necessarily make fishermen more militant, he said, because they would "have more to lose personally than now by striking." His final argument hit a nerve. In the continuing debates about fish versus power, Crutchfield noted, the fishing industry showed no net economic yield because it cost the full value of the catch to land it. Unless the canners could prove they were contributing to the national economy, there would be no incentive to protect their interests at all.

Ottawa was pressing the same point. In a 1962 discussion document, "On the Management of the B.C. Salmon Fisheries," the fisheries department reported that the value of the catch had risen 20 per cent since 1940 while the capital invested had risen 165 per cent. "The present organization of the B.C. salmon fisheries represents a waste of capital and labour resources," the paper said, "which, as well as natural resources, must be conserved." Civil servants, who before the Second World War had taken the canners' word as law, now were pressing the economic imperative of a larger corporate interest. Unless the salmon industry could show net benefits to the economy, the paper warned, it would be "at a fatal disadvantage in schemes for river-basin development."

The government had little patience for the canners' anxieties about the power of fishermen, given their own tight concentration, and neither did James Crutchfield. "As long as there are four firms that buy 90 per cent of the salmon delivered to B.C., you do not have exactly a free competitive situation," he remarked. "For all practical purposes, the major packers own the fisheries and they are willing to allow these people to fish through their willingness to buy. They are just constrained by law from taking full advantage of the situation. You do not have free and open competition for salmon in B.C."

Ottawa continued to push its plans, and fisheries minister Louis Robichaud announced a licence limitation program in 1965, only to withdraw it within the year "because of unforeseen difficulties." He did, however, begin a program of issuing licences for both men and vessels, leaving the door open for either option later. When fisheries deputy minister Alf Needler personally lobbied a meeting of representatives from all industry organizations that summer, he treated them to a lecture on the tragedy of the commons. "Effective maintenance of the resource at its most valuable long-term level is the main reason for moving toward restriction of entry," he told them, and increased licence fees or royalties "by way of economic rent would strengthen the hands of those who would spend more government money to build the resource."

Needler announced three important decisions, each designed to calm processor fears. First, the unit of control was to be the boat, not the fisherman. This was to ensure, Needler said, that there would be "no exclusive use of a public resource by one section," an oblique reference to the fear of strengthening the union's hand. At the same time, fishermen rather than processors would be required to pay the economic rent because, as Needler's assistant put it, "secondary industry is not in the same sense users of the resource." Finally, Needler and his men were considering the concept of a buyback, a government purchase of excess boats financed with money raised by licence fees or royalties. All the basic elements of what was to become the Davis plan were in place.

As the new Liberal administration found its feet, Needler and R. E. McLaren, a top fisheries economist, stepped up the pressure. They promised vague protection for native fishermen and suggested that fishermen would be expelled from the industry if they failed to show minimum landings. Under their plan, vessels could only be replaced with vessels of the same length or less, a move they thought would reduce capitalization. Union opposition remained solid, but worsening conditions in the industry were compelling processors to reconsider their position.

Salmon runs had not increased as quickly as the processors had hoped. In 1966, virtually the entire $30 million value of the harvest was eaten up by fleet operating costs of $25 to $28 million. Although most of this burden was borne by fishermen, the cost squeeze was making them more determined than ever to maintain high fish prices. In a confidential memo to B.C. Packers' vice-president E. L. Harrison, who provided much of the Fisheries Association's leadership during the 1960s, association manager Ken Campbell proposed a radical departure, urging support not only for licence limitation but also to seek "harvesting privileges for buyers in exchange for royalties of some type." In return for this concession, Campbell recommended another revolution in canner policy, an agreement that fishermen were employees of the canners. This would open the door to grant fishermen the same bargaining rights enjoyed by other workers.

The association was not ready for Campbell's proposal, but was facing the reality that it could no longer resist licence limitation. For the first time, the main pressure for limitation was coming from outside the industry. "We have entered a period in which the salmon resource is threatened by other resource use which is the most serious since the fish-power struggle in the 1950s," declared the report to the association's 1967 annual meeting. The canners noted with alarm the attacks of a young economist named Peter Pearse, who had condemned the economic mismanagement of the industry in lectures the previous winter.

When Needler met the canners late in 1967, he found a changed attitude. Far from resisting limitation, the canners now were demanding it. A new element was a proposal long advocated by the UFAWU for a salmonid enhancement program to increase landings as much as 50 per cent in fifteen years. If the fleet was reduced to 5,000 vessels from 8,000 and prices rose 70 per cent, all of which seemed likely, the value of the catch could triple to $90 million. The entire industry would be transformed, Harrison vowed. "The prize is worth the contest."

The association then laid out its own licence limitation plan. Its seven-point program reflected a merger of processor interest with the direction of the government. With two exceptions, its points became government policy. The processors proposed to licence the fleet in three size categories—under 50 feet (15.2 metres), 50 to 65 feet (15.2 to 19.8 metres) and over 65 feet. Licences would be transferable and vessels would be allowed to use any gear. Licences issued to native fishers could be sold only to other native Indians. A minimum level of corporate ownership would be protected "to ensure that a processing and marketing organization can within limits predict its share of the catch." A buyback would reduce the fleet size. Finally, the number of buyers' licences would be frozen, "leading to a reduction in the number of buyers . . . reducing the committal of assets to industry and will tend to stabilize the price and collection system."

Harrison's new ardour in support of licence limitation reflected still-secret changes in B.C. Packers' corporate structure which were to have a dramatic impact on the industry.

B.C. Packers had emerged from the 1950s in strong shape, tied into the province's corporate power structure by the presence of lumber magnate H. R. MacMillan in the presidency. By the early 1960s, however, as MacMillan eased into retirement, the company's structure once again required trimming. A catastrophic fire at Namu in 1962 seemed providential, but the insurance company insisted that the plant be entirely rebuilt. The modern cannery erected at the site proved a costly burden. The troubled firm soon came to the attention of George Weston Co., a growing Canadian-based baking company with greater ambitions.

Weston initiated a clandestine takeover of B.C. Packers in 1962 as part of a long-range and costly expansion that ultimately made it a dominant force in the Canadian food industry, both in processing and retailing. The takeover was a tightly guarded secret, with Weston's Megargy Investment acquiring shares of B.C. Packers to complete the deal. The move made sense for both sides. For B.C. Packers, Weston offered a source of financing and a captive share of the vital domestic market for canned salmon. From Weston's point of view, B.C. Packers was a source of a wide range of products. The key, however, was canned salmon, an important element of grocery marketing. The famous Clover Leaf label was a precious prize.

Although details of the takeover remain locked in corporate archives, the impact on the company's management style soon became evident. No longer just a big fish in a provincial pond, B.C. Packers now responded to a broader corporate strategy that measured success strictly by return on investment. Dissatisfied with returns in B.C., B.C. Packers looked for opportunity elsewhere. Using J. H. Todd as their vehicle, B.C. Packers and Canadian Fishing collaborated to invest heavily in the booming Chilean reduction fishery and sent fleets through the Panama Canal to exploit Atlantic Canadian herring stocks. By 1966, B.C. Packers could report an average annual return on investment of 10 per cent. That year, the revelation that B.C. Packers was a creature of Weston came in hearings of a House of Commons inquiry into food prices.

In 1967, company president Norman Hyland, who had taken over the helm that year, reported profits had doubled to $1.7 million in the previous twelve months. A year later, though, the company's annual report showed a profit of only $9,816 for 1967, just one per cent of the $929,872 profit reported by the company in 1960. (A UFAWU-sponsored analysis suggested the real 1967 figure might be closer to $363,211, and later company reports "adjusted" the profit figure to $651,041.) Despite a dramatic resurgence of profits to a record $1.6 million in 1968, Weston was no longer content to watch its subsidiary from the sidelines. Now ranked as the world's third-largest merchandising group, Weston took direct control of B.C. Packers.

Hyland was a prominent casualty of the Weston coup. Toronto lawyer G. E. Creber was installed as chairman of the board of B.C. Packers and soon was anointed president of Weston. R. I. Nelson, former president of Nelson Bros. Fisheries, became B.C. Packers' new president to retain a sense of local colour. Nelson's appointment shocked the industry. Nelson Bros. had been admired by many fishermen as an independent firm with local roots, an alternative to B.C. Packers' faceless monopoly. But Nelson now confirmed that his company had been a wholly owned B.C. Packers' subsidiary since 1960.

The winds of change were shaking others canners as well. Growing runs of pink salmon were increasing supplies and driving down retail prices, but the canners' operating costs stubbornly refused to decline. As 1968 turned into 1969, the greatest round of corporate concentration since 1928 swept the coast. In the first three months of 1969, mergers and consolidations, including B.C. Packers' absorption of Nelson Bros., reduced the number of Fisheries Association members from seven to five. The five surviving companies, with B.C. Packers dominant, controlled between 80 and 90 per cent of production. The seven other coast canners had to be content with the dregs.

Almost simultaneously, the election of the Trudeau government in 1968 broke the seven-year log jam on licence limitation. With the processors fully committed to action and a majority government at last, Ottawa could move. Within weeks of his appointment, fisheries minister Jack Davis publicly pledged to make licence limitation a top priority.

THE DAVIS PLAN—"A WORLD FIRST,

A WORLD BEATER"

JACK DAVIS UNLEASHED LICENCE LIMITATION ON THE FISHING industry like a sudden storm, keeping his program secret from all but a chosen few until 8 September 1968. He described his scheme as "measures to increase the earning power of B.C. salmon fishermen and to permit more effective management of the salmon resource by controlling the entry of fishing vessels into the fishery." Initially, there was no pretence that the plan was required for conservation reasons. "The new regulations will curtail the size of the fishing fleet, and on a long-term basis, reduce production costs," Davis said. In a move that did much to undermine opposition to his plan, Davis promised that "boats presently fishing for salmon will not be deprived of fishing rights" and that "any person will still be able to buy and sell these salmon vessels." It was touted as a plan in which no one lost and everybody won.

The quick action, the firm and positive tone of the release, and the assurance that the plan would produce the desired results were all hallmarks of Davis. A Rhodes scholar, chemical engineer and former administrator of Atomic Energy of Canada, Davis was someone who had never tasted failure nor confronted a problem that intellect, logic and energy could not solve. Elected to Parliament for the B.C. riding of Capilano in 1962, Davis had tolerated a long apprenticeship on the back benches, serving as parliamentary secretary to Louis Robichaud. Davis had ample opportunity to learn both the problems of the B.C. industry and the solutions long advocated by resource economists.

Designed as a pre-emptive strike, Davis's announcement outlined a multiphase program that would become effective in January 1969. The first phase promised "A" licences to vessels with salmon landings over 10,000 pounds (4536 kilograms) in 1967 or before 7 September 1968. Those with landings less than 10,000 pounds (later clarified to mean the equivalent of $1,250 in salmon earnings) were handed "B" licences, which would expire ten years later. Licence fees were doubled to $10, "the first step in increasing the value of the salmon fishing privilege," and future increases were promised "as the fishing privilege become more valuable due to the reduction of the fleet."

The announcement came at a time when the UFAWU had been engaged on several fronts in struggles that were testing a new leadership. Homer Stevens remained as secretary-treasurer and Steve Stavenes as president, but business agent Alex Gordon had retired to be replaced by Jack Nichol, a veteran of the union's shore section. Rigby, who had died of cancer in 1965, had lived long enough to see his dreams of unemployment insurance and workers compensation for fishermen become a reality, but his proposals for licensing and conservation would have to be developed by others. Those now at the helm were leading a bitter struggle against the Prince Rupert Fishermen's Co-operative Association. A strike of union trawl fishermen had escalated into a serious confrontation when co-op vessel owners attempted to break the strike by delivering a catch across picket lines. Union shoreworkers refused to unload the fish, the catch ultimately spoiled, and the vessel owners obtained sweeping court injunctions which the UFAWU defied. The struggle led ultimately to one-year jail terms for Steve Stavenes and Homer Stevens, and a thirty-day term for Jack Nichol. Stavenes and Stevens had just been released in September 1968 when Davis's announcement was released.

So it fell to Buck Suzuki, acting president of the UFAWU, to answer Davis's announcement. Perhaps recalling the two-class licence systems he had opposed in the 1930s, Suzuki condemned the proposals as unacceptable "because they diminish the rights of men already in the fishery and increase the power of the big companies that now dominate the industry."

This line of thinking was taken up in the daily press, where columnists agreed that Davis had no answer to the charge he was favouring corporate control. One, Norman Hacking, wrote, "Davis is creating all the conditions for monopoly takeover that Garfield Weston or any of his fellow tycoons could ask for."

Past union president Reg Payne predicted that most native fishers would qualify only for "B" licences because of their poor gear and training. The "A" licence system would "completely defeat your avowed purpose," he warned Davis. "The capital investment in the industry is going to increase instead of decrease, because every time a Class A fishing vessel changes hands it will do so at a vastly inflated value." Payne's forecast was borne out to the letter.

The threat of corporate control of a public resource quickly became the dominant issue in the debate. Davis made the most of the pockets of support he found in the fleet. Although the UFAWU and the Native Brotherhood opposed the plan, some small but politically important groups immediately endorsed it. Joining the processors in support of the scheme were the Pacific Trollers' Association and the Fishing Vessel Owners Association, which represented troll and seine vessel owners respectively. The seine owners, in particular, stood to benefit from the plan.

Throughout the autumn of 1968, Davis campaigned tirelessly for his program, tailoring his rhetoric to the occasion but never wavering from his main goal, which to isolate the UFAWU and destroy its support in the fleet. When he addressed a large fishermen's meeting in Prince Rupert, where Liberal party connections ran deep, especially in the Prince Rupert Fishermen's Co-op, he warned against the UFAWU's policy, which he claimed would "have us eliminate people in the industry rather than vessels from the fleet." The union scheme would eliminate the value of a vessel, he claimed, and deny the right of a father to pass his vessel on to his son. "This commercial salmon fishing vessel licensing scheme is unique in the fisheries of the world," Davis concluded triumphantly. "It is a world first. And you, I know, will make it a world beater. Others, I know, will want to copy our system and they will be coming out here to British Columbia to see just how you pulled yourselves up by your boot straps and made our west coast salmon fishery one of the most efficient and effective commercial operations of all time."

Davis's religious fervour failed to impress very many. Callers to an open line program featuring Davis treated the minister to caustic and derisive criticism when he touted the virtues of the scheme. "Can a gillnetter be replaced with a drum seiner?" one caller asked. "Yes," said Davis, "it can." "Well," said the caller, "isn't this foolish, because with a drum seiner you can have the potential of catching ten times as much as a gillnetter, so you can go ahead and use eight or ten or fifty of your gillnet licences and make drum seiners. You call that conservation?"

Davis's counterattacks quieted the mainstream press, but hints of his eccentric understanding of fisheries shocked and frightened many. In an October address to the B.C. Weekly Newspapers Association, Davis likened the fishing industry to a copper mine, in which the best ore is taken first before the miner turns to progressively larger volumes of lower grade ore until the vein is exhausted. "Mr. Davis then turned to the sea and explained the life there is built on the same type of pyramid," reported Port Hardy's *North Island Gazette*. "At the top is the whale and below it such species as the salmon and the tuna. As the base broaden outs it contains fish successively smaller but in greater number until, at the bottom, is the limitless mass of plankton which supports the whole pyramid. The whale, the minister said, has been virtually wiped out and the tuna and the salmon will be the next to go as man works his way down the pyramid to the plankton.

"Now it may be that Mr. Davis was so wrapped up in his main theme that he didn't realize that he had, with the utmost casualness and in a completely offhanded way, accepted the elimination of an entire industry for which he is the man mainly responsible. Does he not realize that with the application of a little common sense the whale need not have been eliminated? Does he not know that other forms of life, like the halibut and the fur seal and the buffalo, have been brought back from the point of extinction because enough people awakened in time to the knowledge that they must be saved? Does he not appreciate the fact that enough is now known to assure that the salmon will not disappear if the proper things are done? If he does not know these things and if he is, indeed, not greatly concerned about whether the salmon survives, he is not the man for the position he is supposed to fill. If he is going to admit defeat before he even starts, it would be better if he quit now and let someone else do the job."

Within weeks of Davis's announcement, however, the giddy winds generated by new money were stirring in the industry. Boats that had been offered for sale at $1,000 in August and found no takers already were selling for between $3,500 and $4,000. Boatyards began to hum with activity as derelict boats were broken up and their formerly worthless licences used for brand-new vessels of the latest design. As the program gathered momentum, Davis hastily introduced regulatory changes which altered it dramatically. On 21 November, he announced that all fish landings, not just salmon landings, would qualify a vessel for an "A" licence. By this stroke of the pen, he increased the salmon fleet by several thousand vessels. For vessels owned by those not interested in the salmon fishery, he created a "C" licence that would not be subject to limitation but would be barred from the salmon fishery.

As the first phase of the Davis plan took effect, the newly reorganized processors extended their rationalization from head office down to the fleet. Just after New Year's Day 1969, venerable ABC Packing announced it would close all its B.C. canning operations, selling to Canadian Fishing its North Pacific cannery on the Skeena and its Phoenix cannery on the Fraser. B.C. Packers and Canadian Fishing split ABC's 150 rental gillnetters, whose licences suddenly had acquired new value with the Davis plan. Within days, B.C. Packers and Canadian Fishing announced they were dismembering J. H. Todd, which they had been operating as a joint venture for more than ten years. Then came the news of Weston's direct takeover of B.C. Packers and the revelation that Nelson Bros. was a secret B.C. Packers subsidiary.

The two majors used the opportunity to carry through a devastating round of plant closures, effectively ending fish processing on the central coast. B.C. Packers closed Sunnyside on the Skeena and its cannery at Klemtu before the

1969 season, and Canadian Fishing shut down Phoenix on the Fraser, as well as both North Pacific and Inverness on the Skeena. More than 1,000 shoreworkers, overwhelmingly native people, were thrown out of work.

This daunting concentration of power underlined UFAWU charges that the industry was being transferred into the hands of a small and powerful group. Throughout 1969, the processors had to fight to save their company fleets from elimination, a tribute to the effectiveness of the UFAWU's campaign against the Davis plan. With the assistance of NDP MPs, the union forced the Davis plan before the House of Commons Standing Committee on Fisheries, which undertook community hearings around the province. The committee hearings were the only public review of the Davis plan.

E. L. Harrison of B.C. Packers and Ken Campbell of the Fisheries Association were leading the corporate campaign in Davis's defence, but the union's charge that the Davis plan simply confirmed corporate control was gaining support. The incessant drumfire of opposition to the plan, which went far beyond union ranks, rattled the government's policy makers, but not Davis. In a comment that fishermen never forgot, he boasted that "if it happened at some point of time that two thirds of the fishermen didn't think it was the best scheme in the world, I would still be concerned about putting it in because I think it is the best, and in the end, will turn out to be the very best."

The union was pounding away at the issue of corporate control and finding receptive audiences. Its attack on conditional sales agreements, which covered more than 800 vessels in 1969, had a devastating impact. In these agreements, a company advanced money to a fisher to buy boats or gear. In return for the loan, he or she agreed to sell fish only to the lender. A commonplace clause in the agreements read that "should the company feel unsafe with respect to the said goods or the unpaid purchase money (of which the company shall be the sole judge)," it could compel the fisher to redeem the loan within twenty days or lose everything. The Fisheries Association did not count boats under such agreements as company-owned, but life told a different story. In 1969, processors directly owned 761 vessels; fully 600 of these vessels were owned by B.C. Packers and Canadian Fishing. But through conditional sales agreements, mortgages and other means, the companies had control of the production of another 1,400 vessels in a fleet of 7,500 boats of all types. In other words, the processors controlled about one-third of the fleet. When Davis found it impossible to defend the conditional sales agreements, the companies grudgingly agreed to his request to delete clauses giving them the right to seize boats on twenty days' notice.

This conflict spilled over into Phase 2 of the Davis plan, which included a number of features for which the canners were unprepared. A year after his first announcement, Davis revealed that an "A" licence owner would require a

$5,000 average annual production to retain a permit, or $20,000 over a four-year period. Licence fees were raised to $25, and owners of vessels not reporting landings for two consecutive years were told their privileges would be scrapped. Finally, Davis proposed to levy a royalty of one per cent of the landed value of the catch. This money was to be used to subsidize a harvest of dogfish, which were deemed a threat to salmon conservation. Davis also proposed to raise the royalty one per cent a year until it amounted to five per cent of the landed value.

The absurdly high quota requirement to keep an "A" licence was a deliberate strategy, the minister told the canners privately, to force half of the fleet into the "B" licence category. The results of the first year of the plan had been mixed, at best. The salmon fleet had been reduced by 571 boats to a total of 6,977 by September 1969. Most of those eliminated had not been actively fishing. The value of the fleet, however, had risen almost 10 per cent to $95.5 million.

In a cutting commentary on the first year of the plan, UFAWU business agent Jack Nichol acidly noted how difficult it would be for a one per cent royalty to reduce the capital value of a fleet increasing by 10 per cent annually in value. "The new fees are expected to generate $1 million next year to put the [buyback] fund at $1.5 million," Nichol wrote. "This two-year total represents greater financial input or investment by fishermen to be used to reduce capital investment by fishermen. Only an economist of Davis's stature can explain—or can he?—this contradiction."

Davis hoped that by forcing thousands of boats into the "B" category, where their licences would expire, he could concentrate the buyback on a core fleet of only 2,500 vessels which accounted for 80 per cent of the landings. To protect the canners' investment, the department decided that the production of two or more "B" vessels could be combined to produce an "A" licence, a direct gift to companies owning scores of dilapidated rental boats. This "pyramiding" of licences, often combining three small gillnetters into a single seiner with ten times the fishing power, was actually increasing the fleet's catching capacity. It was fine with Davis.

As a pure free enterpriser, however, Davis was finally feeling discomfort at the charges he was aiding monopoly. In a confidential memorandum to the processors on 5 November, he dropped a bombshell which enraged them. "I will be proposing that no individual, corporation or agency be permitted to licence more than ten commercial salmon fishing vessels on the west coast in 1980," Davis wrote. He would require the companies to sell 10 per cent of their fleet annually in an effort to ensure that no one group reaped a windfall from licence limitation. It took only a few weeks for the processors to force Davis to back down. A face-saving formula dictated by the minister in front of a delegation of indignant canners reduced the firm targets to a simple "expectation... that outright company ownership would decline in proportion to the total." From then on, Davis and the processors saw eye to eye.

In the months that followed, the political battle over the Davis plan ebbed and flowed. Under union pressure, Davis dropped his royalty plans and repeatedly modified the licensing rules. In the end, however, he never deviated from his basic goal. Although the number of vessels declined, the companies used their right to combine the licences of various boats to roll the total tonnage into a single new boat, usually a seine vessel of vastly increased efficiency. Davis further increased licence fees, then proposed to eliminate vessels that failed to meet minimum quality control standards. Ignoring huge fishermen's meetings, which by now included speakers from the UFAWU, the Pacific Trollers' Association and the Native Brotherhood, he served notice of still more changes—elimination of fishermen's unemployment insurance, creation of a "catch insurance" scheme funded entirely by fishermen and a mysterious Phase 4. In this last and most revolutionary phase, Davis proposed to reshape the fleet, alter the fishing season and resolve many other matters.

On 3 October 1971, the fisheries department sponsored an unusual auction along the dyke which supported West River Road in Ladner. More than 3,000 people scrambled along the shoreline and jammed the area around the auctioneers' tent to bid on fifty-two commercial salmon vessels brought there from around the south coast. The buyback list reflected places, people and companies that made up the fabric and the history of the industry: the crab fisher-gillnetter *Fascination,* the seiners *Pachena* and *William C. Todd,* the gillnetter *Nelbro 18* and many more. They had been purchased from their owners for a total of $714,000, money raised by the government from the licence fees paid by commercial fishermen. They were sold in just three hours for only 40 per cent of their appraised value to buyers who pledged never to use them in the B.C. commercial fishery. At least eight of them were sold to Washington State fishermen who would use them to harvest Fraser-bound salmon stocks. In short, Davis was taxing Canadian fishermen to buy out fishing vessels, then selling the vessels at a loss to competitors of the Canadian fleet.

Nichol's prediction that the buyback would never catch up with the capitalization unleashed by Davis proved accurate. When the buyback auctions ground to a halt in 1974, the program had succeeded in removing 361 boats from the fleet. Vessel purchase costs had exceeded revenues by $130,082. The boats removed had an assessed value of $5.9 million, but the new investment in the salmon fishery already was many times that value. Davis's world first, world beating licence limitation scheme was up and stumbling.

The economic consequences of the Phases 1 and 2 of the Davis plan and the corporate rationalization that followed fell with particular ferocity on coastal native groups. The UFAWU repeatedly called for protection of native employment, and its licensing proposals to protect bona fide fishermen would have averted the disaster that followed. Within days of the plan's announcement, Nisga'a leader Frank Calder spoke against it, warning it would result in "gradual elimination of Native Indian participation in the fishing industry" and would deny aboriginal rights. By placing the emphasis on the fishing record of a particular boat, Calder warned, Davis would eliminate hundreds of native fishermen who were marginal to the canners but vital breadwinners for their communities.

Given the processors' absolute control both of the northern canning industry and of the rental gillnet fleets, the fate of native fishermen and shoreworkers rested in the hands of B.C. Packers and Canadian Fishing. The cannery closures of 1969, which centralized production in Prince Rupert and Vancouver, eliminated shore employment for about 1,000 workers, more than 650 of them native men and women. The Indian Affairs department restricted itself to issuing a warning to native fishermen not to sell their vessels too readily. It set about creating an Indian Fishermen's Assistance Program to help some native fishers stay afloat.

A confidential Fisheries Association analysis conducted in 1972 concluded that wages earned by native workers in the industry had dropped a staggering 20 per cent between 1968 and 1971. The number of northern canneries dropped from seven to three, cutting the number of shore jobs for native men by 37 per cent, or 281 positions. The number of women losing their jobs was even worse, some 450, or 45 per cent of the native workforce. Another 122 native fishermen, or 14 per cent of that section, were thrown out of work.

The canners engaged in a second round of cuts in the fleet in 1971, when both Canadian Fishing and B.C. Packers announced they would withdraw large numbers of their vessels from production because of expected poor runs in the coming season. Homer Stevens estimated 300 native Indians and 100 whites would be out of work.

To these losses, the native community had to add the scores of licences lost for other fisheries, such as halibut, as a result of licence limitation. An investigation in 1978 concluded that the number of native gillnetters had declined 29 per cent in the first two years of the Davis plan. Between 1964 and 1971, gillnetters declined from 400 to 345, trollers from 388 to 197, and seiners from 135 to 57. Nonsalmon vessels had dropped to one per cent of the fleet in 1971 from 12 per cent in 1963. This final and crushing repudiation of the policy proposed by A. C. Anderson some ninety years before, which had sought to ensure native participation in the commercial fishery, would have grave consequences for the industry.

Davis warned the canners in December 1971 that he intended to press ahead soon with Phase 4. A key goal was to "maximize mobility and competition for salmon" and to improve quality by reducing the river catch of salmon to a minimum. The objective was to deliver the best quality fish to the docks at the lowest possible price. So far, every one of Davis's 1970 initiatives had increased the cost of fishing, which was of no consequence to the government or the canners because harvesting costs now had been placed entirely on the backs of fishermen. One-day openings meant fishermen would bear the cost of rushing from one fishery to another or else face days of idleness waiting for a chance to fish. Moving the harvest out to sea could improve quality, but would add to transportation costs.

The renewed economic crisis that hit the industry in 1971 effectively ended Davis's public licensing initiatives. Throughout 1971, he considered the composition of a special committee he proposed to assign the task of shaping the future of the industry. Grandly named the West Coast Fleet Development Committee, it met for the first time in May 1972. It was told to meet in camera and to produce a report within a year.

The committee marked a fundamental shift in Davis's political strategy. Battered by public confrontation, he shifted the debate behind closed doors and made a show of putting the decisions into the hands of the industry. The make-up of the group, however, minimized the union's grassroots influence and gave a strong role to organizations which supported the government's initiatives. As a result, the Prince Rupert Co-op, and the Pacific Trollers' Association, which each represented fewer than 600 fishermen, had one representative apiece. The UFAWU's 3,000 fishermen were given two representatives, but its 3,000 shoreworkers and tendermen were left out of the equation altogether. Chairperson was Rod Hourston, federal fisheries director for the Pacific region. Robert McMynn represented the province of B.C. Also sending single representatives were the Native Brotherhood, the Fishing Vessel Owners Association and the Fisheries Association.

The tenth member of the committee was new to the fishing industry, appointed by Davis to represent the general public. An active Liberal party member, resource economist and University of British Columbia professor, he was Peter Pearse. Young, articulate and ambitious, Pearse quickly assumed control of the committee, which had been given the sweeping task of advising on "the development of the salmon resource, including construction of salmon hatcheries and spawning channels [and] the size and composition of the salmon fishing fleet required to harvest the resource."

Early in 1973, the committee established a subcommittee on fleet rationalization, chaired by Pearse himself. He immediately produced a draft report which urged the department to shift to gear types "of best potential productivity." To this end, he advocated measures to encourage the seine fleet, curb the troll fleet and reduce the gillnet fleet. The report was warmly endorsed by Ken Campbell, the Fisheries Association representative on the committee. Scotty Neish, one of the UFAWU's representatives, was outraged. He charged Pearse with ignoring minority views. The union's anger grew when Walter Ironside, its other representative, reported on the workings of another subcommittee dealing with vessel subsidies. This group had quickly left the issue of subsidies to tackle fishermen's unemployment insurance, which Pearse believed should be changed to "catch insurance... handled by the fishermen themselves." A fishing patterns subcommittee quickly disposed of the union's proposal for allocation based on protection of fishermen's earnings as "too inflexible and inefficient." They urged instead a move to area licensing, which would compel fishermen to opt for a particular fishing area and stay in it.

With the deadline for a report—and a federal election—bearing down on the committee, Pearse revealed that he also had been considering the issue of licence fees. He preferred a system of "royalties on the catch" which would be "more equitable and lead to greater efficiency." Neish and Ironside decided to submit a minority report outlining their objections to the "majority" view. But in a final burst of activity, the West Coast Fleet Development Committee's report was rushed to press. The UFAWU representatives were left to publicize their minority report as best they could.

The majority report, largely drafted by Pearse, was to provide the framework for future industry development. An endorsement of the Davis plan, it urged continued fleet reduction, continued buyback programs, and catch royalties or a landing tax. Pearse also urged elimination of fishermen's unemployment insurance and more research. The only positive recommendation, from the union's point of view, was a call for acceleration of the Salmonid Enhancement Program.

In their minority report, Neish and Ironside tallied the consequences of the Davis plan. It had resulted, they charged, "in the displacement of huge numbers of fishermen, increased capitalization of the primary catching sector with reduced proportional returns, economic redistribution of wealth produced from the fishing industry in favour of the large processing companies and to the detriment of fishermen; and [the] placing of the financial burden for rationalization and administration of the fishing industry onto the backs of fishermen." The brief concluded with a call for "public ownership and management of fisheries resources."

The argument was largely ignored. The Trudeau government had been reduced to a minority in 1972 and its attention was elsewhere. More importantly, it seemed that the Davis plan might be working—the industry was embarking on the biggest boom in its history.

THE BATTLES OF THE

SPAWNING GROUNDS

THE DAVIS PLAN REPRESENTED THE TRIUMPH OF THOSE WHO believed the salmon fishery was simply a question of producing money from fish. The vital first step—producing fish—failed to excite much interest. Enormous efforts were mobilized to stop wealth from leaking out of the industry in "dissipated rents." Almost no resources could be found to ensure that wealth continued to flow into the fishery in the form of healthy stocks.

Almost from the day the Second World War had ended, British Columbia had been seized by an explosion of intensive economic development, as new investment produced sharp increases in production. The lumber industry was convulsed by mergers. The combination of H. R. MacMillan Export and Bloedel and Stewart in 1951 made MacMillan Bloedel the largest forest company in Canada. Exports that previously had flowed to the United Kingdom now moved mostly to the United States. Pulp and paper production almost doubled in the five years after the war, and growing revenues allowed the Social Credit government elected in 1952 to consolidate its popularity with a host of roads, bridges and railroads. Before this onslaught, the salmon could only retreat. Organized fishermen and shoreworkers soon realized that if they hoped to protect fish habitat, they would have to rely on their own resources.

These massive changes in the provincial economy, along with the new integration of B.C.'s corporate sector with its American counterpart, pushed fisheries far down the list of government priorities. This fact had come sharply home to fishermen in 1949, when the provincial government invited the Aluminum Co. of Canada (Alcan) to establish a smelter in B.C. The site selected was Kitimat, near a native community situated at the mouth of the Kitimat

River, an important salmon river on an inlet south of Prince Rupert. The agreement ultimately signed with Alcan horrified the Social Credit party, which was then in opposition. Party president Major A. H. Jukes termed the deal "nothing more or less than communism," but others saw it as the largest resource giveaway ever in the history of a province with some impressive precedents. Once committed to the smelter, Alcan prospected far afield for hydroelectric power, assessing watersheds as far south as the Chilko for a suitable system to drown.

The agreement left no room for doubt that the project would be profitable. Not only did Alcan obtain all necessary crown land for a laughable $1.60 an acre (65 cents a hectare), it received a waiver of all timber royalties and stumpage for resources it planned to flood. In fact, the trees did not even have to be cut. Alcan also obtained all mineral rights and, as a final act of environmental vandalism, was granted permission to build the project without any protection of fisheries resources. Outcry from the fishing industry, bolstered by the International Pacific Salmon Fisheries Commission, drove Alcan off the Chilko, a move the company claimed was a major concession to fisheries interests. The agreement, however, did give Alcan complete control of the flows of the Nanika and the Nechako, rights it retains to this day.

The project was pushed through in short order, and Alcan left no doubt that it took its new rights seriously. In effect, it owned the water resources of the Nanika, which was tributary to the Skeena, and the Nechako, which flowed into the Fraser at Prince George. These rivers, blocked near their main sources, would be backed up against the Coast Range in four large storage lakes. Their flow would be drained through a tunnel to turbines on the other side of the mountains at Kemano and transferred by high-voltage line from there to Kitimat. When the Kenney Dam was completed on the Nechako, it had none of the fish mitigation measures recommended by the fisheries department. Not only did Alcan refuse to implement the improvements, the department declined to prosecute the company for the violations. James Sinclair, then minister of fisheries, became a director of the Alcan board upon his retirement from politics in 1957.

The flooding of the reservoir was also accompanied by uncommon brutality to the native people of Cheslatta, who were rousted out of their homes just days ahead of the flood waters, driven from their land "like coyotes" and offered a pittance in compensation.

Between October 1952 and June 1955, no water was released to the Nechako and only trickles were allowed over the dam between July 1955 and January 1957. The Nechako's famous chinook runs staggered and then collapsed, tumbling from several thousand spawners to just fifty for several years.

Only cool weather prevented elimination of the run in the face of Alcan's refusal to release any cold water to the warm pools remaining on the ravaged Nechako.

The privatization of two river systems at the expense of all their other resource values sounded a warning that was not lost on organized fishermen. The Alcan scheme was just one of the megaprojects encouraged by the provincial government. Fishermen soon found themselves at odds with the entire economic strategy of big business. Engineers of B.C. Electric, later expropriated by the Social Credit government to create B.C. Hydro, had even grander dreams than Alcan. At the fifth National Resources Conference held in Victoria, they described plans to stand the Fraser system on its head, "diverting portions of the Peace, Parsnip and Finlay Rivers into the Fraser at Prince George." Storage dams would hold still more water at Babine Lake, Stuart Lake and Chilko Lake.

The cornerstone of the entire project was the colossal Moran Dam, which would rise 220 metres from the bottom of the Fraser Canyon near Lillooet. The storage area for this project would stretch 320 kilometres north to Quesnel and flood other Fraser tributaries to depths of several hundred metres, taking communities, railways and highways with it. This $500-million project to rival the Columbia dams would eliminate spawning areas for 44 per cent of the Fraser sockeye above the dam, but would undoubtedly also devastate the runs below the dam with drastic temperature and flow changes, as well as new parasites and diseases from remote river systems.

The battle against the Moran dam was to last almost a generation, but the struggle with Alcan was shorter, tougher and nearly lost altogether. Union opposition to the Alcan scheme began in earnest in 1949 with intensive participation in provincial government hearings on Alcan's application for water rights on the Chilko, Nechako and Nanika. The tremendous fish losses suffered on the Columbia already were well known in the Pacific Northwest, and the fish versus dams controversy that raged throughout Washington and Oregon states during the 1950s had its counterpart in Canada. In Canada, however, the battle was harder fought and ultimately more successful.

Other voices were raised against the dams, of course, including that of Roderick Haig-Brown, the Campbell River conservationist and sport fisher. The venerable Henry Doyle saw in the Alcan project both elimination of his beloved salmon runs and the ultimate condemnation of the canners who had driven him from his rightful place in the industry a half-century before. Appalled at the canners' weak-kneed response to the threat of the dams, Doyle issued one last barrage of letters, briefs and analyses from his retirement home in California.

The UFAWU's General Executive Board made habitat protection a key part of a crowded agenda. As corporate pressure to build the Moran dam continued, union organizer Tom Parkin turned his energies to the battle almost full-time. Parkin had joined the UFAWU staff in 1945 at Rigby's urging. An eloquent and popular speaker, he hit the road with a film projector and a wall-sized electrified map of the Fraser watershed. As he described the salmon runs of various tributaries and the locations of the Moran's facilities, he could light up the relevant portion of the map. In scores of community gatherings, labour council meetings and service club luncheons around the province, Parkin preached against Moran. Native groups, unions and conservation groups endorsed the UFAWU position, which in this case had been buttressed by federal and provincial research indicating that fisheries mitigation could cost more than the dam and probably would not work. When the scheme finally crumbled, editorial writers singled out Parkin's campaign as a major reason.

Government agencies charged with stewardship of the resource, however, were an even tougher challenge. When Parkin protested plans in 1960 to spray DDT over Moresby Island in the Queen Charlottes to control spruce budworm, federal officials would agree to eliminate only a controversial emulsifier from the spray. A similar operation in 1957 had reduced the spawning population on the Keogh River to 50 from 20,000. At a panel discussion to discuss the issue, fisheries scientists agreed that "perhaps less is known about pollution than any other major problem affecting the country's fisheries resources." They noted also that funding for such research was declining.

Ottawa was ill equipped, therefore, to demand compensation for the wholesale losses which were occurring in plain view. It neither knew what its existing fisheries resources were nor could it demonstrate that development was causing losses. A prolonged controversy and study were required to squeeze minimum compensation from the B.C. Power Commission for heavy losses on the Puntledge River on Vancouver Island, where spring salmon escapement of between 1,500 and 1,000 in the war years had dwindled to 400 in 1958 despite the construction of fishways.

Lacking any fundamental knowledge of the resource and politically constrained from acting, the department was left with only one option to maintain escapements—fisheries closures. In 1961, the department imposed for the first time a uniform coastwide closure for forty-eight hours a week and closed all salmon fishing from 1 December to 31 January. Quatsino chum runs were weak, so that area was closed for four years. The Queen Charlotte Islands chum fishery was closed for a similar period and, for the first time, trolling for salmon was banned in the Strait of Georgia during Christmas week to avoid undue catches of "tinies."

Fishermen continued to defy the theories of economists about their disinterest in conservation by demanding comprehensive environmental protection for fisheries resources. A UFAWU brief to Victoria in 1961 blamed high-seas fishing and pollution for the decline in runs. Union representatives demanded $5 to $10 million a year for salmon enhancement, including fishways, stream clearing, reforestation and sewage treatment. The fisheries department, union leaders said, appeared "to have only one major solution, which is to impose ever greater restrictions on the commercial fishing fleet in terms of shorter weeks and shorter seasons, combined with four-year closures in certain areas."

The union's call for increased fish production was not new. The issue had first received major emphasis on the union's submission to the Royal Commission of Canada's Economic Prospects in 1955. By 1967, the fisheries service itself had calculated that the runs could be doubled in a seven- to ten-year program worth $265 million.

Although unable to find funds for habitat protection, the department was able to scratch together some cash to answer the siren song of artificial fish production. The sockeye hatcheries which had convinced the canners of the 1890s that the runs could never be overfished had been closed in the late 1930s after it was conclusively proved they were producing no additional fish. Almost thirty years later, research began once more into methods to boost production with existing habitat. Experiments with artificial spawning channels, which doubled or tripled river habitat by twisting new channels of spawning gravel into existing flood plains, proved successful on the Big Qualicum River on the east coast of Vancouver Island. In 1960, the department opened a second channel at Robertson Creek, where chinook and pink salmon spawned after running up Barkley Sound on Vancouver Island's west coast. The International Pacific Salmon Fisheries Commission had spent much of its first twenty-five years rebuilding Fraser runs with the assistance of the Hell's Gate fishways. The commission also played a vital role, because of its relative independence from Canadian political pressures, in providing a scientific basis for opposition to the Alcan project, the Moran Dam and many other major projects. As late as 1974, however, Peter Larkin could state flatly that "there has been no large-scale systematic effort to artificially increase salmon production."

Despite the encouraging successes with spawning channels, hatcheries and fishways, rehabilitation failed to find favour with senior fisheries managers. "One of the best tools for rehabilitation is management of the salmon run itself," Hourston told *The Fisherman* in the spring of 1962, "i.e. putting an adequate number of spawners on the spawning grounds." As for pollution, "we have a biologist employed full-time on this problem [and] we feel that we have pollution problems related to new industries fairly well under control." This astonishing claim was followed just weeks later by a major report from the salmon commission, which proved the devastating impact of untreated pulp waste on salmon.

Hourston was unable to provide satisfaction in any area. When union fishermen questioned logging practices on the Indian River, just north of Vancouver, Hourston conceded he had no way to control the firm involved. For every victory like the defeat of Moran, there were a hundred crippling losses: Gates Creek sockeye lost to hydro turbines in 1962, mysterious losses of natural spawners on the Chilko in the same year, and, tragically, a mere one million Adams sockeye struggling back from the survivors of the electric fence episode of 1958. Appeals for a tough pollution code met government silence.

This public concern was far ahead of government thinking. When union fishermen protested logging and gravel removal from spawning streams on the Queen Charlottes in 1963, the federal fisheries minister stated flatly that "no salmon streams in the Queen Charlotte Islands have been destroyed by logging or gravel removal," although "certain sections may be in need of improvement." J. Angus Maclean could provide no estimate of chum salmon declines because spawning estimates could be in error by as much as 30 per cent. Nor could the department suggest any action against MacMillan Bloedel for releasing toxic waste from its Port Alberni mill. Hourston rejected proposals to enforce waterflow agreements on the Coquitlam, Alouette and Stave rivers, to restore salmon runs depleted by dams in the 1950s and earlier, as offering little potential. He rejected concern about raw sewage, including tampons and condoms, polluting the Kitimat River, nor did he see any reason to change Alcan's discharge of effluent containing calcium, sodium, fluoride, aluminum, iron and sulphate into the same river.

In an effort to deflect some of the criticism, department officials revealed in 1963 they had exacted the supreme penalty from one group posing a threat to the salmon: sea lion herds had been cut in half to 4,300 adults and 1,500 pups between 1956 and 1961 as a result of bounty hunting.

Some industry leaders, stung by the public condemnation, decided the best defence was a good offence. This reached absurd proportions when Senator Tom Reid, chairman of the salmon commission, blamed the bitter disappointment of the low 1963 returns and the forecast of poor 1964 runs on union strikes in 1959 and 1963. These actions had created "havoc," Reid raged, "mainly through upsetting natural factors controlling year class production." In a scathing rebuttal, Homer Stevens traced the troubled history of the 1964 run, which had encountered blistering heat in the summer of 1960, heat which might have been shrugged off had it not been for the continuing losses of water to Alcan and other river users. "It seems a pity the commission is unable to blame the heat wave on the strike," Stevens said, "as that would help cinch its case." (Two years later, salmon commission officials agreed the run had been hit by a "climatic debacle.")

Despite growing public concern, developers continued to advance ·plans that involved the complete destruction of salmon runs. Yet improvement or expansion of the runs was not part of the government's vocabulary. "Maybe I misinterpret conservation," said Hourston, "but in my opinion it is the wise use of the resource." More and more, wise use of the resource seemed to imply its sacrifice to the economic requirements of other industries.

As James Crutchfield told a 1965 conference on pollution, there was no cost to the polluter in the destruction of runs. Forest companies "get away with murder through political blackmail," he said, "and their attitude seems to be 'Why in the hell should we stop polluting if we don't have to?' " The Parsons plan of 1965, which would have diverted Canada's Fraser River south to the American Midwest, compelled salmon commission director Loyd Royal to warn that "you can't have salmon with high dams or with uncontrolled pollution." The Parsons plan would "destroy a vast salmon-producing empire without any conceivable compensating benefits," he said. Until then, he continued, fisheries resources had "been saved in the face of almost unequalled economic development. The public says this is what they want. This is what they will get if all the people representing a stable society can continue to sit down at the water resource planning table. The day the immediate glitter of dollars upsets such a plan, the fisheries as we have them will be gone."

Had the runs been saved? In every area of the coast, they suffered one insult after another. The dumping of toxic mine tailings by Utah Mines in Quatsino Sound poisoned kilometres of the inlet. Pulp mills rose on the Fraser. A full twenty years later, public protest would force fisheries studies which proved that the mills routinely dumped effluent exceeding both in volume and degree of contamination the amounts set out in their permits. Estuary land in the Fraser delta was dyked and filled. In 1970, the provincial government again considered construction of the Moran Dam, but unanimous public outcry once more buried this hydroelectric Frankenstein. Such periodic victories were far outweighed by the steady erosion of fish stocks and fish habitat which threatened the ultimate collapse of the salmon runs.

WHAT PRICE THE DAVIS PLAN

AFTER A FALTERING START, THE 1970S PROVED TO BE ONE of the best decades the fishing industry had ever experienced. Although Jack Davis's initiatives and his own federal political career were ended by his defeat in the election of 1974, dramatic changes in world markets combined to provide B.C. processors and fishermen with their seven best consecutive years from 1973 to 1980. The record earnings and profits of that era could have been used for the permanent improvement of the resource, coastal communities and the industry, but due to the market mechanisms installed by Davis, they were wasted in speculative investment, a grossly overcapitalized fleet and new processing facilities which the resource could not support.

The most startling change was in the value of the salmon itself. Growing demand for the product, particularly in Japan, began pushing up world prices in the early 1970s, a tendency accelerated by the extension of 200-mile (370-kilometre) limits around the North Pacific, which dramatically reduced Japan's high-seas harvest. Despite increases in salmon production from Alaska and the Soviet Union, demand outstripped supply. For the first time in history, fishermen began receiving price increases, sometimes in excess of union-negotiated floor prices, year after year. Davis's assault on the number of fishing vessels had served part of its purpose. A total fleet of 6,104 salmon fishing vessels in 1969 had declined to only 4,707 in 1980. Most of the decline had come in the gillnet and troll fleets, with gillnetters bearing the brunt of the reduction as licences were pyramided into seine vessels. The seine fleet had increased, as Davis had hoped, to 316 salmon vessels from 286. But hidden in the figures was a major increase in the number of combination boats equipped to fish by more than one gear. When combination herring and salmon seine vessels were included, the number of seiners had risen to more than 550, at least double the pre-1968 figure.

Rising prices in the salmon industry had helped to pay for this change. Landings fluctuated during the decade from a low of just under 100,000 tonnes to more than 175,000 tonnes in the bonanza year of 1973. Even in the bleak year of 1980, landings were almost 100,000 tonnes. But landed value, the amount paid to fishermen for their catches, had skyrocketed from $30 million in 1969 to $130 million in 1980. The two banner years of 1978 and 1979 saw landed values exceed $180 million, a six-fold increase over a decade before.

That was not all. The herring fishery, which had closed entirely in the late 1960s after stocks collapsed, was re-established as a roe fishery. The eggs extracted from the spawning herring were exported to a hungry luxury market in Japan. The value of herring landings climbed from nothing in 1972 to $125 million in 1979, before collapsing to $25 million as a new crisis—and a season-long strike—hit in 1980. Processors who had paid out only about $27 million for fish of all types in 1969 were buying almost $250 million worth by 1980.

This gusher of money, combined with the reduced fleet, should have made fishermen very wealthy. Thanks to the Davis plan, however, the industry was built on sand. Declining prices, rising costs, crushing interest rates and a downturn in catches reduced most fishermen to paupers in twelve short months at the end of the decade. In 1980, Peter Pearse estimated that salmon gillnetters had average gross earnings of only $12,750. Trollers earned a more respectable $21,000, and salmon seiners $24,980. Earnings were somewhat higher for combination salmon vessels, but the average earnings for all vessel owners from all fisheries was only $31,000 gross, not much to cover all expenses and then to support a home and family. Davis's elite club had high entry fees but low returns. Where was the money?

The industry had poured hundreds of millions of dollars into the value of the fleet. In the race to keep up with spiralling licence charges, reduced fishing time and the increased cost of gear, fishermen had converted to combination vessels, built new boats to replace old ones and joined the processors to create a massive seine fleet. Between 1969 and 1980, the capital value of the fleet had risen from $91 million to $432 million. The value of licences, which had been nil in 1969, now stood at $150 million. The debt load of the industry, which had stood at $13.4 million in 1969, now was at least $300 million. In sum, the industry had produced a fleet worth about $600 million, financing at least half of that cost with debt. Fisheries economist David Reid spelled out the consequences to fishermen at the 1983 conventions of the UFAWU and the Native Brotherhood. In 1981, when total salmon and herring revenues were $180 million, fishermen had paid out $45 million in interest. This was an amount equivalent to 180 per cent of the total value of landings in 1969. After paying other fixed costs of about $25 million and operating costs of $72 million, fishermen had only $38 million, or about $8,500 each on average, to live for a year.

Yet the $45 million in interest was not all that the fishermen owed, it was just all that they could pay. Reid had learned that two-thirds of all fishermen's accounts with banks were in arrears. Foreclosures had been limited only because there were no buyers for the boats already seized. Total industry investment in the fleet since 1969 had exceeded $500 million, Reid reported, "but that half-billion dollar investment didn't catch any more fish." The catch remained the same.

Even fishermen whose licences had been granted to them by the Davis plan, and thus had little or no debt, were little cheered by the thought that their boats now carried licence values of $10,000 or $20,000. The licence could only produce that value by being sold. Those carrying the massive debts were trying to support a cost equivalent to two, three or four vessels with the earnings of one. And those earnings were not increasing as fast as the value of the pack suggested. Thanks to their continued concentration of economic power, processors and banks were able to keep a disproportionate share of the value of the pack for themselves.

By capitalizing the value of the licences, the Davis plan had opened the fishing industry to bank lending, and the banks were happy to rush in, particularly as the value of licences climbed in the mid-1970s. Even more money came from the federal government's subsidy schemes, which loaned fishermen $133 million, twice as much as had been released under the same programs from 1955 to 1974. Banks and credit unions loaned almost $100 million between 1975 and 1981, with fully 60 per cent of that amount provided by the Royal Bank and the Canadian Imperial Bank of Commerce, both of which had close ties to the major processors. Only four per cent of the credit came from fishermen's credit unions, which, significantly, refused to accept licences as collateral. Had the banks acted as responsibly, the crisis would have been very much lessened.

Although the processors maintained their system of loans and credit, they were no longer the only lenders in the field and so needed new techniques to buy the loyalty of fishermen. The result was a proliferation of bribes in the form of "charter fees" or under-the-table bonuses paid in return for assured delivery of their catch. To do this, the processors needed to hold down the minimum price negotiated with the union. This was achieved in spite of a long and bitter salmon strike in 1975. Processors were able to open up a substantial margin between the union minimum and the actual grounds price. In this margin, processors played favourites, curried loyalty and punished transgressors. As the decade wore on, the bonus came to be regarded as a basic right by seine vessel owners, who could not otherwise have supported their massive investments. The bonus system, which paid seine vessel owners 30 to 100 per cent on top of grounds prices, reinforced the illusion of independence in fishermen while tightening their economic shackles. When the bottom fell out, many found they could neither survive without the bonus nor find another "competitor" prepared to take them on.

The increased prices also presented the illusion of competition. In some marginal fisheries, the illusion was convincing because of the influx of cash buyers, people willing to pay cash for fish right on the grounds. Sometimes backed by small companies looking for fish to fill specialized fresh markets, the cash buyers were more often the agents of major Japanese fish corporations. The arrival of dozens of cash buyers at lucrative fisheries convinced some fishermen and the public that the industry was a model of free competition. The reality was very different.

The four top firms in B.C. took 65 per cent of the salmon production in 1972. More than half of the entire catch was taken by B.C. Packers alone. As a result, the canners were able to increase the spread between what they received for their fish and what they paid fishermen. In 1973, when the price increases began, the export price was 370 per cent of the price paid to fishermen. By 1980, when export prices were nearing their peak and landed values were starting their free-fall, the difference was about the same. But in dollars and cents, that spread now was $2.62, substantially more cash to move around than the $1.55 available in 1973.

Although the UFAWU fought the price cuts with all the resources at its disposal, a second combines investigation and the corrosive divisions in the fleet fostered by the Davis plan were undermining its strength. Even when salmon fishermen struck for five weeks in 1975 and herring fishermen struck for the entire roe herring season in March 1980, processors still were able to get some production to market. Crutchfield's prediction that fishermen would be less able to strike under this form of limited entry had proven correct.

The number of scabs was not enormously greater in the 1970s, but the tremendous efficiency of their gear and the increasing shortness of the season made strikes an "all or nothing" affair. With the assistance of the processors and the Department of Fisheries, nonunion fishermen's organizations were created in various sectors of the fleet. Ostensibly they were advancing the interests of a particular gear, but in most cases fishermen who joined them did so to find encouragement and protection for strikebreaking. For the first time since the 1920s, the corporate sector could again run the fleet on a company-store basis, denying boats, credit or services to those who, through strike action, were unable to make payments.

The Davis plan produced a dramatic intensification of fishing effort, but the costs of this increase were borne on the one hand by the fishermen and on the other by the taxpayers, who were kind enough to cover all research, management, habitat protection and enhancement costs as well as provide a subsidy for the canners' collective marketing efforts.

The first signs of a collapse came in the roe herring fishery in 1979, where cash prices rose in a single season from a previously unthinkable level of $2,500 a tonne to $4,500 and even $5,000. The source of this bonanza was a wild and unpredictable gang of freebooting cash buyers packing bundles of $1,000 bills and bidding $100 a tonne more than the established firms. Their objective was to acquire as much of the lucrative roe harvest as possible and to ship it to the apparently insatiable market in Japan. They were bankrolled, in most cases, by gigantic Japanese trading companies like Mitsubishi and Marubeni, which advanced loans to small Canadian processors to secure a share of the Canadian catch. The Central Native Fishermen's Co-op, which was established to salvage processing jobs at Bella Bella on the central coast, received $7 million in investment from Marubeni. Millions more flowed into other firms. The upward price pressure was compounded by catches which fell thousands of tonnes short of the expected quota. Established processors dropped out of the price war and thousands of shoreworkers watched as their jobs were taken by newcomers working in plants which, in some cases, had been built with government subsidies. The Big Four firms—B.C. Packers, Canadian Fishing, J. S. McMillan and Norpac—saw their share of the catch tumble to less than 50 per cent.

It was the end of seven years of salad days for B.C. processors. As the roe season wound down, B.C. Packers reported that its profits for 1978, up more than 50 per cent from 1977, were $12.5 million. The 1979 profits were $6.5 million, about half that amount.

The bubble burst in March 1980 when the Fisheries Association demanded cuts in minimum roe-herring prices to $285 a tonne from the $1,200 guaranteed in 1979. Association bargaining representative Jerry Spitz conceded it "could very well be true" that the extraordinary highs of the previous year had been the result of market manipulation, but he insisted that fishermen absorb the full shock of the cut. The strike that followed cost the industry the entire herring season. More importantly, it triggered a reorganization in the processing sector which left Weston's B.C. Packers completely dominant among the survivors.

The earthquake began in Seattle, where Canadian Fishing's parent firm,

New England Fish (Nefco), was facing bankruptcy. Nefco officials made a frantic effort to raise funds by selling the majority of their most valuable asset, Canadian Fishing (Canfisco). Phone calls were placed to B.C. Packers' head office in Steveston and a deal was quickly consummated, giving the Weston subsidiary a major new base on the Skeena fisheries.

For about $15 million in American funds, Weston acquired Canfisco's new Oceanside cannery in Prince Rupert, its Atlin cannery and cold storage, 122 rental gillnetters, two shipyards and valuable property along the Steveston waterfront. Nefco retained control of Canfisco's valuable Gold Seal label, its venerable but efficient Home Plant cannery in Vancouver and its seine fleet.

Although chastened by profits that had tumbled to $6.5 million in 1979, the Nelson brothers, who still headed B.C. Packers, had reason for jubilation. Weston had already done exceedingly well by its investment in B.C. Packers. It had acquired a controlling interest in 1962 for about $6 million and raised its stake to just over 80 per cent in 1974 for an estimated cost of about $10 million. This amount was exceeded by Weston's share of B.C. Packers' profits in 1978 alone. The acquisition of the Canfisco assets was just the first step in a long series of moves that used adept real estate deals and political influence to recover all the costs of the purchase and more. In its 1980 annual report, Weston declared its decision to concentrate its efforts in "acquiring processing and marketing areas" while withdrawing from "primary fishing and related fishermen's servicing functions."

This strategy of transferring still more harvesting costs to fishermen would have far-reaching consequences. Richard J. Currie, a Weston director who sat on the B.C. Packers board, spelled them out in a frank interview in 1981. Weston's standard approach, he said, amounted to "boiling the business down." The company concentrated on "moving out redundant assets of all kinds, fixed assets, balance sheet assets or people." The decisions were a straightforward as "a doctor's decision to amputate a gangrenous arm."

The axe fell quickly and mercilessly. In the next thirty-six months, B.C. Packers closed its Seal Cove cold storage in Prince Rupert, its Masset cannery and its Tofino operation, as well as reducing its Namu operations to a shell. Operations in Prince Rupert were consolidated at the modern Oceanside cannery formerly owned by Canfisco. In 1981, the company sold more than two hundred gillnetters, most of them relics of Canfisco's fleet, to the federal government for $12.7 million. The federal government in turn gave the boats to three northern tribal councils, but most of the production continued to flow to B.C. Packers. Layoffs and closures continued in 1982, but B.C. Packers tightened its links to foreign fish supply, sending two modern tuna seiners to its Philippines cannery and purchasing a salmon cannery in Alaska. In 1983, the federal government again came to Weston's aid with the $9.8 million purchase of fishing facilities along the Fraser, which were turned over to the Department of Fisheries and Oceans' Small Craft Harbours Branch. Three years after purchasing Canfisco, Weston had flipped some of the lowest-value assets to the federal government for more than the cost of the entire acquisition, using the proceeds to invest in low-wage areas offshore and in labour-saving technology in B.C. In 1982, the Weston empire had $7.8 billion in sales and a return on invested capital before tax of 14.6 per cent. Its five-year profit growth had been 156.4 per cent, the highest of Canada's ten largest corporations.

The changes at B.C. Packers and Connors Bros., Weston's Maritime fishing industry subsidiary, were designed to fit fish processing into Weston's larger plan for the food industry. Unable to increase its profits in retailing by absorbing its competitors, Weston was working to reduce the cost of the food it sold. The highly monopolized Canadian retail food industry, where 50 per cent of B.C.'s canned salmon was sold, was controlled by three massive grocery-buying groups that distributed to thousands of retail stores. Through its Weston connection, B.C. Packers had guaranteed access to this market and to Weston's internal financing. Smaller competitors like Central Native Fishermen's Co-op found themselves going cap-in-hand to their competitor for access to retail shelves.

As the period of "rationalization" drew to a close, profits failed to rise as quickly as Weston's strategic plan demanded. Richard Nelson himself was unceremoniously dumped from his position at the head of B.C. Packers, and a Weston loyalist from Connors Bros. was installed.

B.C. Packers executives began to question the need for any competition in the processing sector at all. In their submissions to the royal commission probing the wreckage of the 1980 collapse, company officers urged the government to think about a single processing company for the salmon fishery. If necessary, they said, it could be under public ownership. Evidently Weston was so sure of its control of market access that it could contemplate leaving the messy business of fish processing to someone else.

The earthquake that had begun with the fall of Nefco quickly destroyed many of the small "independent" firms that had relied on major Japanese corporations for funding. Eight firms had disappeared completely by 1983, among them canning companies or co-operatives in Victoria and Bella Bella that employed more than a hundred workers each. Norpac Fisheries, at one time a significant second-rank firm, was swallowed up by J. S. McMillan Fisheries and Ocean Fisheries, two rising companies closely held by families in their second generation in the fishing business. The most prominent failure, however, was Cassiar Packing Co., one of the industry's oldest firms, which went out of business on Labour Day weekend in 1983, just before fishermen picked up their season's earnings. Although its assets ultimately provided a foundation for Ocean Fisheries' ascendancy during the 1980s, Cassiar's collapse cost hundreds of shoreworkers their jobs and cost fishermen hundreds of thousands of dollars in earnings.

This was one of the achievements of the Davis plan: economic crises which once had come at intervals of twenty-five or thirty years now were less than a decade apart. The tragedy of the commons began to seem like musical comedy as the boom years of the 1970s faded into what Peter Pearse termed the "exceptionally bleak" circumstances of the 1980s. For not only had the industry's corporate structure disintegrated, there were disquieting signs that the resource itself finally was faltering under the double blows of pollution and habitat loss.

As the first century of commercial salmon harvesting drew to an end, fisheries scientists took stock. Somehow B.C.'s salmon runs had survived, thanks in equal measure to their own astonishing resilience, the vigilance of fishermen and conservationists, and, to be fair, the tenacity of some fisheries managers. But the runs were a shadow of their original abundance and far below the levels scientists believed could be sustained even with the remaining habitat. Average annual landings, which had remained stable at about 20 million fish from the 1930s through to the 1950s, had risen to about 23 million fish during the 1970s, due in large part to the steady rebuilding of Fraser River sockeye by the International Pacific Salmon Fisheries Commission. But the increase in numbers of fish disguised a disturbing contrary trend—the weight of the annual harvest had declined. Average sizes of all salmon species were declining, apparently a genetic response to fishing pressure.

There were other troubling signs. Although fishing had been entirely stopped on threatened chum stocks on north Vancouver Island and the Queen Charlottes, the runs remained weak. Chinook stocks, despite massive hatchery releases, were decreasing in most coastal systems, although the runs had stabilized in rivers like the Fraser and the Skeena. Coho stocks were falling in five major areas, stable or increasing somewhat in six. Steelhead runs were stable in only five of the four hundred known producing streams. Only the fertile pink salmon, which had recolonized most of the Fraser and Thompson system since the opening of the Hell's Gate fishways, were on the upswing. Careful study of the potential capacity of the province's streams confirmed that salmon stocks could be increased to annual runs of 37 million from the 1990 level of 22 million, given appropriate management, habitat protection and investment of public funds.

In theory, such a program already was in place. The continuous public demand for expenditures to increase fish habitat and production had not gone entirely unheeded. Throughout the 1950s and 1960s, the fisheries department had put aside funds for major fishways on half a dozen important salmon rivers. Research biologists had proven the feasibility of artificial spawning channels. By the early 1970s, interest in hatcheries had revived to the extent that Jack Davis approved construction of the Capilano hatchery in his own riding. By 1974, the industry and the department were convinced that a coastwide program could produce enormous dividends.

Salmonid enhancement had compelling economic logic, but the overwhelming public support for the program made it politically attractive as well. In a series of informal public hearings held around the province in 1977, the federal government asked Canadians if they wanted to invest in the protection and improvement of their fish stocks. The resounding answer was yes. In defiance of economic theory which had concluded that the common property nature of the resource produced a situation in which no one considered its welfare, 248 organizations and individuals made submissions to the seventeen meetings held coastwide. They overwhelmingly endorsed a full-scale enhancement program, particularly one that encouraged public participation and natural techniques rather than hatcheries. Only one direct quote from an unnamed intervenor was published in the slim final report, but it conveyed the public mood: "What's at stake today is more than the commodity called fish. . . . What's at stake now is our own attitudes, our hopes, our vision and all of it regarding a very rich, but fragile environment. What's at stake is our determination to live up to our responsibility as guardians of the world we use. What's at stake is our ability to see beyond the stretch of our own greedy arms. What's at stake is our chance to demonstrate that we are able to reject the easy way, the quick way, in favour of what we know in our hearts to be the right way."

When Ottawa concluded that the costs of salmonid enhancement could be recovered from royalties on the catch, the last obstacle was overcome. In the past, the government had tried to impose royalties simply as a necessary discipline—painful but ultimately beneficial. From now on, government officials would insist that royalties had nothing to do with fleet rationalization but were simply a way of paying for enhancement.

Fisheries minister Romeo LeBlanc announced late in 1977 that his government was committing $150 million over five years to the first phase of the program, which was to increase annual salmon production by 25,000 tonnes a year. The second phase was to take production on to the historic levels of more than 100,000 tonnes annually.

From the beginning, however, Ottawa chiselled and chopped at the program. By 1981, the Salmonid Enhancement Task Group, a public board set up to oversee the program, estimated that LeBlanc's decision to extend the first phase to seven years from five, with no increase in funding, slashed buying power by $28 million. Inflation ate up another $75 million. Another $24 million had simply been cut. In effect, the government had spent the equivalent of only $47 million, yet had obtained production of 87 per cent of the target. To the annoyance of the task group, much of the investment had been poured into costly hatcheries, in direct contradiction of the public demand for small-scale stream clearing and natural production.

The department responded to these criticisms by repeated attempts to dismantle the task group, which remained an irritating reminder of the public's deep and abiding concern for the future of the resource. Further evidence of public concern was the massive participation in the program's community projects, which mobilized more than 7,000 volunteers to produce fish from incubation boxes and stream-clearing projects on scores of creeks and rivers. The sad reality was, however, that the increased production from enhancement projects was obscuring the very real losses from a host of causes. Far from rebuilding the stocks, the program was simply slowing their decline.

In 1977, LeBlanc had also sponsored the introduction of important and substantial changes to the Fisheries Act, making it potentially the country's most effective legal weapon against pollution. Revisions to Section 33 of the act made it illegal to pollute or contaminate fish habitat and set out substantial penalties. In reality, however, salmon stocks always came second when other corporate interests were at stake.

One such showdown came in 1979 on Riley Creek, at Rennell Sound in the Queen Charlotte Islands. Provincial authorities at first agreed to exclude a sensitive parcel from logging because of the threat posed to salmon in the creek from siltation and landslides. Then they allowed the company, a subsidiary of C. Itoh of Japan, to proceed. Confronted by this defiance, LeBlanc authorized fisheries officers to charge both the loggers and their employer. Unable to contact senior company officials, the fisheries officers arrested first one logger and then another. For more than a week, the company sent loggers into the firing line in what clearly was a test of the new provisions of the Fisheries Act. After a ten-day showdown, sixteen loggers, the company and a company official faced charges for destruction of fish habitat. When provincial officials, the International Woodworkers of America and the company put pressure on Ottawa, LeBlanc ordered a humiliating retreat. The charges were stayed, logging proceeded, and the fisheries department came away with an agreement to study better ways to log with "a view to minimizing impact on fish habitat." Subsequent slides heavily damaged Riley Creek's salmon runs.

LeBlanc faced further defiance just months later from Alcan, when it ignored a direct order to increase flows from its reservoir to cool the waters of the Nechako River. Claiming that its water licence rights overrode the Fisheries

Act, Alcan reduced flows out of the reservoir by 50 per cent so that it could increase power generation at Kemano. This electricity was sold to B.C. Hydro for export to the United States. The reduced flows to the Nechako resulted in low water levels and high water temperatures throughout much of the Fraser system. Finally, on 1 August, LeBlanc sought an injunction from the B.C. Supreme Court to enforce his order. Fortunately for the salmon, the judge was Mr. Justice Thomas Berger, former provincial leader of the New Democratic Party, who declared that "the minister represents the public interest. The power [to decide water flows] ultimately must be his." Berger's injunction was all that saved the Fraser salmon. Despite overwhelming evidence, backed up by the International Pacific Salmon Fisheries Commission which stated that reduced flows could be devastating for salmon, subsequent federal commentary of Alcan's Kemano completion project claimed that overfishing, not habitat degradation, was the main cause of fish declines on the Upper Fraser. Despite the injunction and the salmon commission research, Alcan was absolved of responsibility for any deterioration of the stocks.

In 1981, LeBlanc himself came under fire for his decision to allow Amax Corp. to dump toxic tailings from its Alice Arm molybdenum mine directly into the inlet. LeBlanc claimed that the marine disposal system had been approved by his environmental experts "pretty well unanimously," but internal department documents released by *The Fisherman* proved otherwise. One extraordinary clause of the special permit issued to Amax allowed dumping of tailings at levels of contamination up to 80,000 times higher than those permitted under the Fisheries Act. These tailings included substantial amounts of heavy metals. World metal markets did for the salmon what the Fisheries Act under the Liberals could not—Amax closed up the project twelve months after metal prices collapsed.

In 1983, the UFAWU joined forces with native bands along the Fraser in an effort to curb Canadian National Railway's massive twin-tracking project along the Fraser Canyon, where its predecessors had done such untold damage seventy years before. To produce enough space to add its second track, CN sought approval to dump tonnes of rock along the river's edge. Convinced that Ottawa's environmental review process would prove useless, the Alliance of Tribal Councils declared in October 1984 that they would deny CN access to their reserves. The UFAWU condemned the department's stance on the project, pleading with Ottawa act on "its mandate to protect salmon habitat and to refrain from conceding to CN or to any proponent that habitat loss is unavoidable." A one-year moratorium on construction was ordered by the newly elected Tories in early 1985, but ultimately CN was able to complete the project everywhere except where the tracks crossed native reserves. (CN created what it said was an equivalent amount of "new" habitat, to ensure the losses were balanced. The ability of the CN habitat to support fish life was unproved.)

These projects were the ones that actually began construction. The Trudeau government, which was committed to an economic strategy based on export of raw materials, studied billions of dollars' worth of megaprojects during the period, despite the clear threat they posed to fish resources. By early 1985, projects with a potential worth of $5 billion were either under construction or waiting for regulatory approval. The $250 million annual landed value of the salmon resource was of little weight in these economic calculations.

Even the impact of these projects, however, was of little importance when placed against the daily erosion of fish habitat throughout the province by logging, urban encroachment, estuary development, pesticide use and sewage dumping. Of all the organizations in the industry, only the UFAWU maintained any sustained environmental program. Desperate to broaden the opposition to fish habitat loss, it founded a charitable foundation named after Buck Suzuki to promote research and education about the value of wild fisheries resources.

The contraction of profits and the decline of salmon stocks placed those who directed the fate of the industry in an uncommonly tough situation. Despite the obvious virtues of the Davis plan, it must have seemed clear to Weston's senior planners that fundamental changes were in order if profits were to revive. Dramatic cuts in fish prices, which had been imposed on fishermen, could go only part way to meeting the company's needs. B.C. Packers' net profit after taxes as a percentage of equity had averaged 4.71 per cent as the boom gathered steam in the early 1970s and then surged to 19.6 per cent in the glory years from 1977 to 1979. Crushing interest rates had transformed that performance into a net loss of 4.5 per cent a year from 1980 to 1982 despite increased total sales. Reduced interest charges would provide some relief, but permanently lower fish prices were crucial to Weston's long-term plans. Yet how could prices be lowered still more with fishermen already staring bankruptcy in the face? A massive restructuring of the salmon fleet seemed the only solution. This time the job must be comprehensive. The stocks, the fishermen, the environment—all had to be subjected to the discipline of the marketplace.

THE TRAGEDY OF THE COMMONS

EARLY IN MAY 1980, B.C. PACKERS' CHAIRMAN R. I. NELSON stood before a shareholders' meeting and reported that the industry was in the midst of "a financial crisis, the fourth since the turn of century. These crises have occurred in 1902, 1928, 1968 and now again in 1980, and have in each case been associated with overcapacity in the processing sector. They have been resolved by a series of mergers and amalgamations of companies and rationalization of processing operations. B.C. Packers Ltd. has participated in these rationalizations since 1902 and in each case has emerged as a stronger company."

The crisis of 1980 may have proved a boon to Weston and B.C. Packers shareholders, but it marked disaster for fishing industry workers and ultimately for salmon stocks. In the space of three years, 1,000 shoreworkers lost their jobs. A dozen fish plants closed. Hundreds of fishermen suffered the loss of their vessels. The general economic crisis that gripped the country was magnified severalfold in coastal communities by cuts in unemployment insurance, rising interest rates, and reduction in government spending for fisheries research and enforcement.

The industry collapse of 1980, which came just weeks after a revitalized Liberal party under Trudeau swept Joe Clark's Conservatives from power, created once more that critical combination of circumstances which produced action—a majority government and an industry-wide demand for change. Fisheries minister Romeo LeBlanc, restored to his portfolio, was being hounded on all sides, including by prominent B.C. Liberal MP Iona Campagnolo and by Senators Jack Austen and Ray Perrault.

Liberal party leaders quickly provided a man with the answers—Dr. Peter

Pearse, defeated Liberal candidate from the riding of Quadra in Vancouver. Since his brush with the West Coast Fleet Development Committee in 1972, he had been keen to submit the fishing industry to his theories. LeBlanc quickly teamed up Pearse with Fern Doucet, an economist with experience on the Atlantic coast, and gave them four weeks to provide answers to the most vexing question he faced in B.C. To the chagrin of fisheries officials, they advocated a freeze on any major initiatives until a complete review of the fishing industry could be carried through.

Pearse left no doubt about where he stood on licensing, parting sharply with regional officials who recently had declared the Davis plan "a tragedy." "The Davis Plan was a much needed initial step," Pearse insisted, a good idea that "wasn't followed through." Fewer than eight weeks later, Pearse was formally appointed to conduct the most sweeping investigation of the Pacific industry in sixty years.

Pearse, only forty-six in 1980, had established his reputation as a resource economist with a massive report on the B.C. forest industry, completed for the New Democratic Party government of Dave Barrett. Pearse had studied forest economics in university but had long been interested in fisheries economics. He was a firm believer in the economic theories of Scott Gordon and Crutchfield. In his writing and comments before and after his inquiry into the fisheries, he made it clear that he was personally offended by the "dissipation" of the industry's wealth.

In fact, Pearse had been considering this question for more than a decade and had outlined all the main aspects of his thinking in a paper on the national regulation of fisheries to a conference of the Fisheries Service of Canada in October 1971, even before his appointment to the West Coast Fleet Development Committee. Significantly, he ranked "economic efficiency in fish harvesting" ahead of "conservation and enhancement of the resource" in his goals, which in turn were ahead of enhancement of fishermen's incomes, maintenance of employment opportunities and minimization of social and economic dislocation. From the beginning, therefore, he was interested in reduced fleet sizes, regardless of economic and social consequences for those dependent on the resource. In this paper, Pearse also argued strongly for catch royalties as superior to any other means of capturing the "economic rents" of the fishery. The only flaw he found with schemes like the Davis plan was that they left the resource as "common property to the individual fishermen. A more fundamental reform would be to avoid regulating independent fishing units by allocating whole fisheries to single enterprise—either private or public. Such a sole ownership policy would eliminate common property in the fishery, along with all its incentives for perverse economic adjustments." He concluded that, unfortunately, "sole ownership must be regarded as politically unacceptable, even if it is technically workable." Finally, he approvingly quoted Crutchfield, who had remarked "the American and Canadian economies have made remarkable progress under a form of economic organization which requires that each enterprise use resources effectively or give them up to those who will. The fishing industry, like any other, must meet that challenge or step aside."

In his marathon eighteen-month investigation of the industry, Pearse heard almost 200 submissions in 67 days of public hearings. Transcripts of his sessions filled 14,000 pages and dozens of researchers produced papers for the most comprehensive review in the history of the industry. The intensive public hearings provided the government with a high-profile and effective symbol of action and concern, but Pearse had long considered what he intended to say, and the public hearings were simply the price he had to pay to say it. As he admitted some months later to a House of Commons committee, he could have written his report without holding even an hour of public hearings.

The commission was confronted with a welter of conflicting suggestions. Nonunion fishermen's groups favoured catch royalties to fund salmonid enhancement. The Native Brotherhood proposed a special corporation to represent native interests in the industry. The UFAWU reiterated its call for comprehensive habitat protection and salmonid enhancement, combined with a return to Bill Rigby's proposed system of licensing fishermen, rather than boats. This seemed as valid as ever to the union, which offered a program it said would eliminate the problem of overcapitalization once and for all. B.C. Packers demanded a 40 per cent reduction in the fleet, a 25 per cent landing tax levied at dockside and a commitment to pull the fishery "toward the destination of returning salmon," the river mouths, where the company favoured installation of fish traps. Most significantly of all, the Weston agents said it was time to consider "consolidation of processing into fewer or even a single organization" with government intervention to buy out and retire "capacity which is obsolete or poorly located." Such a processing corporation, they indicated, could be either privately or publicly owned. Just as B.C. Packers had been content to get out of the fishing end of the business, so Weston was now preparing to leave all but the most lucrative processing. Its assurance of control of the catch was complete.

Despite the tremendous volume of submissions, Pearse was able to issue a substantial interim report just eleven months after undertaking the commission. Taking his lead directly from submissions by B.C. Packers and the Fisheries Association, Pearse urged a massive buyback program, financed by heavy catch royalties, to reduce the fleet "to the maximum extent possible." Halibut and herring fishermen would be issued annual personal quotas—called individual transferable quotas or ITQs—for a share of the allowable catch. These quotas could be bought and sold, allowing further concentration of ownership and fleet reduction. In an unusual twist, he urged the licensing of people as well as boats, "because people can write cheques." Those cheques would be substantial, a "disaster for fishermen" in the words of UFAWU secretary-treasurer George Hewison. Pearse estimated that under his proposals the average gillnetter or troller would have paid $1,646 in royalties in 1979, an amount taken directly from net income regardless of how large or small that net income was. Seine vessel owners would have paid almost $7,000. The silence from nonunion gear organizations that had recommended royalties was deafening. In a November 1981 interview in *The Fisherman,* Pearse said he believed this burden could be borne easily because fleet reduction would increase average annual landings.

Unlike the narrow reviews of previous years, the Pearse Commission was considering the entire industry from spawning gravel to the end of Canada's fishing limits. His terms of reference specifically excluded international treaties and the processing sector, but included questions of habitat, native rights, sport fishing and all the many minor fisheries, from shellfish to sole, which received little attention from intervenors. When the final report was released in September 1982, however, few were prepared for its scope, its detail or its sweeping conclusions. Pearse had drafted a revolutionary strategy for the industry which would integrate fisheries resources into the national economic agenda of the corporate sector.

The key to Pearse's proposals was a commitment to privatize fishing rights. Within ten years, according to a complex licence auction scheme, fishermen would buy up each others' licences until half of them had been eliminated. In 1993, any person or corporation would have the right to purchase fishing rights, which by then would be issued for three coastal regions. Very quickly, Pearse said later, the fleet could be reduced by 80 per cent and "ultimately they might not need any boats at all" as fishing switched to traps and weirs.

Pearse's argument was founded on three critical conclusions. The first was that "the main cause of decline and low abundance of many stocks has been overfishing," not habitat destruction. With that decided, his main emphasis shifted to controls on fishermen, not measures to husband and increase the runs.

His second conclusion was that "stock depletion, poor economic performance and instability result from treating the resource [the fish] as common property and are normal when resources are treated this way. It is the Tragedy of the Commons." This identified the absence of property rights as the reason for fishermen's unfortunate behaviour. Pearse's prose, normally flat and professorial, glinted with anger as he spelled out his objective, which was nothing less than the elimination of common property fishing. In an echo of the B.C.

Packers submission more than a year before, he said that "the free enterprise system depends on someone having control over all the factors of production, including natural resources, and ensuring that they are used in the most profitable way."

This led to Pearse's third conclusion, that the goal of fisheries policy should be to ensure "that the resources are allocated to those who can make the most valuable use of them and that whoever used the resources does use them in the most beneficial way." The goal of licensing, apart from basic conservation, was to ensure "efficient organization of the primary fishing sector to harvest the catch at low cost... and provide the best opportunities for successfully competing in world markets." As a consequence, habitat protection was reduced to a pious wish that the department "ensure that the total fish production capacity in the region will not be diminished as a result of industrial and other activities that impinge upon fish habitat."

In Pearse's view, "identifiable and measurable harm to fish habitat should be tolerated for any particular development only if the damage is fully compensated through expanded fish production capacity elsewhere." This policy, soon named the "no-net-loss" concept, opened the door to corporate cash payments in return for the right to destroy fish habitat. Such payments would only be required, however, where damage was "identifiable and measurable," an impossible test in the case of long-term, low-level destruction. These payments would be put into an enhancement fund for later use by the government. But Pearse, determined to reduce the obstacles to other forms of development that could "yield benefits greater than the value of habitat lost," went even further. He called for the elimination of effluent recommendations and urged that future projects be approved on a site-specific basis, with higher pollution levels allowed on streams "insignificant for fish." The Department of Fisheries would be bound to allow other development—this concept he called "integrated resource use planning"—and would be subject to suit if it sought to tighten controls once a permit was issued.

While Pearse was content to let market forces determine the value of fish habitat, he was determined to have proof of profit before endorsing the Salmonid Enhancement Program. By 1982, enhancement production was just coming onstream. Despite unexpected cost overruns and sharp funding cuts, the program had returned $1.30 to the economy for every dollar expended. But Pearse was deeply disturbed by a host of problems including management conflicts, environmental issues and economic considerations. Ultimately, he concluded, without fleet rationalization, "enhancement as an economic development program is bound to fail." He called for a two-year halt on enhancement work for assessment and planning at the conclusion of the program's first phase. After that, funding should be limited to half of the royalties collected annually—about one-third of the current spending. Finally, further enhancement should emphasize "enhancement by management," the imposition of closures to put extra spawners on the grounds. Fishermen would then be forced to pay for the enhancement, Pearse said, in foregone catches.

While dubious about public expenditure on fish production, Pearse was enthusiastic about private investment in the same field. Proposals for private salmon farms (where fish would be reared in pens) or ocean ranches (where fish would be released from hatcheries to graze on the high seas) were considered "most attractive." Pearse was especially pleased at the prospect that the government could "harness private initiative and ingenuity in producing fish, linking those who would incur the costs directly with those who would benefit." He urged the department to create mariculture leases that would give holders "the exclusive right to fish" for natural or artificial stocks produced in a given area. At the head of the list was a proposal by the government's B.C. Development Corp. to develop the province's first ocean ranch on Kyuquot Inlet on Vancouver Island's northwest coast.

Pearse's enthusiasm for ocean ranching proved his fatal weakness. The vision of an industry reducing itself by auction in a ten-year period to a handful of corporate-owned salmon weirs and hatcheries provoked an unprecedented backlash.

Alerted to Pearse's direction by his own comments and the zealous promotional work of the B.C. Development Corp., the UFAWU undertook an investigation of ocean ranching in Oregon. An eight-page supplement to *The Fisherman,* entitled "Private, for Profit," released just a few weeks before Pearse's final report, revealed that George Weyerhaeuser Ltd., the logging giant that dominated the state economy, was the major producer of Oregon's ranched coho. Wild stock fisheries were being closed to ensure adequate returns to Weyerhaeuser's faltering hatcheries. David Schlip, an Oregon troller, warned B.C. fishermen that "ocean ranching, or private for profit aquaculture, must be stopped because it is not compatible with a natural resource. If it follows true to form in British Columbia, you will go in with a failing public program. Pretty soon it will start to fall apart and as it starts to fall apart, you will see more restrictions imposed on it. After the private sector is well established, you'll see their releases start to sky-rocket and they'll use a policy to conserve wild fish. I'm sure your fishermen will face restrictions to put the ocean ranchers in business. They can't be put in business if you're allowed to fish."

In six years, the Oregon private hatchery system had gone from nothing to annual releases greater than the public program. Corporations like Gulf Oil, Union Carbide, British Petroleum and Crown Zellerbach were vying for permits. The most advanced operation, however, was backed by George Weyer-haeuser, which told shareholders that "aquaculture relates to our land and water ownership. . . . Managing nature is a basic part of our business. Aquaculture builds on that corporate strength." What was good for Weyerhaeuser, however, was proving fatal for Oregon's wild coho stocks.

Weyerhaeuser's fisheries scientists were using waste heat from a pulp mill to accelerate the growth of coho smolts, produced from eggs imported from as far afield as Puget Sound. When the fish were pumped into the ocean, they strayed into rivers 65, 80 and 100 kilometres away, where they interbred with wild stocks. The genetic diversity of Oregon's natural fish was severely eroded. After their time at sea, the ranched coho would straggle back to an artificial watercourse installed at the company's harbourside processing plant. The salmon swam straight into a cage that lifted them out of the water and dumped them onto cleaning tables.

In Canada, the Salmonid Enhancement Program was already moving into private hands. Although it was more costly to do so, the fisheries department was allowing private contractors to take over the operation of important facilities. At the Little Qualicum spawning channels on Vancouver Island, Underwood McClelland Associates held the contract under the supervision of biologist Don Sinclair, who was one of the team that had presented B.C. Development Corp.'s ocean ranching proposal to Pearse.

The optimism that they were riding the wave of history coloured the comments of all the ocean ranchers. Bill McNeil, who managed Oreaqua, had little patience for the fears of critics. "What we're looking at here is a classic transition of public policy away from a hunting gathering philosophy to more of a farming philosophy," he said. "The whole thing is propelled by a requirement for more production from the ocean. Fishermen feel threatened by it because they're the hunters and the gatherers."

Only a single significant industry organization, the Native Brotherhood, had endorsed ocean ranching in any form, but its members, stung by Pearse's refusal to recognize aboriginal title, repudiated that stand in a tense debate at its annual convention just two weeks after Pearse's report came out. Even the Pacific Trollers' Association, which had supported royalties and a number of other changes proposed by Pearse, warned that ocean ranching was "public enemy number one as far as fishermen are concerned." The B.C. Wildlife Federation, which endorsed much of the report, agreed. With ocean ranching, said one spokesman, "they'll push us out and pretty soon we'll have the coast so covered with lines that only special people can get inside to fish." The UFAWU, determined to block the report or win a one-year moratorium at the minimum, found it an easy matter to organize coastwide protest meetings.

Commercial groups, sport groups, labour councils, tribal councils, a number of city and community councils and the B.C. Federation of Labour endorsed the opposition movement. Scores of small businessmen reliant on the industry added their voices, fearful that a 50 per cent reduction in the fleet would spell their demise. A three-day fishermen's conference in Vancouver early in 1983, including representatives of every major fishermen's organization except the Native Brotherhood, condemned the Pearse report and adopted a Fishermen's Charter of Rights founded on protection of the common property nature of the resource. By February, Tory fisheries critic John Fraser had promised his party's support for a one-year moratorium.

As the protest movement grew, LeBlanc moved out of the fisheries portfolio, replaced by Gaspé Liberal Pierre De Bané, an autocratic lawyer who vowed to push ahead with Pearse's recommendations as quickly as possible. Industry representatives, including the processors, quickly reined him in. Soon after his appointment, a chastened De Bané emerged from a meeting with his new Minister's Advisory Council, a body that included representatives of all major industry groups, to declare "the Pearse Report is behind us."

Jack Nichol, president of the UFAWU, who played a critical role in the advisory council, revealed the council had voted unanimously against Pearse's habitat and ocean ranching recommendations and unanimously in favour of full funding for a second phase of the Salmonid Enhancement Plan. De Bané had approval only to proceed with about seventy recommendations of an administrative nature. These unanimous positions came from a body that included only a single union representative. Also casting ballots were representatives of the Fisheries Association and gear organizations with as few as 120 members. Clearly demoralized, De Bané agreed to the demand for a moratorium, giving a new Fleet Rationalization Committee until the first anniversary of the Pearse report's release to provide a palatable plan for fleet reduction. Publicly, De Bané had retreated, pledging to await the recommendations of the Fleet Rationalization Committee and his Minister's Advisory Council before making any further moves. Behind the scenes, however, he took a very different course.

Early in November 1983 NDP fisheries critic Ted Miller obtained a copy of a confidential memorandum to De Bané outlining draconian plans for a 50 per cent fleet reduction to be imposed as soon as possible. The plan was the work of a top-level "policy review committee" headed by De Bané aide Terry O'Reilly. O'Reilly's plan called for area licensing, quota fisheries and heavy royalties. Miller charged that O'Reilly was "knee-capping" the Minister's Advisory Council and Jack Nichol agreed. Following the news of the secret plan, the UFAWU issued a call for a Fishermen's Survival Conference to be held in Vancouver just before Christmas. More than two hundred people turned out for the three-day gathering, which agreed to launch an industry lobby to Ottawa to fight the Liberal plans. They called their movement the Fishermen's Survival Coalition.

It was clear even before the coalition left for Ottawa, however, that De Bané was intent on inflicting massive damage before his government's mandate ran out. Sweeping legislation to restructure the Atlantic fishery was already before the House of Commons, and De Bané had promised a similar package for the Pacific Coast. Claiming that salmon stocks were declining at an annual average rate of 1.5 per cent, the government was proposing drastic catch reductions combined with a fleet rationalization program that De Bané conceded would mean "hardship, pain and sacrifice." Although salmonid enhancement was expected to provide some increased production by 1986, any further increases would have to come from salmon farms and aquaculture. Environmental protection and further funding of the Salmonid Enhancement Program were not among De Bané's options.

Only ninety days after the first emergency meetings in Vancouver, 120 fishermen from every area on the coast were combing the halls of Parliament, tracking down MPs. Wearing bright orange survival suits, they demonstrated on the frozen lawn below the Peace Tower. The Fishermen's Survival Coalition was a grassroots movement that seemed able to move mountains. More than $100,000 was raised in a five-week period to cover the massive costs of the delegation, which was endorsed not only by the UFAWU but also by the Pacific Trollers' Association, the Pacific Gillnetters Association, the Pacific Coast Salmon Seiners Association and members of the Prince Rupert Fishermen's Co-op. It was a good time for coalitions in B.C.—the Solidarity Coalition had erupted during the same period to challenge the restraint program of the province's Social Credit government.

The brief the coalition took to Ottawa represented a new consensus among fishing industry workers about the future of the resource and their industry. The first plank in their program was "protection of the fish as the common property of the people of Canada." Their environmental program included rejection of Alcan's Kemano project, which De Bané was pushing forward, and full enforcement of the Fisheries Act, combined with a $200-million second phase of the Salmonid Enhancement Program. The first point in the coalition's Fishermen's Charter of Rights was "the right to an industry with a future through fisheries habitat protection and enhancement of salmon stocks."

De Bané finally unveiled his Pacific Fisheries Restructuring Act on 19 June 1984, with the warning that it had to be passed within ten days or die with the current session of Parliament. The legislation was so extreme that even Pearse was shocked by its proposals: a 45 per cent fleet reduction within twelve months, funded partly with cash and partly with shares in a new buyback corporation; implementation of royalties; elimination of combination boats, and drastic reductions in fishing time. The new licensing regime would be based on transferable quotas, which would be extended to the salmon fishery within three years. Of the many pernicious aspects of the bill, the buyback corporation caught the fishermen's eye. In reality, the buyback was a bank bail-out that would buy out bank debt partly with cash and partly with shares in the buyback corporation. The banks themselves would sit on this corporation and redeem their shares with the proceeds of future royalties.

Although the Tories waffled on their stance on the bill, NDP fisheries critic Ted Miller vowed to fight to the end. His resistance was enough to destroy the bill's chances for success, and De Bané bitterly denounced his critics as he accepted appointment to the Senate. He, along with LeBlanc, was one of the eleventh-hour patronage appointments that contributed to the doom of the John Turner government, which was swept from office that fall.

For many in the industry, the election of the Conservatives promised a new day.

HEADS THEY WIN, TAILS WE LOSE

WITH THE CONSERVATIVE PARTY'S ECONOMIC POLICY, THE theories of the "tragedy of the commons" gang came full circle. Liberal economists of the Davis era had sought to reconcile the needs of industry workers with the profit requirements of processors. Liberal economists of the 1980s, Pearse pre-eminent among them, had subjugated the resource to the requirements of national corporate policy. With the Conservatives, the fishing industry was to conform to international economic priorities established in the offices of multinational corporations. For more than a century, business had fought for control of the wealth of the wild salmon. By the 1990s, it had concluded the wild fish was not worth the effort.

Because the Conservatives did not expect the support of coastal communities for policies that could shatter their economies, they adopted a very different political style from their predecessors. Where the Liberals had attempted legislation, the Conservatives proceeded by regulation. Where the Liberals had used lengthy public consultations and royal commissions to divide and rule, the Conservatives performed internal reviews and announced the results. The "dissipated rents" that moved economic theorists to despair were now to be gathered by corporations for which national boundaries were irrelevant. For the Conservative government of Brian Mulroney, the waste lay not only in the overcapitalization of the fleet but in the existence of a government agency to regulate it. The new goal was not just to capture the "dissipated rents" of the fleet but also to reduce the government spending that funded enforcement, research and habitat protection. In the Conservatives' brave new world, the links between salmon and their rivers, streams and oceans would be broken once and for all. The destruction of the wild salmon that decades of pollution, corporate greed and government neglect had failed to accomplish, the Conservatives attempted to achieve in a five-year span by Order in Council.

The revulsion with Liberal policies fostered by the Fishermen's Survival Coalition helped the Tory juggernaut to power in the election sweep of 1984. Many in the industry, including some groups that had endorsed the coalition, contributed directly to the campaign of popular Vancouver Conservative John Fraser, whose strong support of the coalition in the last, dark days of De Bané's regime had won widespread respect. There was jubilation when Fraser won the fisheries portfolio in the new Mulroney cabinet. As the senior minister for B.C. and a member of the powerful inner cabinet, Fraser had the levers of power in his hands. He had been explicit about his plans, telling the House of Commons in February 1984 that under his administration there would be "no tampering with the concept of the resource as common property." He vowed a fully funded second phase of the Salmonid Enhancement Program and a $100-million buyback program.

Yet within months of his appointment, those election promises turned to ashes. The second phase of salmonid enhancement was put on hold and enhancement staff was cut by one-third. The $100-million buyback was slashed to $35 million and later dropped altogether. The decline in Fraser's popularity began with his decision to ratify a new Canada–United States salmon interception agreement. Although Canada's goal had been to ensure that its catch was at least equal to its own salmon production, even treaty supporters admitted there would be no real balance in interceptions in their lifetimes. Perhaps appropriately, Fraser accidentally signed on the American side of the treaty, which Brian Mulroney and Ronald Reagan had made a centrepiece of the Shamrock Summit. It was a sign of things to come. Fraser's decline in popularity soon became a collapse.

While Fraser dashed from coast to coast and crisis to crisis, senior bureaucrats remaining from the Liberal administration quickly implemented the majority of the Pearse report recommendations. Deputy minister Art May hastened to assure processors of his commitment to the Pearse report. "Common property is the root cause of the problems," he said. Regional director general Wayne Shinners added that elimination of the common property resource could take three to five years. Fishermen could be forgiven for thinking that election contests amounted to a game of "heads we win, tails you lose."

The comments by May and Shinners were in brazen defiance of Fraser's declared policy, but both knew that Fraser was a broken man. Less than a year after his appointment, he was swept away by the stink of a scandal involving the sale of rotten tuna. Erik Nielsen, the steely ideologue of Brian Mulroney's Conservative government, personally took control of the fisheries ministry. In the brief period he held office before turning the portfolio over to another British Columbia MP, Tom Siddon, he completely cancelled a proposal for the $212-million second phase of salmonid enhancement. Siddon took his cue, telling reporters just days after his installation that private ocean ranching would be an important way "of partially funding enhancement projects."

Siddon had strong prompting from his new deputy minister, dropped into his post on Christmas Eve to replace Art May. Peter Meyboom had no fisheries background, but he had served on the Treasury Board as a member of Nielsen's Task Force Review, a sweeping study of every area of government spending. Within weeks of his appointment, Meyboom began implementing the task force's recommendations, cutting $25 million and two hundred additional jobs from his own budget.

The twenty-one volumes of Nielsen's Task Force Review were tabled in the House of Commons on 11 March 1986. Nielsen's objective was to harmonize departmental actions with the keystone of Tory economic policy—free trade. At the same time, the review gave the bureaucracy new marching orders for the Conservative era, orders to cut spending and to shift government policy toward privatization and deregulation.

The man on Canada's side of the table at the free trade talks had direct knowledge of these issues because he was a member of the B.C. Packers board of directors. As a member of several George Weston Co. boards, Simon Reisman was one of Canada's political and economic elite, a devout partisan of free trade who had participated in plans for a Grand Canal to turn James Bay into a fresh-water lake which drained by pipeline into the United States.

Reisman's appointment was symptomatic of fundamental changes in economic theory in Canada's ruling circles in the late 1980s. Closer economic integration with the United States had become the single most important objective of national economic strategy. Everywhere in national life, government policy sought to put public resources at the disposal of corporate interest. Where once there had been Canadian-based corporations that sought national policies to meet their needs, there now were multinational corporations demanding unlimited access to Canadian markets and resources.

It was corporations like Alcan, the oil companies and CN that ultimately dictated fisheries policy, not canners or fishermen. Moreover, the increasing production of salmon from farms and hatcheries was reducing even the canners' interest in the future of wild stocks. If fish could be produced by private production, then why have any public expenditures for fisheries at all? The Nielsen Task Force and a 1986 review by federal auditor general Kenneth Dye demanded elimination of the common property fishery, not only because it was increasing the cost of fishing but because the very existence of the fisheries department was a heavy charge on the public purse.

Even before Nielsen's 147-page fisheries report became public, the industry was feeling the effects. Siddon cut fishing vessel insurance programs and raised licence charges, wharfage rates and many other fees to avoid American claims of unfair subsidies. The Nielsen report promised to go much further, with deep cuts in fisheries research, a 50 per cent reduction in quality inspection and cuts in a host of other areas. The main element of the program, however, was a major expansion of "enterprise allocations" and privatized fisheries combined with privatization of salmonid enhancement. Under the Nielsen plan, enhancement would be run by private contractors that would recover their costs by direct harvest of stocks.

Both processors and government had finally found a way they could perhaps rid themselves of fishermen and wild salmon altogether.

By 1983, word had crossed the Atlantic of a biological breakthrough in the hatching and rearing of salmon. In Norway, Atlantic salmon stocks had been privately controlled for centuries, but this had not halted their destruction by hydroelectric development, urbanization and, most of all, intensive high-seas gillnetting. In the early 1970s, however, Norway's salmon exports had begun to grow. By the end of the decade, fisheries experts were confidently predicting production of salmon would soon exceed 30,000 tonnes a year, equivalent to one-third of all B.C.'s average annual production. The secret was fish farming, the rearing of Atlantic salmon from egg to adult in sea pens anchored in Norway's deep and icy fjords.

The news sent a ripple of excitement through the Canadian government. The Science Council of Canada sponsored a major conference in New Brunswick in 1983 to test the waters. A press release set the tone for the discussion to come. "The days of common property fishing are over. Given the finite ability of the ocean to produce fish, especially in its polluted state, and the steadily rising costs of hunting the wild schools, as well as the urgent need to restructure our fishing industry, aquaculture [is] a compelling alternative."

For governments seeking a private sector solution to the twin problems of overcapitalization and pollution, aquaculture offered a perfect solution. The pollution could remain, the fishermen could be eliminated, and the fish could be produced by private owners by artificial means. The virtues of this approach were clear in Norway, where Norsk Hydro, the national electric utility, had financed the costly research and development which ultimately made A/S Mowi the dominant force in the Norwegian fish industry. Like Weyerhaeuser in Oregon, Norsk Hydro was capitalizing on the fishery crisis that its other resource activities had helped to create.

During 1983 and 1984, while fishermen and shoreworkers had been holding fundraisers to send the Fishermen's Survival Coalition to Ottawa, would-be fish farmers and their supporters had been working on a government-funded task force, sponsored by the Science Council of Canada. Their report was released at a gala dinner in Vancouver late in 1984. Ottawa had an obligation, the fish farmers said, "to allow the private sector to establish an integrated profitable industry as quickly as possible." They demanded government-funded research, legislation defining their property rights, low interest loans and reorientation of the Salmonid Enhancement Program "to encourage the development of new salmonid stocks suitable for farming and to integrate with the needs of private sector aquaculture." Among those applauding in the black-tie crowd were representatives of B.C. Packers, which had already committed itself to the new industry. There was little wonder why—the Norwegian industry was reaping millions of dollars of profits annually. Gross profits were estimated at 27 per cent of sales.

Within a week of the Science Council report, Ottawa announced it would participate in a $2.64-million aquaculture research facility at the Nanaimo Biological Station. The prostitution of the Salmonid Enhancement Program was well advanced. Nearing the end of the two-year transition phase ordered by Peter Pearse, the program was providing 10 per cent of the annual catch and returning $1.40 to the economy for every dollar spent. But the program required $20 million a year just to run the hardware built in Phase One. To achieve the long-awaited goal of doubled production would require $187 million over a five-year term in addition to the $100 million needed to run Phase One. But Ward Faulkner, the program's director, was unsure if it would be funded for anything above the basic level of $20 million.

Faulkner's political masters gave one order, however. To cut wages from his budget, he was directed to contract out the equivalent of twenty-four positions at a cost of $200,000 to $500,000 more than employing civil servants. Hundreds of thousands of dollars in other contracts were issued to private consultants, including Envirocon, the consulting firm acting for Alcan in its battle with the fisheries department over the Kemano completion project. Faulkner also was directed to give the fledgling fish-farming industry every possible assistance. Eggs surplus to public hatcheries were to be turned over free of charge or for token amounts. As a further assistance, private operators were contracted to rear 150,000 "Expo coho," which the department wanted to release in time for the 1986 world's fair in Vancouver. During the next four years, the Salmonid Enhancement Program was progressively reduced to a shell and finally integrated into the overall budget, where funds could be trimmed and work contracted out away from public scrutiny.

Ottawa's lust for salmon farming was matched by the provincial government in Victoria. As the Salmonid Enhancement Program withered and died, millions of dollars were poured by both provincial and federal governments into promoting this new high-tech dream. Norwegian farmers, hemmed in by tough restrictions designed to control both production levels and corporate concentration, were looking for new fields. B.C. entrepreneurs were keen to stake the necessary foreshore leases. It was a volatile combination of greed and government complicity that set off the most obscene fish grab since the rush for trap licences at the turn of the century. The farmers touted themselves as harbingers of a better future, in which environmentally friendly farms would produce jobs, exports and economic benefits coastwide while supporting and enhancing the commercial fishery. By selling in the off-season, the farmers said, they would sustain wild salmon prices and help existing processing plants to run year-round.

The UFAWU had taken note of the new industry and was wary of the consequences. The union's 1985 convention called for a moratorium on salmon-farming development until the government could guarantee that it would stay out of the hands of major corporations, would not require wild eggs for brood stock, would not delay a full second-phase Salmonid Enhancement Program and would not be used "as a trade-off or as a coverup for the loss of salmon habitat." But a Science Council of Canada policy statement issued the following month pointed to precisely the opposite direction, urging the production of farmed fish to supply markets while commercial fisheries were closed to "enhance" the runs. A federal-provincial agreement on aquaculture signed that month gave British Columbia virtual autonomy to run the new industry with Ottawa's blessing and financial assistance. The rush was officially on.

Within a year, the fisheries department had sold more than one million chinook eggs to would-be farmers. Millions of coho eggs were sold as well. Atlantic salmon eggs were imported from Scotland for rearing at a Rockefeller-controlled operation near Port Hardy. Although the imported eggs were subject to tough screening for disease, Canadian scientists responsible for import controls warned: "None of the benefits of transfer of young Atlantic salmon and salmon eggs into Canadian waters outweigh the threats to native stocks. There are unpredictable genetic risks associated with transferring European salmon stocks to North America." Although Canadian regulations were among the toughest in the world, "they are not infallible," the scientists said, "a fact which, along with the large number of potential pathogenic organisms that are not considered under the Canadian regulations, makes the likelihood of an unwanted pathogen or strain of pathogen entering the country with fish from a certified (disease-free) source a very real possibility." Senior provincial officials, dissenting from the official line, likened the policy to "playing Russian roulette with wild stocks" and raised doubts about the advisability of moving even B.C. stocks from place to place to meet farmers' requirements.

Notwithstanding such clear warnings, the federal government authorized substantial transfers of Atlantic eggs to Canada. Foreshore leases were issued like confetti. On 14 July 1985, Sunshine Coast resident Mac Richardson looked out his window to see tugs pulling a fish farm into place in front of his waterfront property. By going straight to Victoria, the farm's owners had circumvented local authorities and obtained provincial permits within twenty-four hours. Scantech, a firm with Norwegian ties, operated for weeks without federal licences, but suffered no penalty. What the farmers wanted, the farmers got. Foreshore lease applications were issued for existing anchorages, fishing areas, log-booming grounds and even navigational channels. The provincial strategy amounted to a pre-emptive strike against public foreshore, which until then had been held in common by coastal communities. Community protests were ignored. Provincial lands branch spokesman Tom Cockburn told Sechelt residents "the aquaculture industry will be industry-driven. They will tell us where they wish to go rather than us tell them where they should or should not go."

Public outrage grew almost as quickly as the industry. Sport fishermen in Campbell River condemned both federal and provincial governments for "biological insanity" for importing Atlantic salmon eggs, which could carry unknown diseases into Pacific waters. Yet, these fish would be reared in pens adjacent to the province's largest salmon runs. Exotic diseases and genetic alteration of wild stocks resulting from intermingling with hatchery fish could damage or wipe out wild runs. Sunshine Coast residents attending a special seminar on fish farming early in 1986 learned that the average 2-hectare farm produced sewage equal to a town of 4,000. Sea life under the pens often was eradicated by the deposit of hundreds of tonnes of fish feces. The use of antibiotics in fish feed was linked to the production of new strains of bacteria in the food chain which could cause human illnesses ranging from gastroenteritis to cholera. These concerns, some of which had been cited by Peter Pearse as compelling reasons for reconsidering the public hatchery program, were brushed aside by proponents of the fish-farming industry. Provincial authorities refused to consider environmental studies, saying their job was to put aquaculture on a firm footing.

By May 1986, applications for foreshore leases were being gazetted by the provincial government at the rate of two a day. A UFAWU investigation revealed that the industry had grown from 10 farms in 1984 to 40 in mid-1986, with 113 approved sites and 155 more sites pending approval. Two years later, 700 leases and permits had been approved or were pending. Private hatcheries were springing up throughout the Sunshine Coast to feed the growing demand for young fish. Provincial fisheries officials continued to sneer at environmental concerns. Federal fisheries officials were equally cavalier about the minimum distances required between salmon farms and wild salmon streams.

As the B.C. boom continued, troubling news emerged from Norway, which had been touted as the scene of aquacultural economic miracles. The government there was imposing "farm-free zones" around salmon streams to control disease transfer as well as genetic mixing of farmed and wild fish. Norway had also frozen the issuance of licences and confirmed its limit on the size of farms. B.C., by contrast, allowed farms of unlimited size.

The growing conflicts came to a boil in October 1986, when union fishermen were shocked by proposals to install farms right on key salmon-fishing grounds in the Strait of Georgia. The lease applications were a direct violation of fisheries department pledges to prohibit farms in fishing areas. Angry seiners and gillnetters called a news conference to demand an immediate moratorium on further farms. To the surprise of both union fishermen and fish farmers, newly elected Premier Bill Vander Zalm granted the moratorium on 31 October.

Farmers decried Vander Zalm's actions as "sheer lunacy" and claimed to have lost millions of dollars in investment because of his action. But private meetings with Brian Gillespie, the Kamloops lawyer appointed by Vander Zalm to review the industry, soon put their minds at ease. Gillespie rushed through his work in only six weeks, but his hearings were jammed with members of the public who demanded tighter government controls of the new industry. Their fears were heightened by the news that farmed fish sold in Seattle had contained traces of toxic antifouling paint used on fish-farm nets, a fact that Canadian authorities were unable to confirm because they had no inspection facilities for the farm sector. Once again, as intervenors before the Gillespie inquiry made clear, public opinion overwhelmingly favoured natural salmon production and opposed privatization of the resource. Fishermen from every sector of the industry—native and non-native, union and nonunion—demanded a return to habitat protection and salmonid enhancement.

The UFAWU brief spoke for most intervenors, who favoured a continued moratorium, when it warned that "the salmon farming industry in B.C. is in imminent danger of widespread failure from an economic, environmental and social point of view." The union demanded an end to the import of exotic species like Atlantic salmon, tight zoning regulations for foreshore development, strict environmental baseline studies, controls on farmed salmon production, and "a policy commitment to the preservation and enhancement of the wild stock fishery prior to the development of salmon farming." The B.C. Salmon Farmers Association dismissed these concerns as "99.5 per cent silly," but events were to bear out the union's forecast to the letter.

Before the year was out, Gillespie recommended an end to the moratorium. He urged Victoria to grant two hundred licences that had been caught in the freeze and then to implement tighter restrictions on new applicants, a move that ensured most of the industry could proceed without regulation. Victoria approved the two hundred permits in the subsequent week, tripling the size of the industry in the process. The moratorium on new licences was lifted within six months, after the briefest of environmental baseline studies. Gillespie whitewashed the environmental issues involved in salmon farming, claiming that genetic problems were "not likely to occur," that farms had "little impact on water quality" and that "there was no scientific evidence to show any harmful effect" from the use of toxicants and drugs in farm operations.

The defenders of B.C.'s wild salmon were in an extraordinary position. Although the province's natural salmon stocks were an irreplaceable natural resource supporting commercial, sport and native fisheries worth at least $1 billion a year, government agencies insisted that the public must prove actual harm by salmon farming before they would consider action. All the profit of salmon-farming production was private, all the risk of environmental disaster was the public's. Heartened by the end of the moratorium, the salmon farmers stepped up their offensive against the wild stock supporters, charging that the greatest risk of disease originated in wild fish, not farmed.

But cracks were appearing in the fish farmers' public relations offensive. Residents of the Sunshine Coast found tonnes of dead salmon dumped in their landfills, victims of unexpected algae blooms, disease outbreaks and mismanagement. Countless more tonnes were undoubtedly dumped at sea. And crab, prawn and shrimp fishermen in the mainland inlets east of Johnstone Strait found that farms had actually been anchored on top of their traps when they returned for their fishing gear.

A federal review of the industry predicted a prolonged economic crisis for many farmers as they wrestled with salmon genetics, disease problems and unsuitable sites. Disease was of particular concern because the initial supplies of eggs all came from government hatcheries. Some diseases present in wild fish posed little threat under natural conditions but could break out with devastating consequences in the close quarters of a pen, where antibiotic treatment could quickly produce resistant strains. These new variants could in turn ravage passing wild stocks. Shortages of herring meal, with which to feed farmed salmon, were forcing costly imports of fishmeal from as afar away as Chile. The farmers were proving more adept at raising their share prices on the Vancouver Stock Exchange than at raising salmon; their survival rates were equal. to or less than those of public hatcheries which released their fish to the wild, but the lure of profit was so great that 40 per cent of the industry was foreign-owned. Canadian processors were taking control of much of the rest. B.C. Packers, National Sea Products, Canada Packers, J. S. McMillan Fisheries and the Prince Rupert Co-op all invested in the new industry. The ever-shrewd B.C. Packers, however, declined to take much risk, arranging long-term marketing arrangements rather than taking direct ownership of large operations. Despite a host of problems, farmed salmon production in B.C. began to climb, rising from a few hundreds tonnes a year in the early 1980s to about 6,000 tonnes in 1988, far short of the farmers' projections but enough to de-stabilize fresh fish markets for chinook and coho, the farmers' species of choice.

The chief subsidy Ottawa and Victoria offered the aquaculture industry was lack of regulation. When a fish farm employee charged in 1988 that his em-ployer had dumped 100 tonnes of diseased salmon into the sea and sold several hundred tonnes more for human consumption without purging it of antibiot-ics, federal officials said simply that there were no rules against such behav-iour. They downplayed a steady stream of reports that Norway was wrestling with outbreaks of deadly parasites and disease in its wild stocks, claiming that Canada's fish health regulations were the strongest in the world. They dis-missed fears about the genetic diversity of B.C.'s natural salmon stocks, but fi-nanced the capture of chinook brood stock from nine B.C. streams to create a gene pool from which farmers could produce a superior farmed chinook.

This bubble of misinformation was punctured in April 1988, when UFAWU locals and the Pacific Trollers' Association sent six fishermen, spon-sored by the T. Buck Suzuki Foundation, on a fact-finding tour of Norway. Officials of Norway's Directorate for Nature Management briefed the Canadi-ans on the crises of disease, parasites and genetic intermingling that were shaking the Norwegian industry and threatening the extinction of the coun-try's remaining natural salmon stocks. The Canadians learned of a parasite, spread by farming activity, which had afflicted fish in twenty-eight rivers, re-sulting in the total loss of some wild stocks and cutting 300 tonnes a year from the country's meagre 1,600-tonne harvest of wild fish. They heard of disease outbreaks caused by the importation of foreign smolts, compelling the de-struction of tens of thousands of tonnes of farmed fish. They were told about Norway's salmon sperm bank, a desperate effort to retain the diversified genet-ic material of its many small rivers, threatened by the intermingling of es-caped farmed fish with beleaguered wild stocks. This intermingling of hybrid farmed fish with the many distinctive wild stocks was the most pernicious threat of all. "The loss of locally adopted traits (or characteristics) can eventu-ally exterminate the wild salmon as we know it today," Norwegian biologist Dagfinn Gausen told the Canadians.

Norwegian regulations, already incomparably tougher than Canadian laws, were being tightened. The Suzuki Foundation trip demonstrated that provin-cial and federal assurances about the minimal environmental impact of salmon farming were lies. A B.C. government brochure stated that "environmental damage from fish farms was not a concern," but the Norwegians found that sea life under pens was destroyed. Victoria claimed that "there is no evidence to indicate disease is ever transferred from farmed fish to wild stock," despite Norway's twenty-year battle to control a serious disease transferred to the wild from a trout hatchery. Victoria also denied knowledge of Norway's enormous losses in the battle against a parasite transplanted from Sweden by hatchery-reared fish, which required entire rivers to be poisoned with pesticide to eliminate infected fish. The B.C. government's claim that "escaped farmed fish would rarely interbreed with wild stocks, if at all," was directly contradicted by common sense and by Norwegian studies, which found more than 50 per cent of some river's spawners were of farm origin.

Union fisherman Wayne Patterson said on his return to Canada that he now was convinced that without very tough regulations to control salmon farming, "our wild salmon stocks may one day be annihilated." The other fishermen agreed that a massive disease outbreak in B.C. was simply a matter of time. "Disease, parasites and genetic pollution could weaken our wild stocks and ultimately destroy them entirely," said troller Dan Clark. "If such a disaster were to occur on the Skeena or Fraser systems, the results would be devastating environmentally, commercially, recreationally and culturally for the people of B.C."

The delegation's report on the Norway experience, published in a special edition of *The Fisherman,* provoked a violent and hysterical outburst from B.C. salmon farmers and the provincial government. Leading the counterattack was Patrick Moore, former leader of Greenpeace, now president of the B.C. Salmon Farmers Association and operator of a fish farm on Quatsino Inlet. Concerns about loss of genetic diversity were reminiscent of "Hitler race purity theories," Moore said. He and Tom May, whose Royal Pacific Sea Farms was the industry's largest operator, denounced the Suzuki report as "phoney charges, lies and fabrications." The water in his fish pen was "cleaner and safer to swim in than water coming out of the Fraser River," Moore claimed, asking "how can people get worried about fish pooping in the ocean? They've been doing it for thousands of years." May declared that "if what the UFAWU alleges is true, we should not be in business."

Late in 1989, May was out of business. The man who had been hailed as B.C. entrepreneur of the year dropped out of sight as Royal Pacific Sea Farms collapsed in ruins along with a score of other fish farms laid low by disease, algae blooms, crashing prices and poor management. Losses to bacterial kidney disease ran between 20 and 60 per cent on many farms in 1988, but farmers were unsure how much antibiotic to use or even whether antibiotics were effective. In almost every case, the drugs used were also used to treat human illness, ensuring that drug-resistant bacteria would develop in the human food chain.

Grasping for new markets and frantic to dump their production, fish farmers swamped wild salmon markets and depressed prices for wild stock catches to ten-year lows, sowing bankruptcy in troll fisheries from California to Alaska.

In response to continuous public protest, both federal and provincial governments made moves to tighten their regulations. Although Ottawa had officially given Victoria exclusive powers to manage the industry, both levels of government now reversed their earlier view and agreed that protection of wild stocks was essential. No money was provided, however, for enforcement or inspection. Federal disease regulations required farmers to report outbreaks on their own, warning that they stood to lose their permits if found guilty of poor management.

An internal fisheries memorandum early in 1989 documented gross and repeated violations of fish farm regulations. The memo was from federal fisheries biologist Rob Russell, who advised his superiors that all of the concerns raised by the UFAWU's tour to Norway were valid. He documented illegal dumping of dead and diseased fish in the sea, in pits on land and even directly into salmon streams. Such cases obscured an equally serious problem—the sale of diseased fish for human consumption. Union shoreworkers reported they were required to handle diseased fish on a regular basis, sometimes of such poor quality that they were nauseated. Government officials conceded that they had received frequent reports of fish dead of disease being recovered from pens and sold for human consumption. This practice was frowned upon, but the first quality assurance program for farmed fish was not introduced until 1989, and then only on a voluntary basis. Farmers were also on the honour system to ensure fish had undergone appropriate withdrawal from antibiotics, a system the provincial government said allowed "the market [to] enforce a lot of this." In effect, the province was counting on consumers to detect antibiotic residues on their own and punish wayward farmers by refusing to buy their fish.

Russell's memorandum cast a hard light on the honour system as practised on B.C. fish farms. He reported a private hatchery working on a Department of Fisheries and Oceans (DFO) contract which had not installed mandatory effluent controls on pipes dumping into salmon-bearing waters. He warned that existing controls on the movement of eggs and fish were being circumvented and that "transfer compliance is almost impossible to check." He reported an instance in which a helicopter pilot dropped fish into the wrong farm. He warned of the department's inability to control broodstock, stating that it was unable to determine if broodstock was "hatchery, netpen, commercial seine or illegally obtained fish" poached off spawning beds. He recorded apparently deliberate releases of fish to the ocean: "farmed fish have essentially been ocean ranched." Farmers routinely ignored regulations requiring them to report losses from pens. And he reported repeated cases of migrating juvenile herring and salmon passing through farms. Substantial numbers of the juveniles were eaten, Russell said, and "farm staff are concerned that disease transfer is occurring to farm fish. That transfer will occur in the opposite direction is a very real possibility and is of concern to DFO." Most of Russell's information had been supplied by farm fish employees. Almost no provincial or federal enforcement was in place. Since 1988, catches of farmed coho have been commonplace in B.C.'s commercial fisheries and farmed Atlantic salmon have been found on the west coast of Vancouver Island, in the Strait of Georgia and in the intertidal zone of the Fraser River.

Although federal officials hastened to belittle the Russell memorandum as exaggerated and outdated, their denials had little credibility. Late in 1988, biologists in Washington State and British Columbia were alarmed by an outbreak of viral hermorrhagic septicemia, or VHS, in two Washington State hatcheries. This disease, which killed fish with a progressive viral infection that led to internal bleeding, had never before been detected in the Pacific, although it was common in Atlantic salmon. No link to the Atlantic salmon on Puget Sound farms could be detected, but Campbell River sport fisherman and conservationist Rob Bell-Irving recalled government pledges that no new disease could pass through their screening system. "Perhaps the most alarming situation of all is the fact that we really didn't know the source of the disease as soon as it occurred," Bell-Irving wrote. "Somewhere out there, a disease capable of inflicting great disaster on native wild salmon stocks is brewing and growing. Its creators are reluctant to spill the beans, no matter what the cost. That is the real danger."

The outbreak of VHS was just the first in a series of disturbing incidents. The same year, the fisheries department added marine anemia, which killed fish with a general invasion of proliferating, cancerous blood cells, to the list of diseases devastating Sunshine Coast salmon farms. In 1989, scientists isolated infectious pancreatic necrosis in two Atlantic salmon harvested on B.C. farms, the first such occurrences in the province. The discovery was made by U.S. authorities screening fish before import to the United States.

The economic collapse of many salmon farm companies in 1989 and 1990 did not reduce the number of functioning farms. In an echo of Richard Nelson's boast to the B.C. Packers' shareholders meeting of nine years before, Weston's Earl Pearce told his investors in Toronto in 1989 that the 15 to 20 per cent decline in farmed salmon prices combined with skyrocketing production would wipe out many firms, leaving Weston "particularly well-positioned to expand in this new phase." The federal and provincial governments celebrated this marriage of wild stock and farmed interests with a $500,000 study of the impact of farmed salmon on wild fish, an impact they had been insisting for the past six years did not exist. The consequences of fish farm pollution, genetic mixing, antibiotic use and predation of juvenile salmon and herring were to go under the microscope after 150 farms and 45 private hatcheries had been approved and built. Soon after, fisheries minister Tom Siddon approved the experimental farming of sockeye.

Early on the morning of 3 August 1989, flying pickets dispatched from UFAWU strike headquarters in Vancouver flagged down three loaded tractor-trailer truck units as they approached the Canada-U.S. border at the Douglas crossing south of Vancouver. A tell-tale trail of bloody ice water from the back of the rigs told the pickets they had found what they expected—tens of thousands of kilograms of Canadian salmon, caught by strikebreakers, headed for processing plants south of the line.

As television cameras watched, a fisherman pulled open the back of a truck to reveal a dozen Nelson Bros. totes loaded with Canadian sockeye. The crowd fell momentarily silent as he held a dripping fish, destined for a nonunion cannery in Anacortes, Washington, high above his head. The message to the strikers and their supporters was clear—from now on, Weston intended to operate by its own rules, where and as it pleased.

The seventeen-day strike of 1989 was one of the most hard-fought in the industry's history. B.C. Packers, under the free trade agreement negotiated by its now-famous board member Simon Reisman, exploited the elimination of Canada's export controls on raw fish in an effort to smash the union's base in the processing sector. The processors had demanded concessions in the shore agreement that would have rolled conditions back more than twenty years. Smaller operators caught in the conflict could only watch and whine as B.C. Packers used its debt leverage over seine vessel owners to force the largest scab fishery in the industry's history. Fishermen had already been pummelled by some of the sharpest price cuts in the past decade, forced in most cases by the long-predicted overproduction of farmed salmon. Many needed little reminding that a lost week of sockeye fishing could spell their ruin.

Union members were used to battles with scabs, the processors, the courts and the government. They were unprepared, perhaps, for the ferocious onslaught of a multinational corporation determined to reap the profits of global integration. When it was clear that the strike was stalemated and threatened the loss of the season, outstanding issues were referred to an industrial inquiry commission. Union members could take pride in having survived with their organization intact, but it was clear the industry had been changed forever.

The 1989 strike was a direct result of the Conservative government's surrender of export regulations that were the last obstacle to the creation of an integrated Pacific salmon industry. The regulations, more than eighty years old, had been introduced originally to assure canners that Fraser gillnetters would be compelled to deliver on the river, not to American competitors across the line. They had been part of the industry's array of legal weapons to control the salmon harvest. The UFAWU and the Fisheries Council of B.C. (formerly the Fisheries Association) had fought side by side to avert the loss of the regulations, which both agreed would result in the elimination of thousands of shoreworkers' jobs and ultimately threaten the resource itself. There would be little purpose in habitat protection and salmonid enhancement, UFAWU president Jack Nichol pointed out, if the benefits flowed to corporations in a different country. "Why would we produce salmon in B.C. at your expense and mine in order for an American processor to benefit?" asked Mike Hunter, president of the Fisheries Council.

Until the very eve of the strike, companies and union lobbied and campaigned together to save the regulations, conducting trips to Ottawa, Victoria and a score of community councils. The confrontation at the Douglas border crossing proved once and for all that Weston, at least, could not care less whether or not Canada processed salmon.

The elimination of the Canadian border as a factor in salmon processing was simply the last step in a long series of moves to integrate and subordinate the fishing industry to the requirements of the continental economy. The integration of salmon management, which guaranteed the U.S. a share in Fraser salmon and a voice in its management, had been confirmed with the interception agreement signed by John Fraser in 1984. The integration of the corporate sector had been established by Weston's investments in canneries in Alaska and Washington State. These purchases, which gave it an assured supply of farmed and wild salmon from every major salmon-producing area, were largely concluded by 1988. The only major remaining obstacle to the full play of market forces in the fishing industry was the UFAWU, which not only negotiated the fish price and shore plant agreements on the Pacific seaboard but also had delayed implementation of privatized fish rights for more than twenty years.

Heartened by the union's heavy losses in the summer of 1989, the fisheries department embarked on what it hoped would be its final campaign to privatize Canada's Pacific salmon. A long-range planning document called "Vision 2000," which was leaked to fishermen late that year, looked ahead to a new century in which "the commercial fisheries will no longer be driven by the race for fish, they will be based on a harvesting regime which emphasizes the cost effectiveness of the total fleet, the quality of the landed product and management need to accommodate resource conservation." This new fleet, produced by a strategy of "property rights concepts for all fisheries" would see fishing costs halved as a reduced seine fleet worked like a complex floating trap in "terminal fishing areas." Thanks to royalties, gear licensing and quota fisheries, "the costs of Pacific fisheries management will have declined to 70 per cent of the level of the mid-1980s and will be totally recovered from the industry in increased fees and royalties and other user-pay and devolution arrangements by the year 2010." There is no priority on wild salmon, coastal communities or jobs in this twenty-first century version of an economic perpetual-motion machine. By the end of 1989, programs were under way to add the halibut, crab, prawn, shrimp and black cod fisheries to the geoducks and abalone on the list of resources turned over to private quota holders.

The obsession with the sale of our wild stocks has been matched by a deep concern for the welfare of corporate polluters. Fisheries minister Tom Siddon behaved with particular infamy in September 1987 when he concluded an agreement with Alcan to resolve the long-standing dispute over Alcan's water licence. In return for its agreement not to draw water from the Nanika and Kidprice systems, which are tributary to the Skeena, this immensely profitable corporation was granted the right to reduce flows to the Nechako by a further 42 per cent and to complete the entire project without environmental review. Alcan also finally agreed to install the cold water release system to the Nechako that had been demanded by the International Pacific Salmon Fisheries Commission back in 1950. It was a trivial, laughable concession for Alcan, which expected to increase its generating capacity at Kemano to 1,100 megawatts from 785 megawatts, the equivalent of another Site C dam.

It was fitting that Siddon was joined at the news conference to announce the deal by provincial energy minister Jack Davis, who hailed the agreement as a "win, win, win situation for everyone." Holding high a copy of "Our Common Future," the report of the United Nations Committee on the Environment, Siddon declared his pact with Alcan a model of sustainable development and intoned that "history will remember the wisdom of this moment." Siddon's wisdom included a decision to approve a deal with minimum water flows far below those recommended by his department, which in turn were roundly condemned as grossly inadequate by a province-wide coalition opposed to Alcan's plans. In the process, Siddon surrendered his right as a minister of the crown to control the flow of waters over dams on fish-bearing streams. A coalition of groups from around the province, including the UFAWU, later undertook legal action to force the minister to resume his responsibilities. Late in 1990, the federal cabinet passed an Order in Council which retroactively exempted the Alcan project from the threat of a court-ordered federal environmental assessment. In 1991, Alcan was forced to halt the project after a court ordered an environmental review.

Proof that Siddon's action was not an isolated incident came in December 1989, in the wake of coastwide fisheries closures necessitated by the release of dioxin and other toxic organochlorines from pulp mills. In every case, the mills had been dumping effluent far in excess of levels authorized by their permits. In a lengthy memorandum leaked to a Vancouver newspaper, fisheries habitat management head Otto Langer warned his superiors that "should the public discover how we are determining who should or should not be charged [it] would amount to a near scandal." Langer added: "We have determined that DFO-friendly corporations or parties with provincial permits (as well as the B.C. agency issuing the permit allowed the defence) will enjoy relative immunity from the Fisheries Act. . . . A continuation of this philosophy will result in a wholesale loss of fish habitat and a continued degradation of water quality."

In the same week that the memo was leaked, Siddon declined to prosecute either the pulp mills which were in violation of their effluent permits or the parties responsible for the accidental dumping of toxic chemicals into the Fraser at the height of the Horsefly sockeye run of that summer.

WHERE RIVERS RUN FREE

THE PROSPECTS FOR WILD SALMON SEEM DESPERATE EVEN IN their most remote and secure sanctuaries. The perils are most obvious in the huge Owikeno watershed that sustains the Rivers Inlet sockeye run. Here, the commercial fishery has taken place for more than a century, harvesting sockeye produced from spawning streams untouched by any other human activity. Located nearly at the geographic mid-point of the B.C. coast, Rivers Inlet stretches from Queen Charlotte Sound like a broad highway into the mountains of the Coast Range, running almost due north for 30 kilometres before it turns east. Two arms branch north and west, but the main inlet ends abruptly at a narrow shelf between two steep mountains split by the Wannock River. The Wannock is the sole outlet of Owikeno Lake, a 48-kilometre mountain fastness of fresh water fed by more than twenty creeks and rivers. Of these tributaries, ten are sockeye producers, each contributing a distinctive race to the run. The Wannock itself contributes a substantial number of additional sockeye, chinook and chum.

The fabled and mysterious rivers of the Owikeno are an important symbol to the industry of its history and wealth. For a century, Rivers Inlet has been synonymous with the sockeye fishery, its dozen canneries brought to life by the six-week-long rush of salmon to the mouth of Wannock where they awaited some unknown signal to enter the lake. Apart from timber taken in a few small logging shows near the mouth of the inlet, the only trees cut in the Rivers Inlet system were used to build canneries. The magnificent stands in the Owikeno stood untouched, too remote and too costly to be worth the cutting. For generations the valley simply produced fish, with an annual total run averaging one million, of which up to 80 per cent was harvested and canned. It seemed that the Owikeno, if left to care for itself, would run like this forever.

Early in the 1960s, however, small independent loggers penetrated into the Owikeno to harvest lakeside stands of timber. Two operations on the Genesee were small by current standards, but their impact on the salmon was immediate. The only way to get logs to tidewater was via the Wannock, and season after season the forest companies drove their booms down its shallow waters, devastating the river bottom. The fisheries department repeatedly ignored fishing industry protests and approved the drives, which were an annual event from 1963 to 1967. The 1966 drive occurred at the height of the sockeye migration, despite the construction of a haul-road, built by the provincial forest service at taxpayers' expense, to transport logs to tidewater by truck. The logging companies, unwilling to bear the extra handling costs, simply insisted on a log drive and the fisheries department complied.

Industry anger turned to alarm, however, when Crown Zellerbach announced its application in 1967 to convert 8,000 hectares of its leases in the Rivers Inlet Sustained Yield Unit into a Tree Farm Licence, giving it exclusive long-term cutting rights to the Owikeno. Not only did Crown Zellerbach propose to triple the cut in Owikeno alone to about 350,000 cubic metres a year, it intended to use the entire amount for pulp production because it had a surplus of sawlogs.

Ultimately, however, the Owikeno was saved. The Social Credit government rejected the Crown Zellerbach application, partly because of the protests of small logging companies fearful of being locked out of the Owikeno treasure house, but also because of the strong appeal advanced by the UFAWU to treat Owikeno as a salmon reserve.

The gillnetters of Rivers Inlet could take small comfort from the decision because their failure to secure a salmon sanctuary meant the issue was sure to return. In 1979 it did, as B.C. Forest Products moved a major camp onto the flats between the mouths of the Machmell and the Genesee and installed a log dump and a landing strip. Within a six-year period, six of the Owikeno's ten salmon streams were opened to logging.

But just as logging gathered steam in the Owikeno, fishing stopped. Instead of a catch of 500,000 to 800,000 and an escapement of 300,000 to 500,000, fishermen were finding a total run of only 500,000 fish in the 1960s and 1970s. Why? Since the Owikeno's waters were pristine, reasoned the fisheries department, there could be only one answer—overfishing. In 1979, fisheries managers decided to make Rivers Inlet the test case for their conviction that the cheapest and surest form of enhancement was greater escapement. Therefore, in 1980, Rivers Inlet was closed completely to commercial fishing for the first time since 1882 and was kept closed for four years. Fisheries biologists then sat back and waited for a bonanza that never came.

After a disappointing start, the escapements did increase, rising to an estimated 800,000 in 1982. Once fishing resumed in 1984, managers solemnly vowed to continue their drive for the magic one million spawners, confident that the huge runs they had produced would give them that number with ease. For four straight years, however, Owikeno sockeye disregarded theory and returned at precisely the levels achieved before they had been "enhanced." It was not until 1989 that fisheries department biologists conceded defeat and returned the harvest rate to the traditional level. In the meantime, logging companies had begun to change the Owikeno forever.

The Mid-Coast Timber Supply Area, of which the Owikeno is only a fraction, produces only about six per cent of the coast's wood supply annually, but as the remaining south coast stands of old growth are consumed, it is assuming much greater importance. The Owikeno contains an estimated 14.3 million cubic metres of merchantable timber, which will take forty to seventy years to clear out. The trees being cut are a minimum of 250 years old; those replacing them will need at least 80 to 120 years before they, too, are ready for harvest. Who weighs the value of old-growth forests against the risks to a sockeye run over such a term? Some would like to, but, of course, no one does.

The basic decisions about how and where to log are made first around conference tables and then on the site itself. It is not a question of whether or not there will be logging. That has already been decided. All that is left to discuss is where, how and how fast. Fisheries habitat officers must be guided by the government's policy of no net loss as well as the Coastal Fisheries Forestry Guideline, a handbook of good logging practices produced by the forest industry and a federal-provincial working group in the wake of several conflicts like the Riley Creek confrontation on the Queen Charlotte Islands. For the first five years of heavy logging, the sockeye should notice no difference. After that, no one can say. The consequences, whatever they may be, may not occur until everyone involved in the current decisions is dead. Even then, we know so little about the biology of the sockeye that it is doubtful anyone could state with certainty what had occurred.

It is a telling comment on the federal government's research priorities that after a century of commercial fishing on Owikeno stocks, Canada's top fisheries biologists cannot say how much those runs have declined or why. One who has tried to find out is Kim Hyatt, a sockeye specialist at the Pacific Biological Station in Nanaimo, who explained that the sockeye system can be imagined as a closed loop of linked compartments. One compartment is the river system, where fisheries officers on foot, in helicopters and with small seine nets, make an autumn estimate of the number of spawners. The second compartment is the lake, where Owikeno sockeye fry spend a year preparing for the run to the sea. No estimate is made of the number of fish that reach this stage.

The final compartment is the marine environment. Although salmon spend half their lives at sea, we know little of where they go or how they fare.

"To sort out the causes of a decline," said Hyatt, "you have to able to track each compartment, to say what went into each one and what came out. In the rivers, we know what goes in, but not what comes out. In the lake, we have no idea what goes in or what comes out. In the ocean, we don't anything about what goes in, but we know something about what comes out. We have to guess what's taking place, but guesses are not likely to be very accurate, and understanding the interactions between these compartments could take a long time."

Although scientists may know more about the sockeye than any other species of salmon—research on its life history began in the 1930s—no serious efforts to manage the runs was undertaken until the salmon commission tackled the Fraser and the federal Fisheries Research Board undertook management of the Skeena in the late 1940s. Smaller runs, like those in Barkley Sound, received serious attention only in the 1970s. Management of B.C.'s hundreds of stocks of chinook, coho, pinks, chums and steelhead is in its infancy, guided by the general rule that the least amount of fishing which can be politically sustained is the best course to follow.

"Fish are remarkable, miraculous things," said Hyatt. "They do things the greatest computer can't do. Think of the precision of their timing, their fidelity to a spawning location. Are they very choosy about a spawning location or do they pick fairly randomly?" Hyatt has puzzled over a run that will spawn in one 100-metre stretch of gravel but ignore the next 100 metres of apparently identical stream. "The mechanisms that drive fish production are subtle and interactive," he said. "You don't have a two-step causal relationship, where one thing leads to another. You won't find a smoking gun."

The Owikeno and its neighbouring system on Smith Inlet may offer the last large-scale opportunities to preserve the wild salmon's complex and breathtaking life history in a nearly undisturbed environment. In Owikeno, two parallel sets of economic calculations are at work. One claims to weigh the ethical and economic risks of cutting old-growth forest and establishes an annual quota of wood to be consumed. The other claims to protect the fisheries resource and is directed by policy makers who agree that the economic activities supported by fish are running at a loss. They also agree that the protection of fisheries resources must not be carried to the point that logging becomes unprofitable. They refuse to provide the long-term research funding essential to monitoring the survival of the runs. Clearly, these attitudes pose a more deadly threat to salmon than a century of commercial fishing.

Bill Dwyer of Canadian Pacific Forest Products has spent twenty years in the region, many of them logging the Kilbella and Chuckwalla, where he found fish running far upstream from the point at which fisheries officers thought spawning ended. Because there are fish there today, because second-growth timber at the mouth of that watershed is ready for harvest and because he is being much more careful than his predecessors, Dwyer is "absolutely convinced" that trees and fish will flourish in the Owikeno long after he is gone. He may be right. In the meantime, however, these ancient valleys will undergo massive and irrevocable changes. The old-growth forest, whose own internal mechanisms we barely comprehend, will be logged. The salmon, whose complex cycles remain a mystery, will find themselves in an ecosystem fundamentally different from the one to which they seem so perfectly adapted.

Taken separately, the means by which forests and fish are managed each seem shortsighted and even criminal. That both processes occur separately, even though the resources are part of the same watershed ecosystem, must be considered pure folly. In the absence of a salmon sanctuary against which we can measure the survival of wild stocks, scientists of the future will be unable to say what is happening or why. We will simply have to tell our children that we did the math and it seemed like the best deal we could get at the time.

Where salmon streams are clean and rivers run free, the salmon have run back season after season in triumphant defiance of economic theory, political corruption and the tragedy of the commons. As the industry staggered to the end of the 1989 strike, the waters around Vancouver Island came alive with more than 17 million Horsefly River sockeye, the resurgent descendants of the victims of the 1913 Hell's Gate blockade returning in greater numbers than in any year since that catastrophic summer so long ago. In 1941 the Horsefly had received only 1,000 spawners. In 1989 the commercial fishery took almost 7 million fish, still allowing 1.2 million spawners to return to the Horsefly. The Adams River run the following year was even more bountiful, pouring 12 million fish into the industry and almost 3 million into the 21 miracle kilometres of spawning gravel near Salmon Arm.

When the Suzuki Foundation assembled native groups, fishermen, environmentalists and fisheries specialists to consider the future of wild salmon in December 1988, all agreed with Peter Larkin that production could double to 136 million kilograms a year, back to the fabled nineteenth-century run of 30 million sockeye, if the fresh-water environment could be defended from urbanization, dams, pollution and acid rain. Thanks to existing enhancement projects, which now have assumed such importance that they affect and support more than one-third of the coast's production, wild salmon is poised to return to the abundance that once seemed limitless.

Canada's Pacific salmon and the people it sustains now stand at a turning point in their mutual history. In one direction lies the prospect of continued assaults on fishing capacity in a futile contest to outstrip the consequences of habitat degradation and pollution. Corporate interests intent on selling salmon in world markets will continue their drive to farm wild salmon in the marine equivalent of feedlots. The fish in these lots will be fed by the costly and absurd production of fishmeal from the ocean resources of distant countries whose peoples are starving. Salmon farm technicians will employ an arsenal of drugs, hormones and genetic engineering to create fish able to withstand the stresses and rigours of two to three years in a pen. These fish will pollute the sea floor. Many will contract virulent diseases. Some inevitably will escape, with potentially disastrous consequences for the natural stocks.

The natural stocks that survive will be auctioned to the highest bidders, perhaps sold to tourist operators marketing nostalgic fishing expeditions for the rich trophy hunters of the twenty-first century. If B.C.'s privatized geoduck and abalone fisheries are any guide, commercial fishing rights will soon pass into the hands of a few coupon clippers, who will lease the right to harvest the resource to fishers little better than sharecroppers. The best and most valuable fish will be caught and the smaller ones destroyed as the fishers strive to be "economically efficient." Soon the runs will disappear. Late in 1990 the fisheries department announced it was proceeding with individual transferable quotas for the halibut and black cod fisheries. The same day, it announced that the abalone fishery, the first to be privatized in 1984, was closing for five years to allow stocks to rebuild.

The economists who wrote the policy calling for the privatizaton of our fisheries have stated that "common property is repugnant to the principles of a market economy." Until fisheries resources are brought into the system of private property rights, they say, their future is in doubt. But common property is not the absence of rights, as some economists have suggested. It is the existence of a collective right of all the people, a right and a responsibility for stewardship that each participant in a given community holds and may enforce. It is this collective responsibility which has moved native people, commercial fishers and the general public to cry out time and again for controls on unrestricted fishing, for laws against pollution and for limits on the extraction of wealth from renewable resources. The elimination of the commons creates a single private right where a collective public right existed before. The tragedy of the commons is only a tragedy for those who believe society would be best served if all wealth could be concentrated in a few hands. Instead, they lament, it is democratically "dissipated" to thousands of fishers, shoreworkers and average Canadians who cast their lines on a summer long weekend.

The advocates of privatization and the market system have declared themselves champions of conservation. But where in the history of the salmon or any other resource has the market economy conserved or sustained anything that could be exploited for profit? Where now are the private wild salmon runs of Norway? Who now fishes the salmon of northern Europe or the private salmon rivers of New Brunswick and Quebec? Where are the rain forests of the Amazon, or for that matter, of a hundred valleys on our own Pacific coast, where those with property rights have had free reign to practise conservation? Ultimately, conservation is a public responsibility.

Along the way, however, the people of the coast have been able to win important concessions. The conclusion of the first salmon treaty marked a complete defeat of the canners' stand of 1905 that the Fraser could best be rehabilitated by total closure. The Hell's Gate fishways began to undo the damage of the blockades of 1913, and the sockeye and pink salmon runs soon began to rebuild, notwithstanding the "overfishing" which so preoccupied fisheries managers. Massive public protest twice defeated proposals to dam the Fraser Canyon, and it was the sentiment of common people, as well, which led to the creation of the Salmonid Enhancement Program. Native people, commercial fishing industry workers and sport fishers, as well as countless Canadians whose souls were stirred by the story of the salmon, proved to be the salmon's most steadfast supporters. Their efforts delayed implementation of much of the Davis plan for more than ten years and might have defeated the Pearse proposals completely had it not been for the duplicity of the Conservatives. Now they are being asked to give up their common property in order that it might be saved.

While fishermen, native and non-native, argue with each other and with sport fishermen about who should leave the industry so that others may survive, the fate of our salmon runs is in doubt. Given the demonstrated ability of the resource to grow, even to double, there can be no basis for driving any group into unemployment. Given a rational licensing system to protect the resource and employment, many new jobs could be created immediately, even with new allocations to sport and native fisheries. When the enormous challenges of habitat protection and salmonid enhancement are considered, it is clear that a reorganized industry could support hundreds, even thousands, of new workers, particularly if all possible processing is done in this country.

A major obstacle to the realization of any of these dreams is the unresolved issue of aboriginal rights. Through a series of court decisions, native people have won legal confirmation of their aboriginal fishing rights which federal officials at first had tried to regulate, then to deny. Quick and unco-ordinated exercise of these rights would simply add another expulsion, this time of non-native commercial fishermen, to the industry's long saga of injustice. Negotiation of a coastwide agreement on the protection, management and enhancement of the salmon which sets deadlines for the full restoration of aboriginal rights and the protection of existing jobs could open the way to a new "salmon commons" on the coast. To achieve such a dream, a new movement is required as broad and as diverse as the one contesting the future of the forest. A commitment to protect and rebuild salmon stocks would provide the political foundation for a comprehensive resolution of aboriginal claims, including agreement on an economic strategy that would open the door to an integrated management of natural resources, especially timber and fish, on a basis that respects long-term environmental needs. Such changes would necessitate a complete break from the government policies that have dominated fisheries management for generations.

Many lessons can be drawn from the history of the salmon industry. There are stories of great riches, bitter disappointments, heroic acts and grinding toil. What endures, however, is a truth that may apply to all human activity. When resources are reaped for the gain of a few or the profits of a few seasons, they will be destroyed along with those who harvest them. When they are conserved, however, "for the benefit of all the people" and with a commitment to hand them on to coming generations "in a proper state," they can strengthen, inspire and sustain us all.

NOTE ON SOURCES

Research for this book began in the *Sessional Papers* of British Columbia and Canada, which provide a helpful chronological guide to developments. These and the fisheries department papers in RG23 in the National Archives of Canada formed the basis for the early history. Wherever possible, sources are noted in the text.

The comprehensive clipping files of the International Pacific Salmon Fisheries Commission, held in Special Collections at the University of British Columbia, give an overview of events from 1900 to the early 1920s.

In the course of my research, I reviewed documents at the British Columbia Records and Archives Service, the Pacific Salmon Commission and the City of Vancouver Archives (which has the Bell-Irving and Ladner diaries and letterbooks). The main source, however, was Special Collections at the University of British Columbia: it holds the United Fishermen and Allied Workers Union papers, the Fisheries Association of British Columbia archives and numerous related collections (including the Henry Doyle papers). Special thanks are due to George Brandak and his staff for assistance.

For material on the later period, I relied on personal interviews, the records and files of *The Fisherman* and my own notes from covering the industry for twelve years.

The original manuscript for this book contained footnotes. Those interested in specific sources may contact me care of the publisher.

Following is a list of the key books, collections and documents that formed the basis of this work.

ABBREVIATIONS

BCARS: B.C. Archives and Records Service
FABC: Fisheries Association of British Columbia
NAC: National Archives of Canada

UBC: University of British Columbia Library
UFAWU: United Fishermen and Allied Workers Union

DOCUMENTS

Barricades Agreement. Dept. of Marine and Fisheries, Minutes, Memoranda and Transcripts leading up to the Barricades Agreement. Reel 46, file 2235, Special Collections, UBC.
Bell-Irving, Henry. Letterbooks and Diaries, Vol. 1. Vancouver City Archives.
British Columbia. *Sessional Papers,* 1901, 1913, 1914, 1934, 1937.
"B.C. Fisheries Commission Report," *Sessional Papers,* 1893.
Buyback catalogues. FABC
Buyback Committee. "Financial Report for Commercial Fishing Buyback Program," 30 Sept. 1974. Box 27, licence limitation file, FABC.
Canada. Dept. of Marine and Fisheries, Minutes, reel 46, file 2235, Special Collections, UBC.

Canada. *Sessional Papers*, 1871–1878, 1879, 1882, 1885, 1888, 1889, 1891, 1902, 1904, 1905, 1906, 1915.

Colonial Office. *Correspondence Relative to the Discovery of Gold in the Fraser's River District*. London, 1858.

Davis, Jack. "Operation Highline." Speech delivered to Prince Rupert Fishermen's Co-op, 2 November 1968. Box 27, licence limitation file, 1968, FABC.

Davis, Jack. Transcript of Jack Webster radio show, 12 and 13 November 1968. Box 27, licence limitation file, 1968, FABC.

deBeck, Ed Kearny. Add. MSS 346, Box 1, file 19, BCARS.

Doyle, Henry. Notebooks and Papers. Special Collections, UBC.

Eberts inquiry/Barkley Sound investigation. Correspondence and Proceedings. RG23, Vol. 766 and 767, NAC.

Evidence to the Dominion Fisheries Commission in Victoria, 1906.

Fisheries Association of British Columbia. Papers. FABC.

Fisheries and Oceans, Dept. of. "Salmonid Enhancement Program: Report on the Public Inquiries." Vancouver, March 1977.

Found, W. A. Memorandum Re Policy of Placing the Fishing Industry in British Columbia in the Hands of Whites and Native Indians. RG23, Vol. 1045, 721–6–8j[1], NAC.

Gowen, H. H. "Salmon Fishing and Canning on the Fraser River." MS, Northwest Room, Vancouver Public Library.

"Indian Employment Survey." 30 June 1972, marked confidential. Box 27, licence limitation file, FABC.

Japanese-Canadian Citizens Association files, folders 8–2 and 8–4, Special Collections, UBC.

Judgement of the Lords of the Judicial Committee of the Privy Council, 15 October 1929, in RG 23, Vol. 1045, file 721–6– 8[4].

Ladner, Thomas. Letterbooks. Vancouver City Archives.

Licence limitation file. Box 27, FABC.

Licence limitation file. UFAWU.

"Memorandum Re Conference with Indians at Port Essington." RG23, Vol. 932, 721–4–6(27), NAC.

Marine and Fisheries, Dept of. Correspondence, Memoranda and Minutes. RG23, Vol. 542, 678, 741, 766, 767, 929, 930, 932, 933, 935, 936, 942, 1045, 1048, NAC.

Marine and Fisheries, *Sessional Papers*, 1889.

Owikeno Lake files, FABC.

Owikeno Lake files, UFAWU.

Pacific Salmon Commission, 25.2, Vol. 1 c2. Pacific Salmon Commission.

Pearse Paper and Summary. RG23, Vol. 1844, NAC.

Quashela Creek scandal. RG23, vol. 741, file 715–15–2[1]. This and subsequent files contain notes, affidavits and transcripts.

"Report of the B.C. Fishery Commission," *Sessional Papers*, 1892.

"Report of the Dominion Fisheries Commission." Ottawa, 1908.

"Report of the Japanese Fishing Vessels Disposal Committee," Vancouver, December 1942.

"Report of the Royal Commission on Chinese and Japanese Immigration," *Sessional Papers*, 1902.

"Report of the Special Parliamentary Committee to Inquire into the Claims of the Allied Tribes of B.C. as Set Forth in Their Petitions Submitted to Parliament in June 1926," Ottawa, 1927.

"Report on the British Columbia Salmon Industry," 5 December 1901. Henry Doyle Papers. Special Collections, UBC.

"Report Relating to the Use of Trap Nets in the Sooke Area, Purse Seines in a Portion of the Gulf of Georgia in Salmon Fishing in B.C.," Ottawa, 1940.

Rigby, Bill. Papers. UFAWU

"Royal Commission on Indian Affairs for the Province of British Columbia." Memorandum re Fishing Rights and Privileges of Indians in B.C. GR435, Box 65, file 616, BCARS.

"Salmonid Enhancement Program: Report on the Public Inquiries," Dept. of Fisheries and Oceans, Vancouver, March 1977.

Sinclair, James. Speech delivered to UFAWU convention, 22 March 1954. Vol. 134, licence limitation file, UFAWU.

Sloan, William. Memorandum Respecting Salmon Fishery Regulations for the Province of British Columbia, December 1919.

Somerville Cannery Case, Memorandum Re Decision Supreme Court of B.C., RG23, Vol. 1048, file 721–8–4[2].

Victoria Board of Trade. Minute Book. Special Collections, UBC

"Vision 2000: A Vision of Pacific Fisheries at the Beginning of the 21st Century." Pacific Region, Dept. of Fisheries and Oceans.
West Coast Fleet Development Committee, Minutes and Reports, FABC.
Wilmot, Samuel. Report, *Sessional Papers,* 1891.
Wilmot commission testimony, *Sessional Papers,* 1893.

INTERVIEWS BY AUTHOR

Beagle, Mickey. New Westminster, 5 June 1990.
Brown, Emily. Prince Rupert, 4 July 1990.
Dwyer, Bill. Canadian Forest Products, Qualicum Beach, 20 July 1990.
Fretwell, Mike. 11 June 1986.
Gardiner, Ray. Prince Rupert, 3 July 1990.
Gordon, Alex. Parksville, 19 July 1990.
Greenwood, Florence. Prince Rupert, 4 July 1990.
Griffin, Harold. North Vancouver, 28 June 1990.
Grohn, John. Vancouver, 31 Oct. 1986.
Hyatt, Kim. Research biologist, Pacific Biological Station, Nanaimo, 19 July 1990.

Lloyd, Mike. Resource timber officer, B.C. Ministry of Forests, Bella Coola, 24 July 1990.
MacLeod, Ron. North Vancouver, June 1985.
Malyea, Harold. Maple Ridge, 29 Oct. 1986.
Neish, Elgin (Scotty). Victoria, 17 July 1990.
Olsen, Fred. Queen Charlotte City, 7 July 1990.
Orr, Uriah. Fisheries habitat protection officer, Prince Rupert, 4 July 1990.
Payne, Reg. Sydney, 16 July 1990.
Simpson, Julia (Rigby).
Stavenes, Steve. Burnaby, 28 Oct. 1986.
Suzuki, Huck. Delta, 21 June 1990.
Suzuki, Jean. Delta, 21 June 1990.
Vaselenak, Eva. White Rock, 20 June 1990.

PERIODICALS

The Fisherman
New Westminster *Columbian*
New Westminster *Daily News*
New Westminster Mainland Guardian
Pacific Fisherman
Unemployed Worker
Vancouver *Daily Province*
Vancouver *News-Advertiser*

Vancouver *Province*
Vancouver Sun
Vancouver *Daily World*
Vancouver *World*
Victoria *Colonist*
Victoria *Gazette*
The Voice of the Fisherman
Western Fisherman

Campbell, Charles. "Not a Bad Guy for an Academic." *Equity* June 1986.
Gordon, H. Scott. "The Economic Theory of a Common Property Resource: The Fishery." *Journal of Political Economy* Vol. 62.
"Globe 90, An International Forum on Wild Stock Fisheries." *Western Fisherman,* 23 May 1990.
Larkin, Peter. "An Epitaph for the Concept of Maximum Sustained Yield." *Transactions of the American Fisheries Society* Vol. 106, No. 1.
Larkin, Peter. "Play It Again Sam—An Essay on Salmon Enhancement." Fish Resource Board of Canada, Vol. 31(8) 1974.
"New Union, A." Letter to editor. *Coast Seamen's Journal* July 1893.
Ralston, Keith. "John Sullivan Deas: A Black Entrepreneur in British Columbia Salmon Canning." *B.C. Studies* Vol. 32, 1976–77.
Ralston, Keith. "Patterns of Trade and Investment on the Pacific Coast, 1867–1892." *B.C. Studies* Vol. 31, No. 1.
Rickard, T. A. "Indian Participation in the Gold Discoveries." *B.C. Historical Quarterly* Vol. II, January 1938.
Trade Union Research Bureau. "The Export Profit Tax." May 1945, Vol. 134, UFAWU.

PUBLISHED WORKS

Adachi, Ken. *The Enemy That Never Was.* Toronto: McClelland and Stewart, 1979.
Alexander, George. "A Brief Statistical Review of the Sockeye Fishing and Canning Industry in Rivers Inlet," B.C. *Sessional Papers,* 1934.
Assu, Harry, with Joy Inglis. *Assu of Cape Mudge: Recollections of a Coastal Indian Chief.* Vancouver: University of British Columbia Press, 1989.

Bennett, Bill. *Builders of British Columbia*. Vancouver: Broadway Printers, n.d.

Brannon, E. L., and E. O. Salo (eds.). *Proceedings of the Salmon and Trout Migratory Behaviour Symposium*. Seattle: University of Washington Press, 1982.

Canada. *B.C. Fisheries Commission, 1922, Report and Recommendations*. Ottawa: King's Printer, 1923.

Canada. Dept. of Marine and Fisheries. *Report of the Special Fishery Commission 1917*. Ottawa: King's Printer, 1918.

Canada. *Report Relating to the Use of Trap Nets in the Sooke Area, Purse Seines in a Portion of the Gulf of Georgia in Salmon Fishing in B.C.* Ottawa, 1940.

Childerhose, R. J., and Marj Trim. *Pacific Salmon*. Vancouver: Douglas & McIntyre, 1979.

Christy, F. T., and Anthony Scott. *The Common Wealth in Ocean Fisheries*. Baltimore: John Hopkins Press, 1965.

Clement, Wallace. *The Struggle to Organize: Resistance in Canada's Fishery*. Toronto: McClelland and Stewart, 1986.

Crutchfield, J. A., and G. Pontecorvo. *The Pacific Salmon Fisheries: A Study in Irrational Conservation*. Baltimore: John Hopkins Press, 1969.

Drucker, Philip. *The Native Brotherhoods: Modern Intertribal Organizations on the Northwest Coast*. Smithsonian Institution, Bureau of American Ethnology, Bulletin 168. Washington: 1958.

Ewen, Tom. *Fishermen's 1936 Strike*. Vancouver: FCWIU, 1936.

Fisher, Robin. *Contact and Conflict: Indian-European Relations in British Columbia, 1774–1890*. Vancouver: University of British Columbia Press, 1977.

Griffin, Harold. *British Columbia: The People's Early Story*. Vancouver: Tribune Publishing, 1958.

Griffin, Harold. *A Ripple, a Wave: The Story of Union Organization in the B.C. Fishing Industry*.

Hayashi, Rintaro. *Kuroshio no Hate ni (At the Edge of the Black Current)*. Tokyo: Nichi-eki Boekishi, 1974.

Howay, F. W. *Early History of the Fraser River Mines*. Victoria: Banfield, 1926.

Kerr, J. B. *Biographical Dictionary of Well-Known British Columbians*. Vancouver: Kerr and Begg, 1890.

Knight, Rolf. *Indians at Work: An Informal History of Native Indian Labour in British Columbia 1858–1930*. Vancouver: New Star Books, 1978.

Knight, Rolf, and Maya Koizumi. *A Man of Our Times: The Life History of a Japanese-Canadian Fisherman*. Vancouver: New Star Books, 1976.

Ladner, Leon. *The Ladners of Ladner*. Vancouver: Mitchell Press, 1972.

Ladner, T. Ellis. *Above the Sand Heads*. Burnaby: Edna G. Ladner, 1979.

Lamb, W. K. *Simon Fraser, Letters and Journals 1806–1808*. Toronto: Macmillan of Canada, 1960.

Lyons, Cicely. *Salmon: Our Heritage*. Vancouver: B.C. Packers, 1967.

Mackenzie, Alexander. *Alexander Mackenzie's Voyage to the Pacific Ocean in 1793*. New York: Citadel Press, 1967.

Marchak, Patricia, and Neil Guppy and John McMullan (eds.). *Uncommon Property: The Fishing and Fish-Processing Industries in British Columbia*. Toronto: Methuen, 1987.

Marlatt, Daphne. *Steveston Recollected: A Japanese-Canadian History*. Victoria: Provincial Archives of B.C., 1975.

Morice, A. G. *History of the Northern Interior of B.C.* Smithers: Interior Stationery, 1978.

Netboy, Anthony. *The Salmon: Their Fight for Survival*. Boston: Houghton Mifflin, 1974.

Newell, Diane. *The Development of the Pacific Salmon Canning Industry: A Grown Man's Game*. Montreal/Kingston: McGill-Queens University Press, 1989.

Pearse, Peter. *Turning the Tide: A New Policy for Canada's Pacific Fishermen, Final Report of the Commission on Pacific Fisheries Policy*. Ottawa, 1983.

Phillips, Paul. *No Power Greater: A Century of Labour in B.C.* Vancouver: B.C. Federation of Labour, 1967.

Regehr, T. D. *The Canadian Northern Railway: Pioneer Road of the Northern Prairies, 1895 to 1918*. Toronto: Macmillan of Canada, 1976.

Reid, David. *The Development of the Fraser River Canning Industry, 1885–1913*. Vancouver: Dept. of the Environment, 1973.

Rettig, Bruce, and Jay Ginter (eds.). *Limited Entry as a Fishery Management Tool*. Seattle: Washington Sea Grant, 1978.

Robin, Martin. *Pillars of Profits*. Toronto: McClelland and Stewart, 1973.

Rousefell, George, and George Kelez. *The Salmon Fisheries of Swiftsure Bank, Puget Sound and the Fraser River*. Bureau of Fisheries Bulletin No. 27. Washington: U.S. Dept. of Commerce, 1938.

Scott, Jack. *Plunderbund and Proletariat: A History of the IWW in B.C.* Vancouver: New Star Books, 1976.

Sinclair, Sol. *Licence Limitation—British Columbia: A Method of Economic Fisheries Management*. Ottawa: Dept. of Fisheries, 1960.

Sinclair, Sol. *A Licensing and Fee System for the Coastal Fisheries of British Columbia.* Vancouver: Dept. of Fisheries and Oceans, 1973.
Spradley, James P. (ed.). *Guests Never Leave Hungry: The Autobiography of James Sewid, a Kwakiutl Indian.* Kingston/Montreal: McGill-Queens University Press, 1983.
Sracey, Duncan. *Sockeye and Tinplate.* Victoria: B.C. Provincial Museum, 1982.
Stevens, G. R. *Canadian National Railways, Vol. 2, Towards the Inevitable.* Toronto: Clarke Irwin, 1962.
Stewart, Hilary. *Indian Fishing: Early Methods on the Northwest Coast.* Vancouver: Douglas & McIntyre, 1982.
Sugimoto, H. H. *Japanese Immigration, the Vancouver Riots and Canadian Diplomacy.* New York: Arno Press, 1978.
Teit, James. *Mythology of the Thompson Indians* in Franz Boas, *The Jesup North Pacific Expedition,* Memoir of the American Museum of Natural History, Vol. VIII. New York, 1912.
Teit, James. *Traditions of the Thompson River Indians of British Columbia.* New York: American Folk Life Society, 1898.
Tennant, Paul. *Aboriginal Peoples and Politics: The Indian Land Question in B.C., 1849–1989.* Vancouver: University of British Columbia Press, 1990.
Thompson, William F. *Effect of the Obstruction at Hell's Gate on the Sockeye Salmon of the Fraser River.* Bulletin 1. New Westminster: International Pacific Salmon Fisheries Commission, 1945.
UFAWU. *The Future of the B.C. Fishing Industry.* Vancouver: UFAWU, 1983.
Ward, Peter. *White Canada Forever: Popular Attitudes and Public Policy Toward Orientals in B.C.* Kingston/Montreal: McGill-Queens University Press, 1978.

UNPUBLISHED WORKS

Casaday, L. W. "Labour Unrest and the Labour Movement in the Salmon Industry of the Pacific Coast." Ph.D. diss., University of California at Los Angeles, 1938.
Doyle, Henry. "The Rise and Decline of the Pacific Salmon Fisheries." MS. Doyle Papers, Special Collections, UBC.
Gladstone, Percy. "Industrial Disputes in the Commercial Fisheries of B.C." M.A. thesis, University of British Columbia, 1959.
Hudson, Douglas. "Hell's Gate Slide: Subsistence Production and Coping with Disaster." Paper prepared for the Canadian Ethnology Society, Banff, Alberta, February 1979.
Lane, Barbara. "The Barricade Agreement of 1906—A Brief Summary and Analysis." Paper prepared for the Gitksan and Carrier people, 1978.
Lawrence, J. C. "An Historical Account of the Early Salmon Canning Industry in B.C., 1870 to 1900." B.A. thesis, University of British Columbia, 1951.
Lee, Helen. "Corporate Strategy in the British Columbia Fish-Processing Sector." M.A. thesis, Simon Fraser University, 1983.
Pearse, Peter. "National Regulation of Fisheries." Background paper prepared for a seminar on fisheries policy convened by the Fisheries Service of Canada, Vancouver, October 1971. RG23, Vol. 1844, NAC.
Ralston, Keith. "The 1900 Strike of the Fraser River Sockeye Fishermen." M.A. thesis, University of British Columbia, 1965.
Rigby, Bill. Memorandum on licence limitation, n.d. Add. MSS Vol. 134, licence limitation file, 7–8, UFAWU.
Sumida, Regenda. "The Japanese in B.C." M.A. thesis, University of British Columbia, 1935.
Ware, Reuben. "Five Issues, Five Battlegrounds: An Introduction to the History of Indian Fishing in B.C." Paper prepared for the Union of B.C. Indian Chiefs, 1978.
Wigdor, J. *Limited Survey of the Canned Salmon Industry of B.C. Including Cost of Living Data.* Paper prepared for Pacific Coast Labour Bureau of Canada, 1940. Bill Rigby Papers. UFAWU.
Wilson, Reg. "Native Organization in the B.C. Fishing Industry." Term essay, University of British Columbia, n.d.

INDEX